BRAD PITT

SEVEN YEARS IN TIBET

THE JOURNEY
BEGINS
OCTOBER 8

MANDALAY ENTERTAINMENT PRESENTS A REPERAGE AND VANGUARD FILMS/APPLECROSS PRODUCTION A FILM BY JEAN-JACQUES ANNAUD BRAD PITT "SEVEN YEARS IN TIBET" MUSIC BY JOHN WILLIAMS AIRBORNE RICHARD GOODWIN DAVID NICHOLS MICHAEL BESMAN

mandalay DOLBY PRODUCED BY JEAN-JACQUES ANNAUD JOHN WILLIAMS IAIN SMITH SCREENPLAY BY BECKY JOHNSTON DIRECTED BY JEAN-JACQUES ANNAUD TRISTAR

SEVEN YEARS
IN TIBET

JEREMY P. TARCHER/PUTNAM

a member of

PENGUIN PUTNAM INC.

New York

SEVEN YEARS
IN TIBET

HEINRICH HARRER

Translated from the German by
RICHARD GRAVES

With an Introduction by
PETER FLEMING

Jeremy P. Tarcher/Putnam
a member of
Penguin Putnam Inc.
200 Madison Avenue
New York, NY 10016
http://www.putnam.com

Library of Congress Cataloging-in-Publication Data
Harrer, Heinrich, date.
Seven years in Tibet.
Translation of: Sieben Jahre in Tibet.
1. Tibet (China)—Description and travel.   2. Harrer,
Heinrich, date.   I. Title.
DS785.H273   1982   951'.504   81-23244
ISBN 0-87477-888-3   AACR2

Cover design by Kiley Thompson
Book design by Deborah Kerner

THE DALAI LAMA

THEKCHEN CHOELING
McLEOD GANJ 176219
KANGRA DISTRICT
HIMACHAL PRADESH

F O R E W O R D

Prof. Heinrich Harrer is one of those in the West who knows Tibet intimately. His book came at a time when there were much misconceptions about the life and culture of Tibet – and most of the books available then certainly did not help to clear away these wrong impressions.

Having been forced to come to Tibet under unfortunate circumstances, he chose to live among our people and share their simple way of life, thus he made many friends and is regarded with much affection.

I am happy that his book "Seven Years in Tibet" which gives a true and vivid picture of Tibet before 1959 is being reprinted when there is a renewed interest on Tibet.

January 29, 1982

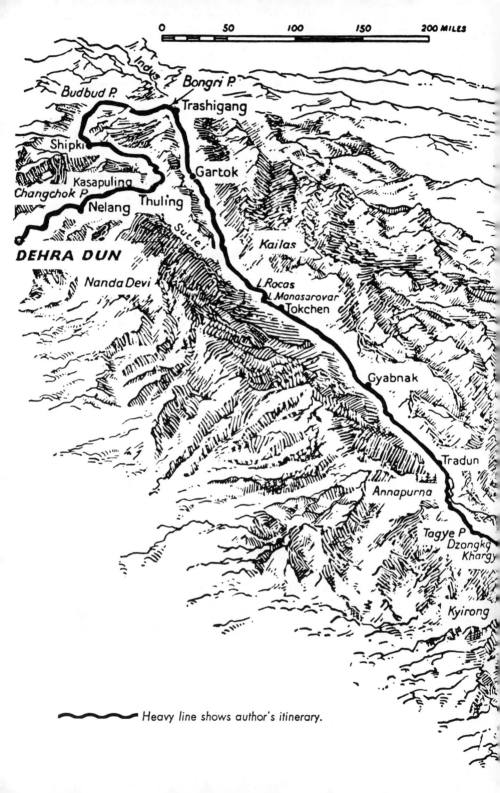

Heavy line shows author's itinerary.

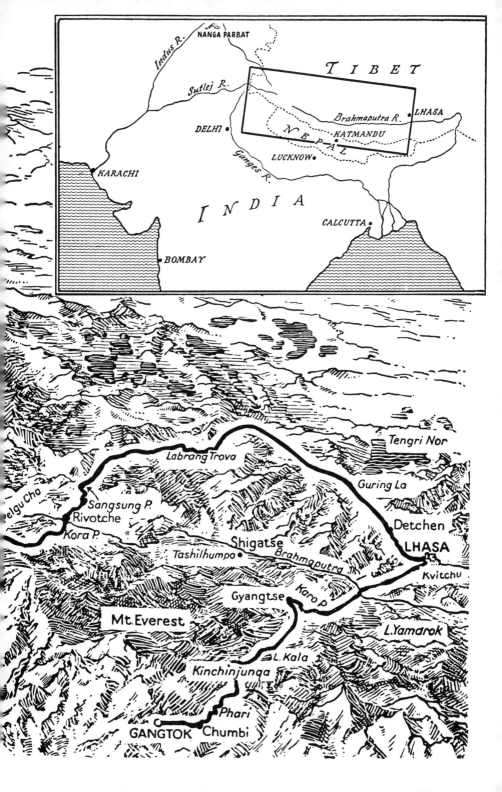

Contents

INTRODUCTION

For the British, and, indeed, I think for most Europeans, Tibet has during the last fifty years held a growing and a particular fascination. In 1904, Younghusband, in a campaign scarcely matched in the annals of war either for its administrative difficulties or for the combination of audacity and humanity with which it was conducted, marched to Lhasa and subdued Tibet. The Tibetans, whose persistent intransigence upon an imperial frontier had at length provoked our incursion, were granted the most chivalrous of terms, and on the remote, mysterious plateau—silhouetted for a time in sharp, painstaking relief by the dispatches that trickled back over the passes from the handful of correspondents with Younghusband's expedition—a veil once more descended.

It was a thick veil, and it did not get much thinner as the years went by. The end of the nineteenth century found Europe's eyes turning toward Asia. The geographical challenge of Africa had been, in its essentials, met, and on that continent the political problems, save in South Africa, appeared in those days to be soluble only in the chanceries of European capitals. In Asia, by contrast, imponderable and exotic forces were on the move. Russia's conquests in Central Asia had fulfilled what was believed to be only the first phase of her territorial ambitions; in the minds of Lord Curzon and of Kipling, her attempts to probe with reconnaissance parties the mountain barrier that separated her armies from India produced apprehensions that the event proved to be disproportionate.

But here again Asia came into the picture, for while Younghusband—bringing artillery into action, for the first and so far the last time in history, at 17,000 feet above sea level—was defeating the Tibetans, the Japanese, with much less of apology in their manner, were defeating the Russians in Manchuria. And only three years earlier, in the Boxer Rebellion, an international expedition had raised the siege of the Legation Quarter in Peking.

Tibet did no more then than she had before, or has since, to gratify Europe's curiosities about Asia. She continued, increasingly, to stimulate them; the extent to which she reciprocated them was inimical. Once four Tibetan boys (in the pages that follow, you will meet briefly the only survivor of a sensible experiment that the Tibetans never got around to repeating) were sent to be educated at Rugby; and until the Chinese Communist forces took the country over, in 1950, the sons of noblemen quite often went to school in India, learning (among other things) the English language. Europe would have welcomed Tibetans gladly, as she has welcomed travelers and students from every other Asiatic country, but whereas—broadly speaking—Europe wants like anything to go to Tibet, Tibet has never evinced the slightest desire to go to Europe.

She has, moreover, made it as difficult as possible for Europeans, or indeed for any non-Tibetans, to set foot on Tibetan territory, however impeccable their credentials. The veil of secrecy, or perhaps rather of exclusiveness, which was lifted by Younghusband and then so tantalizingly dropped again, has in the last fifty years been effectively penetrated by very few, and of these it is safe to say that not one attained to the remarkable position that the author of this book, toward the end of his five years' residence in Lhasa, found himself occupying in the entourage of the young Dalai Lama.

The European traveler is accustomed to seeing Asia, or anyhow the backwoods of Asia, from above. By that I mean that, although at times his situation may be precarious and his resources slender, the European is generally a good deal better off than the primitive people through whose territory he is passing. He possesses things that they do not—money and firearms, soap and medicines, tents and can openers; he has, moreover, in another part of the planet a government that, should he get into trouble, will try to get him out of it. So the foreigner tends to ride upon the high though not very reliable horse of privilege, and to view the backwoods and their denizens from above.

It was otherwise with Herr Harrer. When, in 1943, he made a third and successful attempt to escape from an internment camp at Dehra Dun and headed for Tibet, he was seeing Asia from below. He traveled on foot, carried his few possessions on his back, and slept on the ground in the open. He was a fugitive, with no status, no papers, and very limited funds. For a well-found expedition to follow his circuitous winter route across the Changthang plateau and down to Lhasa would have been a creditable feat; as performed by Harrer and his companion, Aufschnaiter, the journey was an astonishing tour de force. When they reached Lhasa, they were penniless and in rags.

Though there was no shred of justification for their presence in the Tibetan capital, they met with great kindness there, and the various subterfuges that they had practiced upon officials along the route aroused merriment rather than indignation. They had, nevertheless, every reason to expect to be expelled from the country, and although the war was now over, Harrer assumed, on rather slender grounds, that expulsion would mean their reinternment in India. He spoke by now fairly fluent Tibetan, though with a country accent that amused the sophisticates of Lhasa, and he never ceased to entreat permission to stay where he was and to do useful work for the government.

I have not met Herr Harrer, but from the pages that follow, he emerges as a sensible, unassuming, and very brave man, with simple tastes and solid standards. It is clear that from the first the Tibetans liked him, and it must, I think, have been his integrity of character that led the authorities to connive at, if never formally to authorize, his five years' sojourn in Lhasa. During this period he rose—always, it would seem, because of the confidence he inspired rather than because he angled for preferment—from being a destitute and alien vagabond to a well-rewarded post as tutor and confidant of the young Dalai Lama. Of this fourteen-year-old potentate, Harrer, who was certainly closer to him than any foreigner (with the possible exception of Sir Charles Bell) has been to any of his predecessors, gives a fascinating and sympathetic account. When the Chinese Communists invaded Tibet, in 1950, Harrer's parting from this lonely, able, and affectionate youth was clearly a wrench to both of them.

It is unlikely that their conquerors will be able to alter the Tibetan character, so curiously compounded of mysticism and jollity, of shrewdness and superstition, of tolerance and strict convention; but the ancient, ramshackle structure of Tibetan society, over which the Dalai Lama in his successive Incarnations presides, is full of flaws and anachronisms, and will scarcely survive in its traditional form the ideological stresses to which it is now being subjected. It is the luckiest of chances that Herr Harrer should have had, and should have made such admirable use of, the opportunity to study on intimate terms a people with whom the West is now denied even the vestigial contacts that it had before. The story of what he did and what he saw equals in strangeness Mr. Heyerdahl's account of his voyage on the *Kon-Tiki*; and it is told, I am happy to say, in the same sort of simple, unpretentious style.

PETER FLEMING

PREFACE

All our dreams begin in youth. As a child I found the achievements of the heroes of our day far more inspiring than book learning. The men who went out to explore new lands, or with toil and self-sacrifice fitted themselves to become champions in the field of sport, the conquerors of the great peaks—to imitate such men was the goal of my ambition.

But I lacked the advice and guidance of experienced counselors and so wasted many years before I realized that one must not pursue several aims at the same time. I had tried my hand at various forms of sport without achieving the success that might have satisfied me. So at last I determined to concentrate on the two that I had always loved for their close association with nature—skiing and mountain climbing.

I had spent most of my childhood in the Alps and had occupied most of my time out of school climbing in summer and ski running in winter. My ambition was spurred on by small successes, and in 1936, I succeeded after severe training in gaining a place on the Austrian Olympic Team. A year later, I was the winner of the Downhill Race in the World Students' Championships.

In these contests, I experienced the joy of speed and the glorious satisfaction of a victory into which one has put all that one has. But victory over human rivals and the public recognition of success did not satisfy me. I began to feel that the only worthwhile ambition was to measure my strength against the mountains. So for whole months together, I practiced on rock and ice, until I became so fit that no precipice seemed to me unconquerable. But I had my troubles to contend with and had to pay for my experience. Once I fell 170 feet, and it was only by a miracle that I did not lose my life—and, of course, lesser mishaps were constantly occurring.

Return to life at the university always meant a big wrench. But I ought not to complain; I had opportunities for studying all sorts of works on mountaineering and travel, and as I devoured these books there grew in my mind, out of a complex of vague desires, the ambition to realize the dream of all climbers—to take part in an expedition in the Himalayas.

But how dared an unknown youngster like myself toy with such ambitious dreams? Why, to get to the Himalayas one had either to be very rich or to belong to the nation whose sons at that time still had the chance of being sent to India on service. For a man who was neither British nor wealthy, there was only one way. One had to make use of one of those rare opportunities open even to outsiders and do something that made it impossible for one's claims to be passed over. But what performance would put one in this class? Every Alpine peak has long been climbed, even the worst ridges and rock faces have yielded to the incredible skill and daring of mountaineers. But stay! There was still one unconquered precipice—the highest and most dangerous of all—the North Wall of the Eiger.

This 6,700 feet of sheer rock face had never been climbed to the top. All attempts had failed, and many men had lost their lives in the attempt. A cluster of legends had gathered round this monstrous mountain wall, and at last the Swiss government had forbidden Alpinists to climb on it.

No doubt that was the adventure I was looking for. If I broke through the virgin defenses of the North Wall, I would have a legitimate right, as it were, to be selected for an expedition to the Himalayas. I brooded long over the idea of attempting this almost hopeless feat. How, in 1938, I succeeded with my friends Fritz Kasparek, Anderl Heckmair, and Wiggerl Vörg in climbing the dreaded wall has been described in several books.

After this adventure, I spent the autumn in continuing my training with the hope always in mind that I would be invited to join in the Nanga Parbat Expedition planned for the summer of 1939. It seemed as though I would have to go on hoping, for winter came and nothing happened. Others were selected to reconnoiter the fateful mountain in Kashmir. And so nothing was left for me but to sign, with a heavy heart, a contract to take part in a ski film.

Rehearsals were well advanced when I was suddenly called to the telephone. It was the long-desired summons to take part in the Himalaya Expedition, which was starting in four days. I had no need to reflect. I broke my contract without an instant's hesitation, traveled home to Graz, spent a day in packing my things, and on the following day was en route for Antwerp with Peter Aufschnaiter, the leader of the German Nanga Parbat Expedition, Lutz Chicken, and Hans Lobenhoffer, the other members of the group.

Up to that time there had been four attempts to climb this 25,000-foot mountain. All had failed. They had cost many lives, and so it had been decided to look for a new way up. That was to be our job, and the attack on the peak was planned for the following year.

On this expedition to Nanga Parbat I succumbed to the magic of the Himalayas. The beauty of these gigantic mountains, the immensity of the lands on which they look down, the strangeness of the people of India—all these worked on my mind like a spell.

Since then, many years have passed, but I have never been able to cut loose from Asia. How all this came about, and what it led to, I shall try to describe in this book, and as I have no experience as an author, I shall content myself with the unadorned facts.

1

INTERNMENT

By the end of August 1939, we had completed our reconnaissance. We had actually found a new way up the mountain and were now waiting in Karachi for the freighter that was to take us back to Europe. Our ship was long overdue, and the war clouds were growing even denser. Chicken, Lobenhoffer, and I accordingly made up our minds to extricate ourselves from the net that the secret police had already begun to lay for us and to slip away— wherever we found an opening. Only Aufschnaiter was for staying in Karachi. He had fought in the First World War and could not believe in a second.

The rest of us planned to break through to Persia and find our way home from there. We had no difficulty in shaking off the man who was shadowing us, and after crossing a few hundred miles of desert in our ramshackle car, we managed to reach Las Bela, a little principality to the northwest of Karachi. But there fate overtook us, and we suddenly found ourselves taken in charge by eight soldiers, on the grounds that we needed personal protection. We were, in fact, under arrest, although Germany and the British Commonwealth were not yet at war.

Soon we were back with our trusty escort in Karachi, where we found Peter Aufschnaiter. Two days later, England did declare war on Germany. After that, everything went like clockwork. A few minutes after the declaration of war, twenty-five Indian soldiers armed to the teeth marched into a restaurant garden where we were sitting, to fetch us away. We drove in a police car to an already prepared prison camp fenced with barbed wire. But that turned out to be merely a transit camp, and a fortnight later we were transferred to the great internment camp at Ahmednagar, near Bombay. There we were quartered in crowded tents and huts in the midst of a babel of conflicting opinions and excited talk. "No," I thought, "this atmosphere is too different from the sunlit, lonely heights of the Himalayas. This is no life for freedom-loving men." So I began to get busy looking for ways and means of escape.

Of course, I was not the only one planning to get away. With the help of like-minded companions, I collected compasses, money, and maps, which had been smuggled past the controls. We even managed to get hold of leather gloves and a barbed-wire cutter, the loss of which from the stores provoked a strict but fruitless investigation.

As we all believed that the war would soon be over, we kept postponing our plans for escape. But one day we were suddenly moved to another camp. We were loaded onto a convoy of trucks en route for Deolali. Eighteen of us internees sat in each truck with a single Indian soldier to guard us. The sentry's rifle was made fast to his belt with a chain so that no one could snatch it away. At the head and at the tail of the column was a truck full of soldiers.

While we were in the camp at Ahmednagar, Lobenhoffer and I had determined to make a getaway before being transferred to a new camp, where fresh difficulties might endanger our chances of escape. So now we took our seats at the back end of a truck. Luckily for us, the road was full of curves and we were often enveloped in thick clouds of dust—we saw that this gave us a chance of jumping off unnoticed and vanishing into the jungle. We did not expect the guard in the truck to spot us as he was obviously occupied in watching the truck in front. He only occasionally looked around at us. One way and another, it did not seem to us that it would be too difficult to escape, and we postponed an attempt until the latest possible moment, intending to get across into a neutral Portuguese enclave situated very near the route of our convoy.

At last the moment came. We jumped off, and I ran twenty yards off the road and threw myself down in a little hollow behind a bush. Then to my horror, the whole convoy stopped—I heard whistles and shooting and then, seeing the guard running over to the far side of the road, I had no doubt what had happened. Lobenhoffer must have been discovered, and as he was carrying our rucksack with all our gear, there was nothing for me to do but to give up my hopes of escape as well. Fortunately, I succeeded, in the confusion, in getting back into my seat without being noticed by any of the soldiers. Only my comrades knew that I had got away, and, naturally, they said nothing.

Then I saw Lobenhoffer: he was standing with his hands up, facing a line of bayonets. I felt broken with the deadly disappointment of our failure. But my friend was really not to blame for it. He was carrying our heavy rucksack in his hand when he jumped off, and it seems that it made a clatter, which was heard by the guard; so he was caught before he could gain the shelter of the jungle. We learned from this adventure a bitter but useful lesson, namely that in any combined plan of escape, each of the escapers must carry all that he needed with him.

In the same year, we were moved once more to another camp. This time we were conveyed by rail to the greatest POW camp in

India, a few miles outside the town of Dehra Dun. Above Dehra Dun was the hill station of Mussoorie, the summer residence of the British and rich Indians. Our camp consisted of seven great sections, each surrounded by a double fence of barbed wire. The whole camp was enclosed by two more lines of wire entanglement, between which patrols were constantly on the move.

The conditions of our new camp altered the whole situation for us. As long as we were down below in the plain, we always aimed to escape into one of the neutral Portuguese territories. Up here, we had the Himalayas right in front of us. How attractive to a mountaineer was the thought of winning through to Tibet over the passes. As a final goal, one thought of the Japanese lines in Burma or China.

Plans for escape in these conditions and with these objectives needed the most careful preparation. By now we had given up hope of a speedy ending to the war, and so there was nothing for it—if we wished to get away—but to organize systematically. Flight through the thickly populated regions of India was out of the question; for that one would need plenty of money and a perfect knowledge of English—and I had neither. So it is easy to imagine that my preference was for the empty spaces of Tibet. And I thought of being on the Himalayas—and felt that even if my plan failed, it would be worth having a spell of freedom in the high mountains.

I now set to work to learn a little Hindustani, Tibetan, and Japanese, and devoured all sorts of travel books on Asia, which I found in the library, especially those dealing with the districts on my prospective route. I made extracts from these works and took copies of the most important maps. Peter Aufschnaiter, who had also landed in Dehra Dun, had various books and maps dealing with expeditions in Asia. He worked at these with tireless energy, and put all his notes and sketches at my disposal. I copied all of these in duplicate, keeping one copy to take with me when I escaped and the other as a reserve in case the originals were lost.

It was just as important for me, in view of the route by which I proposed to escape, to keep myself physically as fit as possible. So every day I devoted hours to exercising in the open air, indifferent to bad and good weather alike, while at night I used to lie out and study the habits of the guards.

My chief worry was that I had too little money, for although I had sold everything I could do without, my savings were quite insufficient to provide for the necessaries of life in Tibet, let alone for the bribes and presents which are the commonplaces of life in Asia. Nevertheless, I went on working systematically at my plan and received help from some friends, who themselves had no intention of escaping.

I had originally intended to escape alone in order not to have to consider a companion, which might have prejudiced my chances. But one day my friend Rolf Magener told me that an Italian general had the same intentions as myself. I had previously heard of this man, and so one night Magener and I climbed through the wire fence into the neighboring wing, in which forty Italian generals were housed. My future companion was named Marchese and was in outward appearance a typical Italian. He was something over forty years of age, slim of figure, with agreeable manners, and distinctly well dressed; I was particularly impressed by his physique. At the outset we had difficulties in understanding one another. He spoke no German, and I no Italian. We both knew only a minimum of English, so we conversed, with the help of a friend, in halting French. Marchese told me about the war in Abyssinia, and of an earlier attempt he had made to escape from a POW camp.

Fortunately for him, he received the pay of an English general, and money was no problem. He was able to procure for our flight things that I could never have obtained. What he needed was a partner familiar with the Himalayas—so we very soon joined forces on the basis that I should be responsible for all the planning, and he for the money and equipment.

Several times every week I used to crawl out to discuss details with Marchese, and by practice became an expert in penetrating barbed wire. Of course there were various possibilities for the escape, but the one that seemed to me the most promising was based on one important fact—that every eighty yards along the outer fence enclosing the whole camp was a steep, straw-thatched roof that had been put up to protect the sentries against the tropical sun. If we could climb over one of these roofs, we should have crossed the two lines of barbed wire at a single bound. In May 1943, we had completed our preparations. Money, provisions, compass, watches, shoes, and a small mountaineer's tent were all ready.

One night we decided to make the attempt. I climbed as usual through the fence into Marchese's wing. There I found a ladder ready, which we had grabbed and hidden after a small fire in the camp. We leaned it against the wall of a hut and waited in the shadow. It was nearly midnight, and in ten minutes the guard would change. The sentries, waiting to come off duty, walked slackly up and down. A few minutes passed until they reached the point where we wanted them. Just then the moon came up over the tops of the tea plantation.

There we were. It was now or never.

Both the sentries had reached their farthest point from us. I got up from my crouching position and hurried to the fence with the ladder. I laid it against the overhanging top of the fence, climbed up, and cut the wires, which had been bunched together to prevent access to the thatch. Marchese pushed the thicket of wires to one side with a long, forked stick, enabling me to slip through onto the roof. It was agreed that the Italian should follow me immediately, while I held the wire apart with my hands, but he did not come. He lingered for a few ghastly seconds, thinking that it was too late and that the guards were already returning—and, indeed, I heard their steps. I left him no time for further reflection but caught him under the arms and pulled him onto the roof. He crept across and dropped heavily down into freedom.

But all this had not happened in dead silence. The watch was alarmed, and they started shooting, but as their firing broke the stillness of the night, we were swallowed up by the jungle.

The first thing that Marchese did, in expression of his warm southern temperament, was to embrace and kiss me, though this was hardly the moment to give vent to outbursts of joy. Rockets went up and whistles sounded near us, showing that pursuers were on our track. We ran for our lives and moved very fast, using short cuts which I had got to know very well during my outings from the camp. We made little use of the roads and skirted around the few villages we found on our way. At the outset we hardly noticed our packs, but later on they began to feel heavy.

In one of the villages, the natives beat their drums, and we at once fancied they were sounding the alarm. That was one of the difficulties that anyone brought up among our exclusively white population can hardly imagine. In Asia, the sahib invariably travels with an escort of servants and never carries the smallest package himself—what would the natives think, therefore, when they saw two heavily laden Europeans plodding on foot through the countryside!

We decided to march by night, knowing that the Indians are afraid to go through the jungle in darkness on account of the wild beasts. We did not enjoy the prospect particularly ourselves, having often read stories in the newspapers available in the camp of man-eating tigers and leopards.

When day dawned we hid ourselves, exhausted, in a *wadi,* and spent the whole day there, sleeping and eating in the burning heat. We saw only one person during the day, a cowherd; fortunately, he did not see us. The worst thing was that we each of us had only a single water bottle, which had to suffice for the whole day. It was no wonder that when evening came, after a day spent in keeping quiet, we could hardly control our nerves. We wanted to get on as quickly as possible, and the nights seemed far too short for our progress. We had to find the shortest way through the Himalayas to Tibet, and that would mean weeks of strenuous marching before we could feel ourselves in safety.

We crossed the first ridge on the evening after our escape. At the top, we rested for a while and saw 3,000 feet below us the countless twinkling lights of the internment camp. At eleven o'clock, the lights all went out together, and only the searchlights around the camp gave an idea of its enormous extent.

This was the first time in my life that I really understood what it meant to be free. We enjoyed this glorious feeling and thought with sympathy of the two thousand POWs forced to live down there behind the wall of wire.

But we had not much time for meditation. We had to find our way down to the valley of the Jumna, which was completely unknown to us. In one of the smaller valleys, we walked into a cleft so narrow that we could not get on, and had to wait till morning. The place was so lonely and sheltered that I could without misgiving take the opportunity to dye my blond hair and beard black. I also stained my face and hands with a mixture of permanganate, brown paint, and grease, which produced a dark shade. By this means, I acquired some resemblance to an Indian; that was important, as we had decided, if we were challenged, to say that we were on a pilgrimage to the sacred Ganges. As for my companion, he was dark enough not to be noticeable at a distance. Naturally, we did not mean to court close inspection.

On this evening we set out before it was dark, but soon had to rue our haste, for crossing a slope, we found ourselves in the presence of a number of peasants planting rice. They were wading half-naked in the muddy water and stared in astonishment at the sight of two men carrying packs on their backs. They pointed to the slope high up on which one could see a village, which seemed to mean that this was the only way out of the ravine. To avoid awkward questions, we walked straight on, as fast as possible in the direction indicated. After hours of climbing and descending, we at last reached the river Jumna.

Meanwhile, night had fallen. Our plan was to follow the course of the Jumna until we reached one of its tributaries, the Aglar, and then to follow this stream till we came to the watershed. It could not be far from there to the Ganges, which would lead us to the great Himalayan chain. Most of our route up to this point had been across country, and only here and there along water courses had we found paths used by fishermen. On this morning, Marchese was very much exhausted. I prepared cornflakes for him with sugar and water, and on my insisting, he ate a little. Unfortunately, the place where we found ourselves was most unsuitable for camping. It was swarming with large ants that bit deeply into one's skin, and we could not sleep because of them. The day seemed endless.

Toward evening my companion's restlessness increased, and I began to hope that his physical condition might have improved. He, too, was full of confidence that he would be able to cope with the fatigue of the next night. However, soon after midnight, he was through. He simply was not up to the enormous physical effort needed of us. My hard training and condition proved a godsend to us both—I often used to carry his pack strapped over my own. I should say that we had covered our rucksacks with Indian jute sacking to avoid arousing suspicion.

During the next two nights, we wandered upstream, frequently having to wade through the Aglar when our way along the bank was blocked by jungle or rocks. Once as we were resting in the bed of the stream between two rocky walls, some fishermen came by without noticing us. Another time, when we stumbled upon some fishermen whom we could not avoid, we asked in our broken Hindustani for some trout. Our disguise seemed to be convincing enough, as the men sold us the fish without showing mistrust of us—indeed, they cooked them for us—while conversing and smoking those small Indian cigarettes that Europeans find so distasteful. Marchese (who before our getaway had been a great smoker) could not resist the temptation of asking for one, but he had taken barely a couple of puffs when he fell unconscious, as if he had been poleaxed! Luckily, he soon recovered, and we were able to continue our journey.

Later on we met some peasants carrying butter to the town. We were meanwhile becoming more confident and asked them to sell us some. One of them agreed to do so, but as he ladled the almost melting butter, with his dark, dirty hands, from his pot into ours, we both of us nearly vomited with disgust.

At last the valley broadened out, and our way lay through rice and cornfields. It became more and more difficult to find a good hideout for the daytime. Once we were discovered during the morning, and as the peasants kept asking us all manner of indiscreet questions, we packed up our traps and hurried onward. We had not yet found a new hiding place when we met eight men, who shouted to us to stop. Our luck seemed at last to have deserted us. They asked us innumerable questions, and I kept on giving the same answer, namely that we were pilgrims from a distant province. To our great astonishment, we seemed somehow to have stood the test, for after a while they let us go on our way. We could hardly believe that we had done with them, and long after we had moved on, we thought we heard pursuing footsteps.

That day everything seemed to be bewitched, and we had constant upsets. Finally we had to come to the discouraging conclusion that we had indeed crossed a watershed but were still in the valley of the Jumna—which implied that we were at least two days behind our timetable.

So we had to start climbing again, and soon found ourselves in thick forests of rhododendrons that seemed so completely deserted that we could hope for a quiet day and a chance of a long sleep. But some cowherds came in sight, and we had to move camp and bid farewell to the prospect of a good day's rest.

During the following nights, we marched through comparatively unpopulated country. We learned soon enough, to our sorrow, the reason for the absence of human beings. There was practically no water. We suffered so much from thirst that on one occasion I made a bad mistake, which might have had disastrous consequences. Coming across a small pool, I threw myself down and without taking any precautions began to drink the water in mighty gulps. The results were awful. It turned out that this was one of those pools in which water buffaloes are accustomed to wallow in the hot weather, and which contain more mire than water. I had a violent attack of coughing followed by vomiting, and it was long before I recovered from my horrid refreshment.

Soon after this incident, we were so overcome by thirst that we simply could not go on and had to lie down, although it was long before dawn. When morning came, I climbed down the steep slope alone in search of water, which I found. The next three days and nights were a little better; our path lay through dry fir woods that were so lonely that we seldom met Indians in them, and ran very little risk of discovery.

On the twelfth day of our flight, a great moment came. We found ourselves on the banks of the Ganges. The most pious Hindu could not have been more deeply moved by the sight of the sacred stream than we were. We could now follow the Pilgrims' Road up the Ganges to its source—and that would greatly lessen the fatigues of our journey, or so we imagined. We decided that, having got so far and so safely by our system of night travel, we would not risk a change, so we continued to lie up by day and move only by night.

In the meantime we were desperately short of provisions. Our food was practically exhausted, but although poor Marchese was nothing but skin and bones, he did not give in. I, fortunately, was still feeling comparatively fresh and had a good reserve of strength.

All our hopes were centered on the tea and provision stores that were to be found everywhere along the Pilgrims' Road. Some of them remained open late into the night, and one could recognize them by their dull glimmering oil lamps. After attending to my makeup, I walked into the first of these stores that we came to and was driven out with cries of abuse. They clearly took me for a thief. Unpleasant as the experience was, it had one advantage; it was evident that my disguise was convincing.

Arriving at the next store, I walked in holding my money as ostentatiously as possible in my hand. That made a good impression. Then I told the storekeeper that I had to buy provisions for ten people, in order to lend plausibility to an offer to purchase forty pounds of meal, sugar, and onions.

The shop people took more interest in examining my paper money than in my person, and so after a while I was able to leave the shop with a heavy load of provisions. The next day was a happy one. At last we had enough to eat, and the Pilgrims' Road seemed to us, after our long treks across country, a mere promenade.

But our contentment was short-lived. At our next halt we were disturbed by men in search of wood. They found Marchese lying half-naked because of the great heat. He had grown so thin that one could count his ribs, and he looked very sick indeed. We were, of course, objects of suspicion, as we were not in the usual pilgrims' roadhouses. The Indians invited us to their farmhouse, but that we didn't want to do, and used Marchese's ill health as an excuse for not going with them. They went away then, but soon were back, and it was now clear that they took us for fugitives. They tried to blackmail us by saying that there was an Englishman in the neighborhood with eight soldiers looking for a couple of escaped prisoners, and that he had promised them a reward for any information they could give him. But they promised to say nothing if we gave them money. I stood firm and insisted that I was a doctor from Kashmir, in proof of which I showed them my medicine chest.

Whether as a result of Marchese's completely genuine groans or of my playacting, the Indians vanished again. We spent the next night in continual fear of their return and expected them to come back with an official. However, we were not molested.

With things as they were, the days did little to restore our strength, and indeed they laid a greater strain on us than the nights. Not, of course, muscular but nervous strain, as we were in a state of continuous tension. By midday our water bottles were generally empty, and the remainder of the day seemed never-ending. Every evening Marchese marched heroically forward, and in spite of exhaustion caused by loss of weight he could carry on till midnight. After that he had to have two hours' sleep to enable him to march a stage farther. Toward morning we bivouacked, and from our shelter could look down on the great Pilgrims' Road with its almost unbroken stream of pilgrims. Strangely garbed as they often were, we envied them. Lucky devils! They had no cause to hide from anyone. We had heard in the camp that something like sixty thousand pilgrims came this way during the summer months, and we readily believed it.

OUR NEXT MARCH was a long one, but toward midnight we reached Uttar Kashi, the temple town. We soon lost our bearings in the narrow streets, so Marchese sat down with the packs in a dark corner, and I set off alone to try and find the way. Through the open doors of the temples, one could see lamps burning before the staring idols, and I had often to leap into the shadow to avoid being noticed by monks passing from one holy place to another. It took me more than an hour before I at last found the Pilgrims' Road again, stretching away on the other side of the town. I knew from the numerous travel books I had read that we should now have to cross the so-called "Inner Frontier." This line runs parallel to the true frontier at a distance of something between 60 and 120 miles. Everyone traversing this region, with the exception of normal residents, is supposed to have a pass. As we had none, we had to take particular care to avoid police posts and patrols.

The valley up which our way led us became less and less inhabited as we progressed. In the daytime we had no trouble in finding suitable shelters, and I could often leave my hiding place and go in search of water. Once I even made a small fire and cooked some porridge—the first hot meal we had eaten for a fortnight.

We had already reached a height of nearly 7,000 feet and during the night we often passed camps of Bhutia, the Tibetan traders who in summer carry on their business in southern Tibet and in winter come across into India. Many of them live during the hot weather in little villages situated above the 10,000-foot level, where they grow barley. These camps had a very disagreeable feature in the shape of the powerful and savage Tibetan dogs—a shaggy-coated, middle-sized breed—which we now encountered for the first time.

One night we arrived at one of these Bhutia villages which are inhabited only in summer. It looked very homelike with its shingle- and stone-covered roofs. But behind it an unpleasant surprise was awaiting us in the shape of a swiftly running stream that had overflowed its banks and turned the adjacent ground into a swamp. It was absolutely impossible to cross it. At last we gave up trying to find a way over, and determined to wait till day and observe the ground from a shelter, for we could not believe that the Pilgrims' Road broke off short at this point. To our utmost astonishment, we observed next morning that the procession of pilgrims continued on their way and crossed the water at precisely the spot at which we had spent hours of the night vainly trying to get over. Unfortunately we could not see how they managed it, as trees interrupted our sight of the actual place. But something else equally inexplicable occurred. We observed that later on in the morning the stream of pilgrims stopped. Next evening we tried again to cross at the same place and again found that it was impossible. At last it dawned on me that we had in front of us a brook, fed by melted snow and ice, which carried its highest head of water from noon till late into the night. Early in the morning the water level would be lowest.

It turned out to be as I had guessed. When in the first gray of dawn we stood beside the stream, we saw a primitive bridge of half-submerged tree trunks. Balancing ourselves carefully we got across to the other side. Unfortunately there were other streams which we had to cross in the same laborious manner. I had just crossed the last of these when Marchese slipped and fell into the water—luckily on top of the trunks, or he would otherwise have been carried away by the torrent. Wet to the skin and completely exhausted, he could not be induced to go on. I urged him to move at least into cover, but he just spread out his wet things to dry and started to light a fire. Then for the first time I began to regret that I had not listened to his repeated requests to leave him behind and carry on alone. I had always insisted that since we had escaped together we should stay together.

As we were arguing, an Indian stood before us, who after a glance at the various objects of obviously European origin spread out on the ground began to ask us questions. Only then did Marchese realize what danger we were in. He quickly put his things together, but we had hardly gone a couple of steps when we were stopped by another Indian, a distinguished-looking fellow, leading a section of ten strapping soldiers. In perfect English he asked for our passes. We pretended not to understand and said we were pilgrims from Kashmir. He thought this over for a moment and then found a solution which spelled finis to our hopes of escape. There were, he said, two Kashmiris in the neighboring house. If we could make them understand us, we could go on our way. What devilish ill luck had brought two Kashmiris into the neighborhood at just that moment? I had used this alibi only because it was the most unlikely thing to find Kashmiris in this region.

The two men of whom he spoke were flood-damage experts who had been called in from Kashmir. As soon as we stood before them we realized that the moment of our unmasking had come. As we had agreed to do in such a case, I began to speak to Marchese in French. Immediately the Indian broke in, speaking also in French, and told us to open our packs. When he saw my English-Tibetan grammar, he said we might just as well say who we were. We then admitted that we were escaped prisoners but did not give away our nationality.

Soon after, we were sitting in a comfortable room drinking tea, but all the same I felt bitterly disappointed. This was the eighteenth day of our flight, and all our privations and efforts had gone for nothing. The man who had questioned us was the chief of the Forestry Department in the state of Tehri-Garhwal. He had studied forestry in English, French, and German schools and knew all three languages well. It was on account of the flood, the worst catastrophe of the kind in the last hundred years, that he had come on an inspection to this region. He smilingly regretted his presence, adding that as ours had been reported to him, he was obliged to do his duty.

Today when I think of the chain of circumstances that led to our capture, I cannot help feeling that we were victims of something worse than ordinary ill luck, and that we could not have averted our fate. All the same, I did not for a minute doubt that I would escape again. Marchese, however, was in a condition of such complete exhaustion that he had given up all idea of another attempt. In a very comradely manner, he made over to me the greater part of his money, knowing how short I was. I made good use of an enforced leisure to eat hearty meals, as we had eaten hardly anything for the last few days. The forest officer's cook kept us continuously supplied with food, half of which I tucked away in my knapsack. Early in the evening, we said we were tired and wanted to sleep. Our bedroom door was locked on the outside, and the forest officer had his bed put on the veranda in front of our window to prevent any attempt at escape that way. However, he was away for a short while, and Marchese and I took the opportunity to start a mock quarrel. Marchese took both parts, so to speak, shouting abuse in a high and then a low key, while I swung myself through the window, rucksack and all, onto the forest officer's bed, and ran to the end of the veranda. Darkness had fallen, and after waiting a few seconds till the sentries had vanished around the corner of the house, I dropped down twelve feet to the ground below. The soil into which I fell was not hard, and I made little noise; in a moment I was up and over the garden wall and had vanished into the pitch-black forest.

I was free!

Everything was quiet. In spite of my excitement, I could not help laughing at the thought that Marchese was still abusing me according to plan, while the forest officer was keeping watch on us from his bed in front of our window.

However, I had to go on and ran, in my haste, into a flock of sheep. Before I could get back, a sheepdog fastened on to the seat of my trousers and did not let go till he had bitten a piece out. In my terror I dashed away but found that the road I had chosen was too steep for me, and so I had to go back and creep around the sheep till I found another way. Soon after midnight I had to admit that I had again gone wrong. So once more I had to go back a few miles in breathless haste. My aimless wanderings had lost me four hours, and the day was already dawning. Turning a corner I caught sight of a bear about twenty yards away. Luckily he shuffled off without seeming to take any notice of me.

When it was fully light, I hid myself again, although the country showed no trace of human habitation. I knew that before reaching the Tibetan frontier I should come to a village at the other side of which lay freedom. I marched through the whole of the next night and gradually began to wonder why I had not reached the fateful village. According to my notes, it lay on the far bank of the river and was connected with the near side by a bridge. I wondered if I had not already passed it but consoled myself with the reflection that one could hardly miss a village. So I marched on carefree, even after daylight had come.

That was my undoing. As I came around a heap of boulders, I found myself right under the houses of a village, in front of which stood a swarm of gesticulating people. The place was wrongly indicated on my map, and as I had twice lost my way during the night, my pursuers had had time to come up with me. I was at once surrounded and summoned to surrender, after which I was led into a house and offered refreshment.

Here I met for the first time with the real Tibetan nomads, who wander into India with their flocks of sheep and loads of salt and return laden with barley. I was offered Tibetan butter tea with *tsampa*, the staple food of these people on which later I lived for years. My first contact with it affected my stomach most disagreeably.

I spent a couple of nights in this village, which was called Nelang, playing vaguely with the idea of another attempt to escape, but I was physically too tired and mentally too despondent to translate my thoughts into action.

The return journey, in comparison with my previous exertions, seemed a pleasure trip. I did not have to carry a pack and was very well looked after. On the way I met Marchese, who was staying as a guest with the forest officer in his private bungalow. I was invited to join them. And what was my astonishment when a few days later, two other escaped members of our company in the POW camp were brought in—Peter Aufschnaiter, my comrade on the Nanga Parbat Expedition, and a certain Father Calenberg.

Meanwhile I had begun to occupy my mind with plans for escaping once more. I made friends with an Indian guard who cooked for us and seemed to inspire confidence. I handed him my maps, my compass, and my money, as I knew that we should be searched before being readmitted to the camp, and that it would be impossible to smuggle these things in with us. So I told the Indian that I would come again in the following spring and collect my possessions from him. He was to ask for leave in May and wait for me. This he solemnly promised to do. So now we had to go back to the camp, and it was only my resolve to get free once more that enabled me to endure the bitterness of my disappointment.

Marchese was still sick and could not walk, so they gave him a horse to ride. We had another agreeable interruption, being entertained on our way by the Maharajah of Tehri-Garhwal, who treated us most hospitably. Then we returned to our barbed-wire entanglements.

The episode of my flight had left a visible mark on my person, which appeared when on the way back I bathed in a warm spring. There I found my hair coming out in handfuls. It appears that the dye I had used for my Indian disguise was deleterious.

As a result of my involuntary depilation and all the fatigues I had gone through, my comrades in the camp found it hard to recognize me when I arrived.

2

ESCAPE

"You made a daring escape. I am sorry I have to give you twenty-eight days," said the English colonel on our return to the camp. I had enjoyed thirty-eight days of freedom and now had to pass twenty-eight in solitary confinement. It was the regular penalty for breaking out. However, as the English took a sporting view of our bold attempt, I was treated with less than the usual rigor.

When I had finished my spell of punishment, I heard that Marchese had endured the same fate in another part of the camp. Later on we found opportunities to talk over our experiences. Marchese promised to help me in my next attempt to get loose but would not think of joining me. Without losing any time, I at once began to make new maps and to draw conclusions from the experience of my previous flight. I felt convinced that my next attempt would succeed and was determined to go alone this time.

Busy with my preparations, I found the winter passing swiftly, and by the time the next "escape season" came around I was well equipped. This time I wanted to start earlier, so as to get through the village of Nelang while it was still uninhabited. I had not counted on getting back the kit I had left with the Indian, so I supplied myself afresh with the things I most needed. A touching proof of comradeship was the generosity of my companions, who, hard up as many of them were, spent their money freely in contributing to my outfit.

I was not the only POW who wanted to get away. My two best friends, Rolf Magener and Heins von Have, also were engaged in preparing to escape. Both spoke fluent English, and they aimed to work their way through India to the Burma front. Von Have already had escaped two years before with a companion and almost had reached Burma, but was caught just before the frontier. During a second attempt, his friend had a fatal accident. Three or four other internees, it was said, planned to escape. Finally the whole seven of us got together and decided to make a simultaneous breakout on the grounds that successive individual attempts increased the vigilance of the guards, and made it more and more difficult to get away as time went on. If the mass escape succeeded, each of us, once out of the camp, could follow his own route. Peter Aufschnaiter, who this time had as his partner Bruno Treipel, from Salzburg, and two fellows from Berlin, Hans Kopp and Sattler, wished, like me, to escape to Tibet.

Our zero hour was fixed as 2 P.M. on April 29, 1944. Our plan was to disguise ourselves as a barbed-wire repairing section. Such working parties were a normal sight. The reason for them was that white ants were always busy eating away the numerous posts that supported the wire, and these had to be continually renewed. Working parties consisted of Indians with an English overseer.

At the appointed time, we met in a little hut in the neighborhood of one of the least closely watched wire corridors. Here makeup experts from the camp transformed us in a trice into Indians. Von Have and Magener got English officers' uniforms. We "Indians" had our heads shaved and put on turbans. Serious as the situation was, we could not help laughing when we looked at one another. We looked like masqueraders bound for a carnival. Two of us carried a ladder, which had been conveyed the night before to an unguarded spot in the wire fencing. We had also wangled a long roll of barbed wire and hung it on a post. Our belongings were stowed away under our white robes and in bundles, which did not look odd as Indians always carry things around with them. Our two "British officers" behaved very realistically. They carried rolls of blueprints under their arms and swung their swagger canes. We had already made a breach in the fence through which we now slipped one after another into the unguarded passage that separated the different sections of the camp. From here it was about three hundred yards to the main gate. We attracted no attention and stopped only once, when the sergeant major rode by the main gate on his bicycle. Our "officers" chose that moment to inspect the wire closely. After that we passed out through the gate without causing the guards to bat an eyelid. It was comforting to see them saluting smartly, and obviously suspicious of nobody. Our seventh man, Sattler, who had left his hut rather late, arrived after us. His face was black and he was swinging a tar pot energetically. The sentries let him through, and he caught up with us only outside the gate.

As soon as we were out of sight of the guards, we vanished into the bush and got rid of our disguises. Under our Indian robes we wore khaki, our normal dress when on outings. In few words we bade each other good-bye. Von Have, Magener, and I ran for a few miles together, and then our ways parted. I chose the same route as last time and traveled as fast as I could in order to put as long a distance as possible between me and the camp by the next morning. This time I was determined not to depart from my resolve to travel only by night and lie up by day. No! this time I was not going to take any risks. My four comrades, for whom Tibet was also the objective, moved in a party and had the nerve to use the main road, which led via Mussoorie into the valley of the Ganges. I found this too risky and followed my former route through the Jumna and Aglar valleys. During the first night I must have waded through the Aglar forty times. All the same, when morning came I lay up in exactly the same place that it had taken me four days to reach in the previous year. Happy to be free, I felt satisfied with my performance, though I was covered with scratches and bruises, and owing to my heavy load, had walked through the soles of a pair of new tennis shoes in a single night.

I chose my first day camp between two boulders in the riverbed, but I had hardly unpacked my things when a company of apes appeared. They caught sight of me and began to pelt me with clods. Distracted by their noise, I failed to observe a body of thirty Indians who came running up the riverbed. I noticed them only when they had approached dangerously near to my hiding place. I still do not know if they were fishermen or persons in search of us fugitives. In any case, I could hardly believe that they had not spotted me, for they were within a few yards of me as they ran by. I breathed again, but took this for a warning and remained in my shelter till evening, not moving till darkness had fallen. I followed the Aglar the whole night long and made good progress. My next camp provided no excitements, and I was able to refresh myself with a good sleep. Toward evening I grew impatient and broke camp rather too early. I had been walking for only a few hundred yards when I ran into an Indian woman at a water hole. She screamed with fright, let her water jar fall, and ran toward the nearby houses. I was no less frightened than she was and dashed from the track into a gully. Here I had to climb steeply, and though I knew I was going in the right direction, my diversion represented a painful detour that put me back by several hours. I had to climb

Nag Tibba, a mountain over 10,000 feet high, which in its upper regions is completely deserted and thickly covered with forest.

As I was loping along in the gray of dawn, I found myself facing my first leopard. My heart nearly stopped beating, as I was completely defenseless. My only weapon was a long knife, which the camp blacksmith had made expressly for me. I carried it sheathed in a stick. The leopard sat on a thick branch fifteen feet or more above the ground, ready to spring. I thought like lightning what was the best thing to do; then, masking my fear, I walked steadily on my way. Nothing happened, but for a long time I had a peculiar feeling in my back.

Up to now I had been following the ridge of Nag Tibba, and now at last I tumbled onto the road again. I had not gone far when I got another surprise. In the middle of the track lay some men—snoring! They were Peter Aufschnaiter and his three companions. I shook them awake, and we all betook ourselves to a sheltered spot, where we recounted what had befallen us on the trek. We were all in excellent shape and were convinced that we should get through to Tibet. After passing the day in the company of my friends, I found it hard to go on alone in the evening, but I remained true to my resolve. The same night I reached the Ganges. I had been five days on the run.

At Uttar Kashi, the temple town that I have mentioned in connection with my first escape, I had to run for my life. I had just passed a house when two men came out and started running after me. I fled headlong through fields and scrub down to the Ganges and there hid myself between two great blocks of boulders. All was quiet, and it was clear that I had escaped from my pursuers, but only after a longish time did I dare to come out into the bright moonlight. It was a pleasure for me at this stage to travel along a familiar route, and my happiness at such speedy progress made me forget the heavy load I was carrying. It is true that my feet were very sore, but they seemed to recover during my daytime rest. I often slept for ten hours at a stretch.

At length I came to the farmhouse of my Indian friend to whom I had in the previous year entrusted my money and effects. It was now May, and we had agreed that he was to expect me at midnight any day during the month. I purposely did not walk straight into the house, and before doing anything else I hid my rucksack, as betrayal was not beyond the bounds of possibility.

The moon shone full upon the farmhouse, so I hid myself in the darkness of the stable and twice softly called my friend's name. The door was flung open, and out rushed my friend, who threw himself on the ground and kissed my feet. Tears of joy flowed down his cheeks. He led me to a room lying apart from the house, in the door of which an enormous key was hanging. Here he lit a pinewood torch and opened a wooden chest. Inside were all my things, carefully sewn up in cotton bags. Deeply touched by his loyalty, I unpacked everything and gave him a reward. You can imagine that I enjoyed the food that he then set before me. I asked him to get me provisions and a woolen blanket before the following night. He promised to do this and in addition made me a present of a pair of handwoven woolen drawers and a shawl.

The next day I slept in a neighboring wood and came in the evening to fetch my things. My friend gave me a hearty meal and accompanied me for a part of my way. He insisted on carrying some of my baggage, undernourished as he was and hardly able to keep pace with me. I soon sent him back and after the friendliest parting found myself alone again.

It may have been a little after midnight when I ran into a bear standing on his hind legs in the middle of my path, growling at me. At this point the sound of the swiftly running waters of the Ganges was so loud that we had neither of us heard the other's approach. Pointing my primitive spear at his heart, I backed up step by step so as to keep my eyes fixed on him. Around the first bend of the track, I hurriedly lit a fire, and pulling out a burning stick, I brandished it in front of me and moved forward to meet my enemy. But coming around the corner, I found the road clear and the bear gone. Tibetan peasants later told me that bears are aggressive only by day. At night they are afraid to attack.

I had already been on the march for ten days when I reached the village of Nelang, where last year destiny had wrecked my hopes. This time I was a month earlier, and the village was still uninhabited. But what was my delight to find there my four comrades from the camp! They had overtaken me when I was staying with my Indian friend. We took up our quarters in an open house and slept the whole night through. Sattler unfortunately had an attack of mountain sickness; he felt wretched and declared himself unequal to further efforts. He decided to return but promised not to surrender till two days were up, so as not to endanger our escape. Kopp, who in the previous year had penetrated into Tibet by this route in company with the wrestler Krämer, joined me as a partner.

It took us seven long days of marching, however, before we finally reached the pass that forms the frontier between India and Tibet. Our delay was due to a bad miscalculation. After leaving Tirpani, a well-known caravan center, we followed the most easterly of three valleys but eventually had to admit that we had lost our way. In order to find our bearings, Aufschnaiter and I climbed to the top of a mountain from which we expected a good view of the country on the other side. From here we saw Tibet for the first time, but were far too tired to enjoy the prospect, and at an altitude of nearly 18,000 feet, we suffered from lack of oxygen. To our great disappointment, we decided that we must return to Tirpani. There we found that the pass we were bound for lay almost within a stone's throw. Our error had cost us three days and caused us the greatest discouragement. We had to cut our rations and felt the utmost anxiety about our capacity to hold out until we reached the next inhabited place.

From Tirpani our way sloped gently upward by green pastures, through which one of the baby Ganges streams flowed. This brook, which we had known a week back as a raging, deafening torrent racing down the valley, now wound gently through the grasslands. In a few weeks the whole country would be green, and the numerous camping places, recognizable from their fire-blackened stones, made us picture to ourselves the caravans that cross the passes from India into Tibet in the summer season. A troop of mountain sheep passed in front of us. Light-footed as chamois, they soon vanished from our sight without having noticed us. Alas! our stomachs regretted them. It would have been grand to see one of them stewing in our cooking pot, thereby giving us a chance, for once, to eat our fill.

At the foot of the pass, we camped in India for the last time. Instead of the hearty meat dinner we had been dreaming of, we baked skimpy cakes with the last of our flour mixed with water and laid on hot stones. It was bitterly cold, and our only protection against the icy mountain wind that stormed through the valley was a stone wall.

At last on May 17, 1944, we stood at the top of the Tsangchokla Pass. We knew from our maps that our altitude was 17,200 feet.

So here we were on the frontier between India and Tibet, so long the object of our wishful dreams.

Here we enjoyed for the first time a sense of security, for we knew that no Englishman could arrest us here. We did not know how the Tibetans would treat us, but as our country was not at war with Tibet, we hoped confidently for a hospitable welcome.

On the top of the pass were heaps of stones and prayer flags dedicated to their gods by pious Buddhists. It was very cold, but we took a long rest and considered our situation. We had almost no knowledge of the language and very little money. Above all, we were near starvation and must find human habitation as soon as possible. But as far as we could see, there were only empty mountain heights and deserted valleys. Our maps showed only vaguely the presence of villages in this region. Our final objective, as I have already mentioned, was the Japanese lines—thousands of miles away. The route we planned to follow led first to the holy mountain of Kailas and thence along the course of the Brahmaputra till at last it would bring us to Eastern Tibet. Kopp, who had been in Tibet the year before and had been expelled from that country, thought that the indications on our maps were reasonably accurate.

After a steep descent we reached the course of the Opchu and rested there at noon. Overhanging rock walls flanked the valley like a canyon. The valley was absolutely uninhabited, and only a wooden pole showed that men sometimes came there. The other side of the valley consisted of slopes of shale up which we had to climb. It was evening before we reached the plateau, and we bivouacked in icy cold. Our fuel during the last few days had been the branches of thorn bushes, which we found on the slopes. Here there was nothing growing, so we had to use dry cow dung, laboriously collected.

BEFORE NOON THE NEXT DAY, we reached our first Tibetan village, Kasapuling, which consisted of six houses. The place appeared to be completely deserted, and when we knocked at the doors, nothing stirred. We then discovered that all the villagers were busy sowing barley in the surrounding fields. Sitting on their haunches, they put each individual grain of seed into the ground with the regularity and speed of machines. We looked at them with feelings that might compare with those of Columbus when he met his first Indians. Would they receive us as friends or foes? For the moment they took no notice of us. The cries of an old woman, looking like a witch, were the only sound we heard. They were not aimed at us, but at the swarms of wild pigeons that swooped down to get at the newly planted grain. Until evening the villagers hardly deigned to bestow a glance on us, so we four established our camp near one of the houses, and when at nightfall the people came in from the fields, we tried to trade with them. We offered them money for one of their sheep or goats, but they showed themselves disinclined to trade. As Tibet has no frontier posts, the whole population is brought up to be hostile to foreigners, and there are severe penalties for any Tibetan who sells anything to a foreigner. We were starving and had no choice but to intimidate them. We threatened to take one of their animals by force if they would not freely sell us one, and as none of the four of us looked a weakling, this method of argument eventually succeeded. It was pitch dark before they handed to us for a shamelessly high price the oldest billy goat they could put their hands on. We knew we were being blackmailed, but we put up with it, as we wished to win the hospitality of this country.

We slaughtered the goat in a stable, and it was not till midnight that we fell to on the half-cooked meat.

We spent the next day resting and looking more closely at the houses. These were stone built with flat roofs on which the fuel was laid out to dry. The Tibetans who live here cannot be compared with those who inhabit the interior, whom we got to know later. The brisk summer caravan traffic with India has spoiled them. We found them dirty, dark-skinned, and shifty-eyed, with no trace of that gaiety for which their race is famous. They went sulkily to their daily work, and one felt that they had settled in this sterile country only in order to earn good money from the caravans for the produce of their land. These six houses on the frontier formed, as I later was able to confirm, almost the only village without a monastery.

The next morning we left this inhospitable place without hindrance. We were by now fairly well rested, and Kopp's Berlin native wit, which during the last few days had suffered an eclipse, had us laughing again. We crossed over fields to go downhill into a little valley. On the way up the opposite slope to the next plateau, we felt the weight of our packs more than ever. This physical fatigue was caused mainly by a reaction to the disappointment that this long-dreamed-of country had up to now caused us. We had to spend the night in an inhospitable sort of depression in the ground, which barely shielded us from the wind.

At the very beginning of our journey, we had detailed each member of the party for special duties. Fetching water, lighting fires, and making tea meant hard work. Every evening we emptied our rucksacks in order to use them as foot bags against the cold. When that evening I shook mine out, there was a small explosion. My matches had caught fire from friction—a proof of the dryness of the air in the high Tibetan plateau.

By the first light of day, we examined the place in which we had camped. We observed that the depression in which we had bivouacked must have been made by the hand of man, as it was quite circular and had perpendicular walls. It had perhaps been originally designed as a trap for wild beasts. Behind us lay the Himalayas with Kamet's perfect snow pyramid; in front, forbidding, mountainous country. We went downhill through a sort of loess formation and arrived toward noon in the village of Dushang. Again we found very few houses and a reception as inhospitable as at Kasapuling. Peter Aufschnaiter, in vain, showed off all his knowledge of the language acquired in years of study, and our gesticulations were equally unsuccessful.

However, we saw here for the first time a proper Tibetan

monastery. Black holes gaped in the loam walls, and on a ridge we saw the ruins of gigantic buildings. Hundreds of monks must have lived here once. Now there were only a few living in a more modern house, but they never showed themselves to us. On a terrace in front of the monastery were ordered lines of red-painted tombstones.

Somewhat depressed we returned to our tent, which was for us a little home in the midst of an interesting but oddly hostile world.

In Dushang, too, there were—when we came—no officials to whom we might have applied for leave to reside or travel. But this omission was soon to be rectified, for the officials were already on their way to find us. On the next day, we resumed our march with Kopp and myself in front, and Aufschnaiter and Treipel a little way behind us. Suddenly we heard the tinkling of bells, and two men on ponies rode up and summoned us in the local dialect to return to India by the same way as we had come. We knew that we should not do any good by talking, and so to their surprise we just pushed them aside. Luckily they made no use of their weapons, thinking no doubt that we too were armed. After a few feeble attempts to delay us, they rode away, and we reached without hindrance the next settlement, which we knew was the seat of a local governor.

The country through which we passed on this day's march was waterless and empty with no sign of life anywhere. Its central point, the little town of Tsaparang, was inhabited only during winter months, and when we went in search of the governor we learned that he was packing his things for the move to Shangtse, his summer residence. We were not a little astonished to find that he was one of the two armed men who had met us on the way and ordered us to go back. His attitude, accordingly, was not welcoming, and we could hardly persuade him to give us a little flour in exchange for medicine. The little medicine chest that I carried in my pack proved our salvation then, and was often to be of good service to us in the future.

At length the governor showed us a cave where we could pass the night, telling us once more that we must leave Tibet, using the road by which we had come. We refused to accept his ruling and tried to explain to him that Tibet was a neutral state and ought to offer us asylum. But his mind could not grasp this idea, and he was not competent to make a decision, even if he had understood it. So we proposed to him that we should leave the decision to a high-ranking official, a monk whose official residence was in Thuling, only five miles away.

Tsaparang was really a curiosity. I had learned from the books I had studied in the camp that the first Catholic mission station in Tibet had been founded here in 1624. The Portuguese Jesuit Antonio de Andrade had formed a Catholic community and is said to have built a church. We searched for traces of it but could not find any remains of a Christian building. Our own experience made us realize how difficult it must have been for Father Antonio to establish his mission here.

The next day we marched to Thuling to lay our case before the monk. There we found Aufschnaiter and Treipel, who had followed a different route. We all visited the abbot of the cloister, who happened to be the official we wanted, but found him deaf to our prayers to be allowed to proceed on our way eastward. He agreed to sell us provisions only if we promised to go back to Shangtse, which lay on our road to India. There was nothing to do but agree, as we were without food.

There was also a secular official in Thuling, but we found him even less accommodating. He angrily refused all our attempts to approach him and went so far as to arouse the hostility of the people against us. We had to pay a high price for some rancid butter and maggoty meat. A few faggots cost us a rupee. The only pleasant memory that we took with us from Thuling was the picture of the terraced monastery with its gold-pointed roof pinnacles gleaming in the sunlight and the waters of the Sutlej flowing below. This is the largest monastery in West Tibet, but it has a very deserted aspect and we heard that only twenty out of 260 were actually in residence.

When we had finally promised to return to Shangtse, they gave us four donkeys to carry our baggage. At first we wondered at their letting us go without any guards and only accompanied by the donkey man, but we soon came to the conclusion that in Tibet the simplest method of supervision is to forbid the sale of provisions to strangers unprovided with a permit.

The presence of the asses did not add to the pleasure of the journey. It took us a full hour to wade across the Sutlej because the beasts were so tiresome. We continually had to urge them on so as to reach the next village before dark. This place was called Phywang and had very few inhabitants, but looking up at the hillside we saw, as in Tsaparang, hundreds of caves.

We spent the night here. Shangtse was a full day's march distant. On our way there the next day, we had the most glorious views of the Himalayas to compensate us in some measure for the barren landscape through which we were driving our donkeys. On this stretch we first met the kiang, a sort of wild ass, which lives in Central Asia and enchants travelers by the gracefulness of its movements. This animal is about the size of a mule. It often shows curiosity and comes up to look at passers-by—and then turns and trots off in the most elegant manner. The kiang feeds on grass and is left in peace by the inhabitants. Its only enemy is the wolf. Since I first saw them, these untamed, beautiful beasts have seemed a symbol of freedom.

Shangtse was another hamlet with only half a dozen houses built of weather-dried mud bricks and cubes of turf. We found the village no more hospitable than the others. Here we met an un-friendly official from Tsaparang, who had moved into his summer quarters. He would on no consideration allow us to proceed any farther into Tibet, but gave us the choice of traveling via Tsaparang or taking the western route over the Shipki Pass into India. Only if we agreed to one of these routes would he consent to sell us provisions.

We chose the Shipki route, firstly because it was new country for us, and secondly because we hoped in our hearts to find some way out. For the moment we could buy as much butter, meat, and flour as we wanted. All the same we felt dejected at the unenliven-ing prospect of landing once more behind the barbed wire. Treipel, who found nothing pleasant about Tibet, was ready to give up and to cease from further attempts to stay in this barren land.

We spent the next day mostly in satisfying our appetites. I also brought my diary up to date and attended to my inflamed tendons, which had been caused by my forced night marches. I was deter-mined to take any risk to avoid going back to confinement, and Aufschnaiter was of my way of thinking. The next morning we got to know the true character of the local governor. We had cooked meat in a copper pot, and Aufschnaiter must have been slightly poisoned, as he felt very ill. When I asked the governor to allow us to stay a little longer, he showed more ill will than ever. I quarreled with him violently, and to some effect, for he finally con-sented to supply Aufschnaiter with a horse to ride as well as putting two yaks at our disposal to carry our baggage.

This was my first acquaintance with the yak. It is the regular Tibetan beast of burden and can live only in high altitudes. This long-haired species of ox needs a lot of training before you can make use of him. The cows are considerably smaller than the bulls and give excellent milk.

The soldier who had accompanied us from Shangtse carried a letter for our safe conduct, and this entitled us to buy whatever provisions we needed. It also entitled us to change our yaks without payment at each halting place.

The weather by day was pleasant and comparatively warm, but the nights were very cold. We passed a number of villages and inhabited caves, but the people took little notice of us. Our donkey driver, who came from Lhasa, was nice and friendly to us and enjoyed going into the villages and swaggering about. We found the population less mistrustful; no doubt it was the influence of our safe conduct. While we were trekking through the district of Rongchung, we found ourselves following Sven Hedin's route for a few days, and as I was a great admirer of this explorer, lively memories of his descriptions were kindled in my mind. The terrain we traversed remained very much the same. We continued to cross plateaux, climb down into deep valleys, and climb painfully up the other side. Often these were so narrow that one could have called across them, but it took hours to walk across. These constant ups and downs, which doubled the length of our journey, got on one's nerves, and we thought our own thoughts in silence. Nevertheless we made progress and had not to bother about our food. At one point, when we had the idea of changing our menu, we tried our luck at fishing. Having had no luck with the hook, we stripped and waded into the clear mountain brooks and tried to catch the fish in our hands. But they seemed to have better things to do than to end up in our cooking pot.

So we gradually approached the Himalaya range and sorrowfully the Indian frontier. The temperature had become warmer, as we were no longer so high up. It was just here that the Sutlej breaks its way through the Himalayas. The villages in this region looked like little oases, and around the houses there were actually apricot orchards and vegetable gardens.

Eleven days from Shangtse, we came to the frontier village of Shipki. The date was June 9—we had been wandering about Tibet for more than three weeks. We had seen a lot, and we had learned by bitter experience that life in Tibet without a residence permit was not possible.

We spent one more night in Tibet, romantically encamped under apricot trees whose fruit unfortunately was not yet ripe. Here I succeeded in buying a donkey for eighty rupees on the pretext that I would need a baggage animal for my things in India. In the interior of Tibet I could never have managed this, but near the frontier it was different and I felt that a baggage animal was absolutely essential to the successful accomplishment of my plans.

Our donkey man left us here and took his animals with him. "Perhaps we shall meet again in Lhasa," he said with a smile. He had spoken to us enthusiastically about the pretty girls and good beer to be found in the capital. Our road wound up to the top of the pass, where we reached the frontier, but there were no frontier posts, Tibetan or Indian. Nothing but the usual heaps of stones and prayer flags, and the first sign of civilization in the shape of a milestone that said: SIMLA 200 MILES.

We were in India once more, but not one of us had the intention of staying long in this land in which a wire-fenced camp was waiting to receive us.

3

Into Tibet

My plan was to seize the first opportunity to slip over the frontier again into Tibet. We were all of us convinced that the minor officials we had hitherto encountered were simply not competent to decide about our case. This time we had to approach some higher authority. To find what we wanted, we should have to go to Gartok, the capital of Western Tibet, which was the seat of the governor of the region.

So we marched down the great, much used trade road a few miles till we came to the first Indian village. This was Namgya. Here we could stay without arousing suspicion, as we had come from Tibet and not from the plains of India. We passed ourselves off as American soldiers, bought fresh supplies, and slept in the public resthouse. Then we separated. Aufschnaiter and Treipel went down the trade road that flanked the Sutlej, while Kopp and I drove our donkey into a valley that ran in a northerly direction toward a pass that led over into Tibet. As we knew from our maps, we had first to go through the Spiti Valley, which was inhabited. I was very glad that Kopp had attached himself to me, as he was a clever, practical, and cheerful companion, and his vein of Berlin wit never petered out.

For two days we tramped upward on the bank of the Spiti River; then we followed one of the nearby valleys, which would clearly bring us over the Himalayas. This region was not well marked on our maps, and we learned from the natives that we had already passed the frontier when we crossed a certain bridge known as Sangsam. During all this part of our journey, we had on the right of us Riwo Phargyul, a beautifully shaped peak more than 22,000 feet high on the crest of the Himalayas. We had reached Tibet at one of the few places where Tibetan territory extends into the Himalaya range. Of course we now began to be anxious and to wonder how far we should get this time. Luckily no one knew us here, and no unkind official had warned the people against us. When questioned, we said we were pilgrims bound for the holy mountain of Kailas.

The first Tibetan village we reached was called Kyurik. It consisted of two houses. The next, Dotso, was considerably larger. Here we ran into a number of monks—more than a hundred of them—in quest of poplar trunks, which they were going to carry over the pass to Trashigang and there use for one of the monastery buildings. This monastery is the largest in the province of Tsurubyin, and the abbot is at the same time the highest secular officer. We began to fear that our journey might come to a premature end when we met this dignitary. However, when he questioned us, we said we were the advance party of a large European force that had obtained official permission to enter Tibet from the central government at Lhasa. He appeared to believe us, and much relieved, we continued our journey. We had a grueling climb to the top of a pass called by the Tibetans Bud-Bud La. This pass must be over 18,000 feet high. The air was unpleasantly rarefied, and the ice tongues of a neighboring glacier projected over the route.

On the way we met a few Bhutias, who also wanted to go into the interior. They were nice, friendly people, and they invited us to share their fire and drink a cup of rancid butter tea with them. As we had pitched our camp near them, they brought us in the evening a tasty dish of nettle spinach.

The region through which we were traveling was completely unpopulated, and during the next eight days of our march, we met only one small caravan. I have a vivid recollection of one person whom I encountered on this stretch of road. This was a young nomad, muffled in a long sheepskin coat and wearing a pigtail, as all Tibetan men who are not monks do. He led us to his black tent made of yak's hair, where his wife was waiting for him. She was a merry creature, always laughing. Inside the tent we found a treasure that made our mouths water—a haunch of venison. Our host gladly sold us a portion of the meat for an absurdly low price. He begged us to say nothing about his hunting, or he would get into trouble. Taking of life, whether human or animal, is contrary to the tenets of Buddhism, and consequently, hunting is forbidden. Tibet is governed on a feudal system, whereby men, beasts, and land belong to the Dalai Lama, whose orders have the force of law.

I found I was able to make myself understood by these pleasant companions, and the feeling that my knowledge of the language was improving gave me great pleasure. We arranged to go hunting together the next day, and meanwhile made ourselves at home in the tent of the young couple. The nomad and his wife were the first cheerful and friendly Tibetans we had met, and I shall not forget them. The highlight of our host's hospitality consisted in his producing a wooden bottle of barley beer. It was a cloudy, milky liquid that bore no resemblance to what we call beer, but it had the same effect.

The next morning the three of us went hunting. Our young friend had an antediluvian muzzle loader and in a breast pocket carried leaden bullets, gunpowder, and a quick match. When we saw the first flock of wild sheep he managed laboriously to light the quick match by using a flint. We were anxious to know how this museum piece of a gun would function. There was a report like thunder, and by the time I had got clear of the smoke, there was no sign of a sheep to be seen. Then we saw the flock galloping away in the distance; before they vanished over the rocky ridge, some of them turned around to eye us with a mocking glance. We could only laugh at our own discomfiture, but in order not to return with empty hands, we picked wild onions, which grow everywhere on the hillsides and which go so well with venison.

Our friend's wife apparently was used to her husband's bad luck in the hunting field. When she saw us returning without any game, she received us with screams of laughter, and her slit eyes almost disappeared in her merriment. She had carefully prepared a meal from the game her husband had killed a few days before and now got down enthusiastically to cooking it. We watched the operation and were somewhat astonished when she slipped off the upper half of her great fur mantle, around the waist of which she wore a bright colored belt, without a trace of shyness. The heavy fur had hindered her movements, so she stripped to the waist and carried on happily. Later on we often encountered similar examples of natural simplicity. It was with real regret that we parted from this friendly couple, when fully rested and with our bellies full of good fresh meat we set out on our way. As we traveled we often saw the black forms of wild yaks grazing far away on the mountainside. The sight of them prompted our donkey to make a bid for independence: he dashed through a widish stream and before we could reach him had shaken our packs off his back. We followed him, cursing and swearing, and eventually caught him.

Then, as we were busy drying our things on the farther side of the water, two figures suddenly came into view. We recognized the first at once from his regular, slow, mountaineer's stride—it was Peter Aufschnaiter, with a hired bearer. It may be thought that such a meeting in such a place sounds farfetched, but it is only by certain valleys and passes that one comes over the mountain ranges, and we and Peter had chosen the most well-trodden route.

After warm greetings Aufschnaiter began to tell us what had happened to him in the interval. On June 17, he had parted from Treipel, whom he left riding into India on a horse, meaning to pass himself off as an Englishman. He bought the horse with the last of his money. Aufschnaiter himself had been ill, but when he had recovered had followed us. He had on the way heard some of the latest war news to which, though we were living in another world, we listened greedily.

At first Aufschnaiter did not want to go with us to Gartok, as he believed that we would be turned out of the country again. He thought it would be wiser to press straight on into Central Tibet and join up with the nomads there. Finally we all went on together, and Aufschnaiter and I were not to part company again for years. We knew that if everything went smoothly we needed about five days to get to Gartok. We had to cross another high pass, the Bongru La. Camping these days was no pleasure. It was very cold by night at 17,000 feet!

Small incidents provided variety. Once it was the spectacle of a fight between wild asses. The combatants were two stallions, probably fighting for the lordship over the mares in the herd. Chunks of turf flew, and the earth shook under their hoofs. The duelists were so absorbed in their struggle that they did not notice us onlookers. Meanwhile the mares, greedy for sensation, danced around, and the arena was often hidden in a thick cloud of dust.

After crossing the two passes, we had the Himalayas behind us once more, and I was glad to be away from them, as we were at last reaching warmer regions. Coming down into the Indus Valley, we met numbers of yak-drawn caravans bearing wool to India. We were struck by the size and strength of these beasts. Their drivers, too, were well-set-up youths, who despite the fierce cold were naked to the waist. Both men and women wore their fur coats inside out with the fur against their bare bodies. They keep their arms out of the sleeves, so as not to hamper their freedom of movement. The drivers start the yaks off by slinging stones at them and keep them on the track by the same method. They seemed in no way interested in us foreigners, and we pursued our way unmolested.

We marched for five successive days along the upper waters of the Indus before we arrived at Gartok. The scenery was unforgettable. It was the colors that enchanted the eye, and I have seldom seen all the hues of a painter's palette so harmoniously blended. Alongside the clear waters of the Indus were light yellow fields of borax, with the green shoots of springtime springing up near them (for spring in these regions does not come until June). In the background were the gleaming snow peaks.

The first village on the far side of the Himalayas is Trashigang, consisting of just a few houses grouped around a fortress-like monastery surrounded by a moat. Here we again found an ill-disposed population, but they showed no astonishment at seeing us and gave us no real trouble. This time we had arrived just in the season in which Indian traders stream into the country to buy up the wool. We had no difficulty in obtaining provisions from these people. Aufschnaiter tried in vain to turn his gold bracelet into cash. Had he done so, he would have been able to afford to push on directly into Inner Tibet without touching Gartok. During the whole of our march, we were repeatedly stopped by prosperous-looking mounted Tibetans, who asked us what we had to sell. As we had no servants and were driving a pack donkey, they could not imagine that we were anything but traders. We became convinced every Tibetan, whether poor or rich, is a born trader, and exchange and barter his greatest passion.

From our reading we know that Gartok was the capital of Western Tibet, and the seat of the viceroy; our geography books had told us that it was the highest town in the world. When, however, we finally set eyes on this famous place, we could hardly help laughing. The first thing we saw were a few nomads' tents scattered about the immense plain; then we caught sight of a few mud-brick huts. That was Gartok. Except for a few stray dogs, there was no sign of life.

We pitched our little tent on the bank of the Gartang-Tchu, a tributary of the Indus. At last a few curious individuals came up, and we learned from them that neither of the two high officials was in the town and only the "second viceroy's" agent could receive us. We decided to submit our petition to this personage at once. Going into his office we had to bend low, for there was no door, only a hole in front of which hung a greasy curtain. We came into a dimly lit room with paper gummed over the windows. When our eyes had grown accustomed to the twilight, we discerned a man who looked intelligent and distinguished, sitting like a Buddha on the floor before us. From his left ear dangled an earring at least six inches long as a sign of his rank. There was also a woman present, who turned out to be the wife of the absent official. Behind us pressed a crowd of children and servants who wished to see these peculiar foreigners from close at hand.

We were very politely requested to sit down and were immediately offered dried meat, cheese, butter, and tea. The atmosphere was cordial and warmed our hearts, and conversation flowed fairly freely with the aid of an English-Tibetan dictionary and supplementary gestures. Our hopes rose quickly, but we abstained from revealing all our preoccupations at this first interview. We said that we were fugitive Germans and begged for the hospitality of neutral Tibet.

The next day I brought the agent some medicines as a present. He was much pleased and asked me how to use them, whereupon I wrote out directions. At this point we ventured to ask him if he would not grant us a travel permit. He did not directly refuse but bade us await the coming of his chief, who was on a pilgrimage to Mount Kailas but who was expected to return in a few days.

In the interval we made good friends with the agent. I gave him a burning glass, an object of which one can make good use in Tibet. The customary return gift was not long in coming. One afternoon some bearers carried a present of butter, meat, and flour to our tents. And not long after came the agent himself, accompanied by a retinue of servants, to return our visit. When he saw how primitively we were lodged in our tents, he could not get over his astonishment that Europeans led such simple lives.

However, as the time came near for the return of his chief, his friendliness began to flag, and he withdrew himself almost entirely from our society. Responsibility began to oppress him. Indeed, he went so far as to refuse to sell us provisions; luckily, however, there were Indian traders here, ready to help us out for good money.

One morning we heard the sound of bells in the distance as a huge mule-drawn caravan approached the village. Soldiers rode ahead followed by a swarm of male and female servants, and after them members of the Tibetan nobility, also mounted, whom we now saw for the first time. The senior of the two viceroys, whom they call *garpons* in Tibet, was arriving. He and his wife wore splendid silk robes and carried pistols in their girdles. The whole village assembled to see the spectacle. Immediately after arriving, the garpon moved in solemn procession into the monastery to give thanks to his gods for his safe return from the pilgrimage.

Aufschnaiter composed a short letter begging for an audience. As no answer came, we set out in the late afternoon to visit the garpon. His house was not essentially different from that of his agent, but inside it was cleaner and of better quality. The garpon, a high official, is invested for the duration of his mission with the fourth rank in the hierarchy of the nobles. He is in charge of five districts, which are administered by nobles of the fifth, sixth, and seventh rank. During his period of office, the garpon wears a golden amulet in his piled-up hair, but he may wear this ornament only while on duty in Gartok. In Lhasa he is reduced to the fifth rank. All the nobles in Tibet are ranked in seven classes, to the first of which only the Dalai Lama belongs. All secular officials wear their hair piled up on their heads, monks are shaven, and the ordinary people wear pigtails.

At last we came into the presence of this potentate. We explained our case to him in all its details, and he listened to us with friendly patience. Often he could not refrain from smiling at our defective Tibetan, while his retainers laughed out loud. This merriment added a spice to the conversation and created a friendly atmosphere. The garpon promised to consider our case carefully and to talk it over with the representative of his colleague. At the end of the audience, we were hospitably entertained and received tea made in the European fashion. Afterward the garpon sent presents to our tents, and we began to hope for a happy issue.

Our next audience was rather more formal but still cordial. It was a regular official meeting. The garpon sat on a sort of throne, and near him on a lower seat was the agent of his colleague. On a low table lay a file of letters written on Tibetan paper. The garpon informed us that he could give us passes and transport only for the province of Ngari. We would in no circumstances be allowed to enter the inner provinces of Tibet. We quickly took counsel together and suggested that he should give us a travel permit to the frontier of Nepal. After some hesitation he promised to communicate our request to the government in Lhasa, but he explained to us that the answer might not arrive for some months. We were not anxious to wait all that time in Gartok. We had not given up the idea of pushing on to the east and were anxious to continue our journey at all costs. As Nepal was a neutral country situated in the direction which we wished to go, we felt that we could be satisfied with the result of the negotiations.

The garpon then kindly asked us to remain for a few days longer as his guests, as pack animals and a guide had to be found. After three days our travel pass was delivered to us. It stipulated that our route should pass through the following places—Ngakhyu, Sersok, Möntse, Barga, Thokchen, Lholung, Shamtsang, Truksum, and Gyabnak. It was also laid down that we had the right to requisition two yaks. A very important clause required the inhabitants to sell us provisions at the local prices, and to give us free fuel and servants for the evenings.

We were very glad to have obtained so much in the way of facilities. The garpon invited us to a farewell dinner in the course of which I managed to sell him my watch. Afterward he made us give him our word of honor not to go to Lhasa from his territory.

At last, on July 13, we bade farewell to Gartok and started on our way. Our little caravan, now of decent proportions, consisted of our two yaks with their driver and my small donkey, which was now in good shape and carried no more than a teakettle. Then came our guide, a young Tibetan named Norbu, on horseback, while we three Europeans modestly brought up the rear on foot.

NOW AGAIN for weeks we were on the way. During the whole of the next month, we passed no inhabited place of any size—only nomad camps and isolated *tasam* houses. These are caravansaries in which one can change the yaks and find a lodging.

In one of these tasams I succeeded in exchanging my donkey for a yak. I was very proud of this bargain, which greatly multiplied my assets, but my satisfaction was short-lived—the beast turned out to be so refractory that I would have been glad to be rid of him. I was actually able to exchange him later for a younger, smaller animal. This creature also gave trouble, and it was only after having his nose pierced and fitted with a ring of juniper wood tied to a rope that I was able to keep him on the road. We called him Armin.

The country through which we had been traveling for days had an original beauty. The wide plains were diversified by stretches of hilly country with low passes. We often had to wade through swift-running ice-cold brooks. While in Gartok, we had had occasional showers of hail, but now the weather was mainly fine and warm. By this time we all had thick beards, which helped to protect us against the sun. It was long since we had seen a glacier, but as we were approaching the tasam at Barka, a chain of glaciers gleaming in the sunshine came into view. The landscape was dominated by the 25,000-foot peak of Gurla Mandhata; less striking, but far more famous, was the sacred Mount Kailas, 3,000 feet lower, which stands in majestic isolation apart from the Himalaya range. When we first caught sight of it, our Tibetans prostrated themselves and prayed. For Buddhists and Hindus, this mountain is the home of their gods, and the dearest wish of all the pious is to visit it as pilgrims once in their lives. The faithful often travel thousands of miles to reach it and spend years on the pilgrimage. During their journey they live on alms and hope that their reward will be a higher incarnation in a future life. Pilgrims' roads converge here from all points of the compass. At the places from which the first sight of the mountain can be obtained are set up heaps of stones, grown through the centuries to giant proportions, expressing the childlike piety of the pilgrims, each of whom, following ancient observance, adds fresh stones to the heaps. We, too, would have liked to travel around the mountain as the pilgrims do, but the unfriendly master of the caravansary at Barka prevented us by threatening to stop our future transport facilities unless we continued on our way.

For two whole days, we had the glaciers to look at. We mountaineers were more strongly attracted to the majestic Gurla Mandhata, mirrored in the waters of Lake Manasarovar, than by the Sacred Mountain. We pitched our tents on the shore of the lake and feasted our eyes on the indescribably beautiful picture of this tremendous mountain, which seemed to grow out of the lake. This is certainly one of the loveliest spots on earth. The lake is held to be sacred, and around it one finds many small monasteries in which the pilgrims lodge and perform their devotions. Many pilgrims creep around the lake on their hands and knees, and carry home jars of the holy water. Every pilgrim bathes in its icy cold water. We did likewise, though not from piety. Here I nearly came to grief. After swimming out some little way from the shore, I got into a boggy place from which I extricated myself only with a tremendous effort. My comrades had not noticed my desperate struggle to get clear of the mud.

As we were, at this time of year, a little in advance of the pilgrimage, most of the people we met were traders. We saw also many suspicious-looking people, for this region is notorious as the El Dorado of robbers, who find it hard to resist the temptation to attack the traders frequenting the markets. The biggest market in the region is that of Gyanyima. Here hundreds of tents form a huge camp given over to buying and selling. The tents of the Indians are made out of cheap cotton material, while those of the Tibetans are woven from yak's hair and are so heavy that it takes one or even two yaks to carry them.

We wandered for some hours in an easterly direction along the lake and felt as if we were on a seaside walk. Our pleasure in the beauty was disturbed only by the midges, which we did not get rid of till we were clear of the lake.

Proceeding toward Thokchen we met an important-looking caravan. It was the new district governor of Tsaparang on the way to his post from Lhasa. We halted by the roadside, and our guide, with whom we had never got on really friendly terms, made a deep, stiff obeisance and put out his tongue in greeting—a perfect picture of submissiveness. He explained our presence: weapons which had threatened us were put away and we were handed dried fruit and nuts.

In our persons there was no longer any sign of European superiority to be seen. We lived like nomads; for the past three months we had been sleeping mainly in the open air, and our standards of comfort were lower than those of the native population. We camped and cooked and made our fires in the open whatever the weather, while the nomads could find shelter and warmth in their heavy tents. But if we looked as if we had come down in the world, our wits were not blunted and our minds were continually occupied. Very few Europeans had been in these regions, and we knew that everything we observed might have a value later on. We still thought then that we should be returning to civilization within a measurable time. Common dangers and struggles had linked us in a close bond of companionship; each knew the others' virtues and failings, and so we were able to help one another in times of depression.

On we went over low-lying passes till we came to the source of the Brahmaputra, which the Tibetans call the Tsangpo. This region is not only of religious significance to Asiatic pilgrims, it is also highly interesting geographically, for it contains the sources of the Indus, the Sutlej, the Kaxnali, and the Brahmaputra. For the Tibetans, who are accustomed to give a symbolical religious sense to all designations, the names of these rivers are associated with the sacred animals—the lion, the elephant, the peacock, and the horse.

For the next fortnight, we followed the Tsangpo. Fed by numerous streams from the nearby Himalayas, this river grows larger all the time, and the bigger it gets the more tranquil is its stream. Now the weather was continually changing. Within minutes one was alternately freezing or roasting in the sunshine. Hailstorms, rain, and sunshine followed each other in quick succession—one morning we awoke to find our tent buried in snow, which in a few hours melted in the hot sunshine. Our Europeans clothes were unsuited to these continual changes of temperature, and we envied the Tibetans their practical sheepskin cloaks, belted at the waist and with long wide sleeves to take the place of gloves.

Despite these inconveniences we made good progress, stopping whenever we came to a roadhouse. From time to time we had a view of the Himalayas, which surpass in natural beauty anything I have ever seen. We met fewer and fewer nomads, and the only living creatures we saw on the right bank of the Brahmaputra were gazelles and onagers. We were now approaching Gyabnak, the last name on the list of places mentioned on our travel permit. Further than this the authority of our friend in Gartok did not extend. The decision as to what to do next was taken out of our hands, for on the third day of our stay at Gyabnak a messenger arrived in breathless haste from Tradün and summoned us to go at once to that place. Two high officials wanted to see us. We had no regrets about leaving Gyabnak, which was so small that it hardly deserved to be called a place. It consisted of a single house belonging to a monastic official of the province of Bongpa. The nearest nomad tent was over an hour's march away. We started at once and spent the night in a lonely place inhabited only by wild asses.

I shall always remember the next day for one of the most beautiful experiences I have ever had. As we marched forward we caught sight, after a while, of the gleaming golden towers of a monastery in the far distance. Above them, shining superbly in the morning sun, were tremendous walls of ice, and we gradually realized that we were looking at the giant trio Dhaulagiri, Annapurna, and Manaslu. As Tradün and the filigree towers of its monastery lay at the far end of the plain, we had many hours in which to enjoy the view of these mighty mountains. Not even the necessity of wading through the icy waters of the Tsachu dampened our exuberance.

IT WAS EVENING when we marched into Tradün. In the last rays of the setting sun, the red monastery with its golden roof looked like a fairy palace on the hillside. The houses of the inhabitants, the usual mud-brick dwellings, were built behind the hill to shelter them from the wind. We found the whole population assembled and waiting for us in silence. We were at once taken into a house that had been made ready for us. Hardly had we unloaded our baggage when several servants arrived and invited us most courteously to come to their masters. Full of expectation we followed them to the house of the two high officials.

We walked through a whispering crowd of servants into a good-sized room, where in the highest seats sat a smiling, well-fed monk and by him, at the same level, his secular colleague. A little lower down were seated an abbot, the monastery official from Gyabnak, and a merchant from Nepal. The merchant spoke a few words of English and acted as interpreter. They had prepared a bench with cushions so that we did not have to sit crosslegged on the floor like the Tibetans. Tea and cake were pressed upon us and questioning politely postponed. At last we were asked to show our travel permit. This was passed around and carefully studied by all present. There was a period of oppressive silence. The two officials slowly came out with their misgivings. Could we really be Germans? It was simply incredible that we should be escaped prisoners of war and much more probable that we were British or Russians. They made us fetch our baggage which was unpacked and spread out on the floor of the courtyard and then carefully examined. Their chief worry was the idea that we might have weapons or a transmitting set, and it was difficult to persuade them that we had neither. The only things among our possessions to arouse suspicion were a Tibetan grammar and a history book.

It was stated in our travel permit that we wanted to go to Nepal. The idea seemed to please our questioners, and they promised to help us in every way. They said we could start on the following morning and by crossing the Korela Pass would be in Nepal in two days. This did not altogether suit us. We wished, at all costs, to remain in Tibet and were determined not to give up the idea without a struggle. We begged for right of asylum, hammered on the theme of Tibetan neutrality, and compared the situation of Tibet with that of Switzerland. The officials stubbornly, if courteously, insisted on the conditions laid down in our travel document. However, during the months of our sojourn in Tibet, we had become better acquainted with the mentality of Asiatics and knew that to give way early was against the rules. The remainder of our discussion passed off in perfect calm. We all drank endless cups of tea, and our hosts informed us modestly that they were there on a tax-raising journey and that in Lhasa they were not such exalted persons as they seemed to be in Tradün. They were traveling with twenty servants and a great number of pack animals, so that one got the impression that they were, at the least, ministers.

Before taking our leave, we stated clearly that we wished to remain in Tradün a few days longer. The next day a servant brought an invitation to luncheon from *bönpos*—as all high personages are called in Tibet. We had a wonderful meal of Chinese noodles and I think we must have appeared to be starving, to judge from the masses of food they piled on our plates. We were greatly impressed by the skill with which the Tibetans handled their chopsticks, and our astonishment was great to see them picking up individual grains of rice with them. Mutual wonder helped to create a friendly atmosphere, and there was much hearty laughter. At the end of the meal, beer was served and added to the cheerfulness of the gathering. I noticed that the monks did not drink it.

Gradually the talk veered toward our problems, and we heard that the authorities had decided to send a letter to the central government in Lhasa, communicating our request for permission to stay in Tibet. We were told to compose a petition in the English language, which the two officials desired to forward with their letter. This we did on the spot, and our petition was in our presence affixed to the official letter, which had already been prepared. This was sealed with due ceremony and handed to a courier, who immediately started for Lhasa.

We could scarcely realize the fact of our friendly reception and that we should be allowed to stay in Tradün until an answer arrived from Lhasa. Our experience with junior officials had not been satisfactory, so we asked for written confirmation of the verbal consent to our residence in Tradün. This we obtained. At length we returned to our quarters, happy that things had gone so well. We had hardly arrived when the door was opened, and a regular procession of heavily laden servants trooped in. They brought us sacks of flour, rice, and tsampa as well as four slaughtered sheep. We did not know from whom the gifts had come until the mayor, who had accompanied the servants, explained to us that the two high officials had sent them. When we tried to thank him, the mayor modestly disclaimed all credit, and no one seemed willing to admit the generous action. As we parted, the easygoing Tibetan said something that was to serve me in good stead. The haste of Europeans has no place in Tibet. We must learn patience if we wished to arrive at the goal.

As we three sat alone in our house looking at all the gifts, we could hardly believe in our change of luck. Our request for permission to reside in Tibet was on its way to Lhasa, and we had now enough supplies to last us for months. For shelter we had a thick roof instead of a flimsy tent, and a woman servant—alas, neither young nor beautiful—to light the fire and fetch water. We regretted that we possessed nothing of worth which we might have sent to the bönpo in token of our gratitude. We had nothing but a little medicine to offer him, but we hoped for an occasion to express our thanks in due form. As in Gartok, we had here had occasion to encounter the courtesy of the nobles of Lhasa, in praise of which I had read so much in Sir Charles Bell's books.

As we were to stay for months here, we made plans for passing the time. We must without fail make expeditions in the Annapurna and Dhaulagiri regions and in plains to the north. But, a little later, the abbot, whose assistance the mayor had tried to enlist on our behalf, came to see us. He told us that our stay in Tradün had been approved only on the condition that we must never go further away from the town than one day's march. We could go on excursions wherever we liked, provided we were back before night. If we did not comply with these instructions, he would have to report to Lhasa, and that would no doubt prejudice our whole case.

The village consisted of about twenty houses dominated by the hill on which the monastery stood. It housed only seven monks. The village houses were narrow and crowded together, but, nevertheless, every house had its own courtyard, in which wares were stored. All the inhabitants of the village were in some way connected with trade or transport; the real nomads lived scattered over the plain. We had occasion to attend several religious festivals, the most impressive of which was the harvest thanksgiving. We were now on a friendly footing with all the inhabitants and used to doctor them, being particularly successful in our treatment of wounds and colic.

The monotony of life in Tradün was varied now and again by the visits of high functionaries, and I have a vivid recollection of the arrival of the second garpon on his way to Gartok.

Long before there was any sign of his convoy, soldiers arrived to announce his coming. Then came his cook, who at once began to prepare his food, and it was only the next day that the garpon himself arrived with his caravan and retinue of thirty servants. The whole population, including ourselves, crowded to see him come in. The great man and his family rode on splendid mules, and the elders of the village each conducted a member of the family, holding his animal's bridle, to the quarters prepared for them. We were less impressed by the garpon than by his daughter. She was the first soignée young woman we had seen since 1939 and we found her very pretty. Her clothes were of pure silk and her nails lacquered red. Perhaps she had slightly overdone the rouge, powder, and lipstick, but she exhaled freshness and cleanliness. We asked her if she was the prettiest girl in Lhasa, but she modestly said no, and declared that there were many far prettier girls in the capital. We were very sorry to lose her charming company when the party moved on the next day.

We had a new guest in Tradün soon after—a state official from

Nepal who came to see us but posed as a pilgrim. We felt that he wished to persuade us to go to Nepal against our wishes. He said we should be well received in Katmandu, the capital, and find occupation there. Our journey would be organized by the administration and three hundred rupees already had been allocated for our expenses. That all sounded very attractive—perhaps too attractive—for we knew how great was British influence in Asia. We did not take his advice.

After months we began to lose patience and to get on each other's nerves. Kopp kept on saying that he would gladly accept the invitation to go to Nepal. Aufschnaiter as usual went his own way. He bought four sheep as pack animals and wanted to go to Changthang. It is true that this was contrary to our original decision to await the letter from Lhasa, but we greatly doubted getting a favorable answer.

Aufschnaiter, losing patience, marched out one afternoon with his loaded sheep and pitched his camp a few miles away from Tradün. We helped him to carry his things there and intended to visit him the next day. Kopp also began to pack and the local authorities promised to give him transport. They were very pleased that he had decided to go to Nepal, but they disapproved of Aufschnaiter's behavior. From that day on, guards slept in front of our door. But the next day, to our surprise, Aufschnaiter came back to us with his baggage. His sheep had been attacked by wolves, which had eaten two of them. This compelled him to return, and so we three spent one more evening together.

On the following morning, Kopp bade us farewell. The whole population collected to see him off. So now, out of the seven of us who had broken out of the internment camp, five of whom had made for Tibet, only Aufschnaiter and I remained. We were the only mountaineers in the group, and consequently physically and mentally best fitted for the lonely and strenuous life in this bleak land.

It was now late November, and the caravan routes were no longer much frequented. The monastic official sent us some sheep and twelve loads of yak's dung for fuel—and we needed it, for the temperature was already −12 degrees Centigrade.

4

THE

VILLAGE

OF HAPPINESS

In spite of the wintry weather, we were more than ever determined to leave Tradün, with or without a letter of authorization. We started hoarding provisions and bought a second yak. But just in the middle of our preparations, the abbot arrived with the news that the long-awaited letter had come from Lhasa. What we had secretly feared had come true. We were forbidden to travel into Inner Tibet. The letter was not handed to us personally. We were merely told that we must go by the shortest route to Nepal, but that we might march in Tibetan territory as far as Kyirong. From there it was only eight miles to the Nepalese frontier and seven days' march to the capital, Katmandu. We would be given transport and servants for the journey. We agreed at once to this ruling, as our route would take us somewhat further into Tibet, and the longer we remained on the right side of the law the better.

On December 17, we left Tradün, which had sheltered us for four months. We felt no grudge against the Tibetans for not allowing us to go to Lhasa. Everyone knows how hard it is for foreigners without passports to get a footing in any country. By giving us presents and providing us with transport, the Tibetans had shown hospitality far exceeding that customary in other countries. Although I did not then appreciate our good fortune so much as I do now, Aufschnaiter and I were still thankful for the eight months we had passed outside the barbed wire.

Now we were on the march again. Our convoy consisted of Aufschnaiter and myself accompanied by two servants. One of these carried, wrapped up like a sacred relic, the letter of the government to the district officer at Kyirong. We were all mounted, and our two yaks were kept moving by a driver. One could see from far off that our caravan belonged to persons of consequence—very different from the three down-at-heel vagabonds who had crossed the Himalayas into Tibet some months before.

Our road took us again over the Himalayan watershed toward the southeast. The Tsangpo was already frozen when we crossed it, and the nights in the tent were bitterly cold.

After riding for a week, we reached Dzongka, which was visible from a long way off by reason of a thick cloud of smoke which hung over the houses. Dzongka really deserved to be called a village. It contained about a hundred mud-brick houses grouped about a monastery, and around the village were cultivated fields. The village was situated at the junction of two streams that form the river Kosi and, penetrating the Himalayas, flow into Nepal. The place was enclosed by a thirty-foot rampart and commanded by a splendid peak, some 20,000 feet high, called by the natives Chogulhari. It was Christmas Day when we came into Dzongka— our first Christmas since we had escaped. We were lodged in surprisingly comfortable quarters. The tree line was only two days away, and wood was no longer an expensive luxury; it could be used for building and for all household needs. A contraption of tin built around the stove in which we burned crackling juniper wood warmed the whole room very agreeably. When evening came we lit some Tibetan butter lamps, and to celebrate the day we soon had a leg of mutton stewing in our cooking pot.

As in every other place in Tibet, there were no public inns here. Billets in private houses are assigned to travelers by the authorities. This is done by rotation, so that the population is not too badly inconvenienced, and the arrangement forms part of the taxation system.

We had not planned to stay here long, but we were kept in Dzongka a whole month by heavy snowfalls. All day thick snowflakes fell and communications were interrupted. We were glad of our rest here, and interested ourselves in some of the activities of the monks and enjoyed as spectators the performances of a group of dancers from Nyenam.

A number of aristocratic officials lived here, and we soon made friends with them. By now we spoke good Tibetan and carried on long conversations through which we got to know much about the manners and customs of the country. St. Sylvester's Eve passed uncelebrated, but our thoughts dwelt more than ever on home.

Whenever we could, during this period of waiting, we made short expeditions in the neighborhood and found many sandstone caves, a mine of interest to us, containing as they did idols of wood or clay and leaves from Tibetan sacred books—offerings no doubt to the saints who used to live in these caverns.

On January 19, the roads were sufficiently passable to allow us to start off in company with a huge yak caravan. Ahead of us went a herd of yaks, carrying no loads, which acted as snowplows and seemed to enjoy the exercise very much. The country was intersected by valleys and ravines, and in the first two days we crossed no fewer than twelve bridges over the Kosi. My yak, which came from Changthang, was unused to bridges and jibed vigorously when he had to cross one. It was only by pushing behind and pulling in front—an operation in which the drivers enthusiastically assisted us—that we could get him across. I had already been warned not to bring him to Kyirong as he would not be able to stand the hot summer climate, but I had not wanted to leave him behind in view of our plans for flight, which we had not abandoned. Throughout all this time my thermometer showed an unvarying temperature of −30 degrees Centigrade. There were no lower markings on the instrument!

We were deeply impressed by a rock monastery in the neighborhood of the village of Longda. Seven hundred feet above the valley, red temples and countless cells were perched like birds' nests on the rocks. Despite the danger of avalanches, Aufschnaiter and I could not refrain from climbing the rock face, and so obtained another wonderful view of the Himalayas. We also met some monks and nuns and learned from them that this was the monastery founded by Milarepa, the famous Tibetan saint and poet, who lived in the eleventh century. We could easily understand that the glorious surroundings and the loneliness of the place were peculiarly adapted to meditation and the making of poetry. We left this place regretfully and determined to revisit it one day.

Every day we found less snow and after reaching the tree line soon found ourselves in a really tropical region. In this atmosphere the winter garments given us by the Tibetan government were too warm for us. Now we came to Drothang, the last stopping place before Kyirong. I remember that all the inhabitants of this place had highly developed goiters, which one rarely sees in Tibet. We took a week to get to Kyirong, which when the road is good is only three days' march from Dzongka, and can be reached in a single day by a fast courier.

THE NAME KYIRONG means "the village of happiness," and it really deserves the name. I shall never cease thinking of this place with yearning, and if I can choose where to pass the evening of my life, it will be in Kyirong. There I would build myself a house of red cedarwood and have one of the rushing mountain streams running through my garden, in which every kind of fruit would grow, for though its altitude is over 9,000 feet, Kyirong lies on the twenty-eighth parallel. When we arrived in January the temperature was just below freezing; it seldom falls below −10 degrees Centigrade. The seasons correspond to what we have in the Alps, but the vegetation is subtropical. One can go skiing the whole year round, and in the summer there is a row of 20,000-footers to climb.

There are about eighty houses in the village, which is the seat of two district governors who administer thirty villages. We were told that we were the first Europeans who had ever come to Kyirong, and the inhabitants watched our entry with astonishment. This time we were quartered in the house of a farmer, which reminded me of out Tyrolese houses. As a matter of fact, the whole of the village might have been transplanted from the Alps, except that instead of chimneys the roofs of the houses were decorated with prayer flags. These were always in the five colors which represented different aspects of life in Tibet.

On the ground floor were the stables for cows and horses. They were separated by a thick ceiling from the living rooms of the family, which are approached by a ladder from the courtyard. Thick stuffed mattresses served as beds and easy chairs, and near them were small, low tables. The members of the household kept their clothes in brightly painted wardrobes, and before the inevitable carved wooden altar, butter lamps were burning. In winter the whole family sit on the deal floor boards around a huge open log fire and sip their tea.

The room in which Aufschnaiter and I were put was rather small, so I soon shifted to the hay barn next door. Aufschnaiter carried on our unceasing struggle with rats and bugs, while I had to cope with mice and fleas. I never got the better of the vermin, but the view over glaciers and rhododendron forests made up for my discomfort. We had a servant allotted to us, but preferred to do our cooking ourselves. We had a fireplace in our room and were given wood to burn. We spent very little money; our provisions did not cost us more than £2 10s. a month each. I had a pair of trousers made, and the tailor charged half a crown.

The staple food in this region is tsampa. This is how they prepare it. You heat sand to a high temperature in an iron pan and then pour barleycorns onto it. They burst with a slight pop, whereupon you put the corns and the sand in a fine meshed sieve through which the sand runs; after this you grind the corn very small. The resulting meal is stirred up into a paste with butter tea or milk or beer, and then eaten. The Tibetans make a special cult of tsampa and have many ways of preparing it. We soon got accustomed to it, but never cared much for butter tea, which is usually made with rancid butter and is generally repugnant to Europeans. It is, however, universally drunk and appreciated by the Tibetans, who often drink as many as sixty cups in a day. The Tibetans of Kyirong, besides butter tea and tsampa, eat rice, buckwheat, maize, potatoes, turnips, onions, beans, and radishes. Meat is a rarity, for as Kyirong is a particularly holy place no animal is ever slaughtered there. Meat appeared on the table only when it had been brought in from another district or, more often, when bears or panthers left part of their prey uneaten. I never understood how this doctrine could be reconciled with the fact that every autumn some fifteen thousand sheep are driven through Kyirong bound for the slaughterhouses in Nepal and that the Tibetans levy export duty on them.

At the very beginning of our stay we paid a call on the district authorities. Our travel document had already been delivered by a servant and the bönpo thought that we would go straight on into Nepal. That was by no means our intention, and we told him that we would like to stay for a while at Kyirong. He took this very calmly and promised, at our request, to report to Lhasa. We also visited the representative of Nepal, who described his country in the most attractive terms. We had meanwhile learned that Kopp, after staying a few days in the capital, had been pushed off to an internment camp in India. The seductions of automobiles, bicycles, and moving pictures which, we were told, we should find in Katmandu, made no appeal to us.

We could not really hope to get a residence permit from Lhasa, and if we went to Nepal we expected to be expelled into India. Accordingly, we decided to recruit our strength in this fairylike village and stay there till we had worked out a new plan of escape. We could not foresee then that we would stay nearly nine months in Kyirong.

We were not in the least bored. We filled exercise books with notes on the manners and customs of the Tibetans. On most days we went out to explore the neighborhood. Aufschnaiter, who had been secretary of the Himalaya Institute in Munich, used his opportunities for mapmaking. There were only three names on the map of the region we had brought with us, but we now filled in more than two hundred. In fact we not only enjoyed our freedom but made practical use of it.

Our excursions, which at first were limited to the immediate neighborhood, gradually extended further and further. The inhabitants were quite accustomed to us, and no one interfered with us. Of course it was the mountains that attracted us most, and after that the hot springs around Kyirong. There were several of these, the hottest of which was in a bamboo forest on the bank of the ice-cold river Kosi. The water bubbled out of the ground nearly at boiling point and was led into an artificial basin, where it still had a temperature of about 40 degrees Centigrade. I used to plunge alternately into the hot pool and into the glacial waters of the Kosi.

In the spring there is a regular bathing season in this place. Swarms of Tibetans came along and bamboo huts sprang up everywhere in this usually lonely spot, two hours distant from Kyirong. Men and women tumbled naked into the pool, and any signs of prudishness provoked roars of laughter. Many families pay holiday visits to this spa. They set out from their homes, with sacks full of provisions and barrels of beer, and settle down for a fortnight in bamboo huts. The upper classes also are accustomed to visit the springs and arrive with caravans and a staff of servants. But the whole holiday season lasts only a short time as the river, swollen with melting snow, overflows the springs.

In Kyirong I made the acquaintance of a monk who had studied in the school of medicine in Lhasa. He was much respected and was able to live richly on the provisions that he received as fees for his services. His methods of treatment were diverse. One of them was to press a prayer stamp on the spot affected, which seemed to succeed with hysterical patients. In bad cases he branded the patient with a hot iron. I can bear witness to the fact that he thus restored a seemingly hopeless case to consciousness, but this treatment affected many of his patients adversely. He also employed this drastic treatment on domestic animals. As I was reckoned a sort of half-doctor and am greatly interested in everything connected with medicine, I used to have long conversations with this monk. He confessed to me that his knowledge was limited, but he did not worry himself unduly about that and managed to avoid unpleasant incidents by frequently changing his place of residence. His conscience was relived by the fact that the fees derived from his dubious cures served to finance his pilgrimages.

IN THE MIDDLE of February, we had our first Tibetan New Year. The year is reckoned by the lunar calendar and has two names, one of an animal and the other of an element. The New

Year festival is, after the birth- and death-days of Buddha, the greatest event of the year. During the previous night we already heard the voices of singing beggars and wandering monks going from house to house in quest of alms. In the morning fresh-cut pine trees decked out with flags were stuck on the roofs, religious texts were solemnly recited, and tsampa offered to the gods. The people bring an offering of butter to the temples, and soon the huge copper caldrons are overflowing. Only then are the gods propitiated and ready to grant favors in the New Year. White silk veils are draped around the gilded statues as a special mark of respect, and the worshipers reverently lay their foreheads against them.

Rich or poor, all come full of devotion and with no inner misgivings to lay their offerings before the gods and to pray for their blessing. Is there any people so uniformly attached to their religion and so obedient to it in their daily life? I have always envied the Tibetans their simple faith, for all my life I have been a seeker. Though I learned, while in Asia, the way to meditate, the final answer to the riddle of life has not been vouchsafed to me. But I have at least learned to contemplate the events of life with tranquillity and not let myself be flung to and fro by circumstances in a sea of doubt. The people did not pray only at the turn of the year. For seven days they danced, sang, and drank under the benevolent eyes of the monks. In every house there was a party, and we, too, were invited.

It is sad to remember that the festal celebrations in our house were overclouded by a tragedy. One day I was called into the room of our hostess's younger sister. The room was dark, and only when hot hands gripped mine did I realize that I was standing near her. When my eyes had got accustomed to the darkness, I looked toward the bed and recoiled in a horror that I could hardly conceal. There lay completely transformed by sickness one who two days before had been a pretty, healthy girl. Though a layman, I instantly saw that she had smallpox. Her larynx and tongue were already attacked, and she could only cry out with thick articulation that she was dying. I tried to tell her that it was not so, and then escaped from the room as quickly as possible to have a thorough wash. There was nothing to be done, and one could only hope that an epidemic would not break out. Aufschnaiter also visited her and agreed with my diagnosis. Two days later she died.

So after the joys of the festival, this mournful event made us acquainted with the ceremonies of a Tibetan burial. The decorated pine tree that stood on the roof was removed, and the next day at dawn the body was wrapped in white grave cloths and borne out of the house on the back of a professional corpse carrier. We followed the group of mourners, who consisted of three men only. Near the village on a high place recognizable from afar as a place of "burial" by the multitude of vultures and crows which hovered over it, one of the men hacked the body to pieces with an ax. A second sat nearby, murmuring prayers and beating on a small drum. The third man scared the birds away and at intervals handed the other two men beer or tea to cheer them up. The bones of the dead girl were broken to pieces, so that they too could be consumed by the birds and no trace of the body should remain.

Barbaric as all this seems, the ceremony draws its origin from deep religious motives. The Tibetans wish to leave no trace after death of their bodies, which, without souls, have no significance. The bodies of nobles and high-ranking lamas are burned, but among the people the usual way of dealing with them is by dismemberment, and only the bodies of very poor people, for whom this form of disposal is too costly, are thrown into the river. Here the fishes perform the function of the vultures. When poor people die of contagious diseases, they are disposed of by special persons paid by the government.

Fortunately, the cases of smallpox were few, and only a small number died. In our house there was mourning for forty-nine days, and then a fresh tree with prayer flags was hoisted onto the roof. At this ceremony appeared many monks who said prayers to the accompaniment of their own peculiar music. All this naturally costs money, and when deaths occur in the family the Tibetans usually sell some of their jewelry or the possessions of the defunct, the proceeds of which pay for the obsequies performed by the monks and the oil used in their countless little lamps.

During all this time, we continued our daily walks, and the excellent snow gave us the idea of making skis. Aufschnaiter got hold of a couple of birch trunks which we stripped of their bark and dried before the fire in our room. I started making sticks and straps, and with the aid of a carpenter we succeeded in producing two pairs of decent-looking skis. We were delighted with their workmanlike appearance and looked forward to trying them with great excitement. Then, like lightning from a clear sky, came an order from the bönpo forbidding us to leave Kyirong except for walks in the immediate neighborhood. We protested energetically, but were told that Germany was a powerful state and that if anything happened to us in the mountains, complaints would be made in Lhasa and the authorities in Kyirong held responsible. The bönpo remained unshaken by our protestations and did his best to convince us that in the mountains we should be in great danger of attacks by bears, leopards, and wild dogs. We knew that their anxiety about our safety was all humbug, but conjectured that they had adopted their attitude in deference to the requests of the superstitious population, who possibly believed that our visits to the mountains might make the gods angry. For the moment we could do nothing but submit.

During the next few weeks, we obeyed orders, but then we could not resist the temptation to go skiing. The attraction of the snow and the ice slopes was too much for us, and one day we had recourse to a stratagem. I took up my quarters provisionally by one of the hot springs only half an hour distant from the village. A few days later, when the people had got accustomed to my absence, I fetched our skis and carried them by moonlight some way up the mountainside. Early on the following morning, Aufschnaiter and I climbed up over the tree line and enjoyed ourselves on a splendid snow surface. We were both astonished at being able to ski so well after being so long away from it. As we had not been spotted, we went out again another day, but this time we broke our skis and hid the remains of these weird instruments. The people of Kyirong never found out that we had been snow riding, as they called it.

Springtime came, work in the fields began, and the winter corn came up in lovely green shoots. Here, as in Catholic countries, the cornfields are blessed by the priests. A long procession of monks, followed by the villagers, carried the 108 volumes of the Tibetan bible round the village accompanied by prayers and sacred music.

As the weather grew warmer, my yak fell sick. He had fever, and the local vet declared that only the gall of a bear would do him good. I bought the stuff, and dear it cost me, not so much from a belief in its properties as to give satisfaction to the "doctor." I was not astonished at the lack of results. I was then advised to try goat's gall and musk, and hoped, subconsciously, that the long experience of the Tibetans in the treatment of sick yaks would save my precious beast. However, after a few days I was obliged to have poor Armin slaughtered, as I wanted at least to save his meat.

For such cases the people use a slaughterer, a man obliged to live as an outcast on the fringe of the village like the blacksmith, whose craft ranks lowest in Tibet. The slaughterer receives as pay the feet, the head, and the intestines of the yak. I found the manner in which he dispatched the animal to be as speedy as, and more humane than, the methods of our slaughterers. With one swift stroke, he slit open the body, plunged his hand in, and tore out the cardiac artery, causing instant death. We took away the meat and smoked it over an open fire, thus providing a basis for the stock of food we should need when we next escaped.

About this time an epidemic had broken out in Dzongka, causing a number of deaths. The district officer with his charming young wife and four children came over to Kyirong to escape the danger. Unfortunately, the children brought with them the germs of the disease, a kind of dysentery, and one by one went down with it. At that time I still had some *yatren*, reckoned to be the best remedy for dysentery, and offered it to the family. This was a considerable sacrifice for Aufschnaiter and myself, as we had been keeping the last few doses for ourselves in case of need. Unfortunately, it did no good, and three of the children died. There was no yatren for the fourth, the youngest, who fell ill after the others. We were desperately anxious to save him and advised the parents to send a messenger in all haste to Katmandu with a specimen of the stools to find out what was the proper medicine to give. Aufschnaiter wrote a letter in English for this purpose, but it was never sent. The child was treated by the monks, who went so far as to call in a reincarnated lama from a distant spot. All their efforts were fruitless, and after ten days the child died. Sad as this business was, it acquitted us, in a way, of blame, for if the last child had recovered, we should have been held responsible for the deaths of the others.

The parents of these children and several other adult persons also fell ill, but recovered. During their illness they ate heartily and drank large quantities of alcohol, which may have accounted for their getting well. The children had refused food during their illness, and their strength had quickly ebbed away.

Afterward we became very friendly with the parents, who though they felt their loss very deeply, consoled themselves in some measure by their faith in reincarnation. They stayed on for some time at Kyirong in a hermitage and we often visited them there. The father was called Wangdüla and was a progressive and open-minded man. He was very anxious to acquire knowledge and made us tell him any things about life outside Tibet. Aufschnaiter, at his request, drew him a map of the world out of his head. His wife was a twenty-two-year-old beauty from Tibet; she spoke fluent Hindi, which she had learned at school in India. They made a very happy couple.

After several years we heard of them again. They had had a tragic fate. Another baby was born, and the mother died in childbirth. Wangdüla went mad with grief. He was one of the most likeable Tibetans I ever met, and his melancholy story moved me deeply.

During the summer the authorities sent for us again and summoned us to leave Kyirong. In the meantime we had learned from merchants and the newspapers that war was over. It was known to us that after the First World War the English had kept the POW camps going in India until two years after hostilities were over. We had clearly no wish to lose our freedom now and were determined to make another attempt to penetrate into Inner Tibet. The fascination of the country was growing on us, and we were ready to stake everything to satisfy our ambition to know it better. Our knowledge of the language was now good, and we had acquired a lot of experience. What was to hinder us from going farther? We were both mountaineers, and here we had a unique opportunity of surveying the Himalayas and the nomad districts. We had long ago given up all hope of returning home soon, and now wished to push through to China over the northern plains of Tibet, and, maybe, to find work there. The termination of the war had made our original project of getting through to the Japanese lines pointless.

So we promised the bönpos to leave in the autumn if they would in return allow us freedom of movement. This was approved, and from that time on the chief aim of our excursions was to find a pass through which we could reach the Tibetan plateau without touching Dzongka.

During these summer expeditions, we got to know the fauna of the region. We came across a great variety of animals, including species of monkeys that must have migrated here through the deep valley of the river Kosi. For some time leopards used to kill oxen and yaks nightly, and the villagers tried to catch them in traps. As a precaution against bears, I used to carry in my pocket a snuffbox full of red pepper. The bear, as I have mentioned, is dangerous only by day, when he will attack a man. Several of the woodcutters had bad face wounds as a result of encounters with bears, and one had been blinded by a blow from a bear's paw. In the nighttime one could drive these animals away with a pine torch.

On the tree line I once found deep footprints in the newly fallen snow, which I could not account for. They might have been made by a man. People with more imagination than I possess might have attributed them to the Abominable Snowman.

I made a point of always keeping fit and had no lack of strenuous occupation. I helped in the fields or at the threshing. I felled trees and cut torches from the resinous pinewood. The bodily toughness of the Tibetans is due to the bracing climate and the hard work they do.

They are also addicted to competitive sports. Every year a regular athletic meeting is held in Kyirong. It lasts several days. The principal events are horse racing, archery—distance and height of shot—foot races, and long and high jump. There is also an event for strong men, who have to lift and carry a heavy stone for a certain distance.

I contributed to the enjoyment of the public by competing in some events. I nearly won the foot race, having led, after a massed start, for most of the way, but I had not reckoned with the local methods. In the last and steepest bit of the track one of the competitors grabbed me by the seat of my trousers. I was so surprised that I stopped dead and looked around. That was what the rascal was waiting for. He passed me and reached the winning post first. I was not prepared for that sort of thing and amid general laughter received the rosette awarded as second prize.

There was a good deal of variety in life at Kyirong. In summer caravans came through every day. After the rice harvest in Nepal, men and women brought rice in baskets and exchanged it for salt, one of the most important exports of Tibet. It is brought from the lakes in Changthang, which have no exit.

Transport from Kyirong to Nepal is effected by means of coolies, as the road goes through narrow ravines and is often cut into stairways. Most of the carriers are women from Nepal wearing cheap dresses and showing their stout muscular legs below their short skirts. We witnessed a curious drama when the Nepalese came to gather honey. The Tibetan government has officially forbidden Tibetans to take honey, because their religion does not allow them to deprive animals of their food. However, here, as in most other places, people like to circumvent the law, and so the Tibetans, including the bönpos, allow the Nepalese to have the honey they collect, and then buy it back from them.

This honey taking is a very risky adventure as the bees hide the honeycomb under the projecting rocks of deep ravines. Long bamboo ladders are dropped, down which men climb sometimes two or three hundred feet, swinging free in the air. Below them flows the Kosi, and if the rope that holds the ladder breaks it means certain death for them. They use smoke balls to keep the angry bees away as the men collect the honeycomb, which is hoisted up in containers by a second rope. A condition of the success of this operation is perfect and well-rehearsed combination, as the sound of shouts or whistles is lost in the roar of the river below. On this occasion eleven men worked for a week in the ravine, and the price at which they sold the honey had no relation to the risks they ran. I much regretted that I had no ciné-camera with which to take a picture of this dramatic scene.

When the heavy summer rains were over, we began to explore the long valleys systematically. We often stayed out for several days, taking provisions, drawing materials, and compass with us. At these times we camped on the high pastures alongside the herdsmen, who, just as they do in the Alps, spend the summer months grazing their cattle on the luxuriant mountain meadows. There were hundreds of cows and female yaks feeding on the green stretches of pasture in the middle of a world of glaciers. I often helped with the buttermaking, and it was a pleasure to receive a slab of fresh golden butter for my pains.

By all the inhabited huts are found fierce, pugnacious dogs. Mostly they are chained up and by their barking at night protect the cattle from leopards, wolves, and wild dogs. They are very powerfully built, and their usual diet of milk and calves' flesh gives them enormous strength. They are really dangerous, and I had several disagreeable encounters with them. Once one of these dogs broke loose from his chain as I came up and sprang at my throat. I parried his attack, and he sank his teeth into my arm and did not let go till I had wrestled him down. My clothes hung in rags from my body, but the dog lay motionless on the ground. I bound up my wounds with what remained of my shirt, but I still bear deep scars on my arm. My wounds healed very quickly as a result of prolonged baths in the hot springs, which at this season of the year are more frequented by snakes than by Tibetans. The herdsmen told me later that I was not the only sufferer from this battle. The dog had lain in his corner and refused to eat for a week afterward.

During our excursions we found masses of wild strawberries,

but where we found the best we also found the most leeches. I knew from my reading that these creatures are the plague of many Himalayan valleys, and now learned from personal experience how helpless one is against them. They drop from trees on men and animals and creep through all the openings in one's clothes, even the eyelets in one's shoes. If one tears them off, one loses more blood than if one lets them drink their fill, when they fall off by themselves. Some of the valleys are infested to such a degree by leeches that one simply cannot protect oneself against them. The best way of keeping them out is by wearing socks and trousers steeped in salt.

Our excursions gave us many opportunities of mapmaking and sketching, but we found no pass that would have provided us with a line of escape. Without ropes and other mechanical aids, we could not hope to cross any of the high mountain ridges, heavily laden as we should be. And neither of us was enthusiastic about the idea of returning by the Dzongka road, which we knew already. We sent a petition to Nepal to ascertain whether, if we went there, we would be handed over to the British or not, but got no answer. At this time we had still about two months to run before we should have to leave Kyirong, and we spent our days in preparing for our journey. In order to increase my capital, I lent it to a merchant at the usual 33 per cent rate of interest. I was to regret this later, as my debtor delayed repayment and this nearly prevented our departure.

Our contact with the peaceable, industrious villagers had become more and more intimate. They did not reckon their work by the hour, but used every minute of daylight. As there was a shortage of labor in the agricultural regions, hunger and poverty were unknown. The numerous monks, who do no manual work and occupy themselves with spiritual matters, are supported by the community. The peasants are well-off, and their wardrobes contain enough tidy clothes for the whole family to wear on feast days. The women weave their own cloth, and all the clothes are made at home.

There are no police in our sense of the word. Evildoers are publicly sentenced. The punishments are pretty drastic, but they seem to suit the mentality of the population. I was told of a man who had stolen a golden butter lamp from one of the temples in Kyirong. He was convicted of the offense, and what we would think an inhuman sentence was carried out. His hands were publicly cut off and he was then sewn up in a wet yak skin. After this had been allowed to dry, he was thrown over a precipice.

We never saw any punishments as cruel as this. As time has gone on, the Tibetans seem to have become more lenient. I remember witnessing a public flogging, which I thought was not severe enough. The condemned persons were a monk and a nun belonging to the Reformed Buddhist Church, which enforces celibacy. The nun had cohabited with the monk and had had a child by him, which she killed when it was born. Both were denounced and put in the pillory. The guilt was publicly announced and they were condemned to a hundred lashes each. During the flogging the inhabitants begged the authorities to show mercy, offering them presents of money. This produced a reduction of the sentence, and sobs and sighs of relief were heard among the crowd of onlookers. The monk and the nun were exiled from the district and deprived of their religious status. The sympathy shown by the whole population toward them was, to our notions, almost inconceivable. The sinners received numerous presents of money and provisions, and left Kyirong with well-filled sacks to go on a pilgrimage. The reformed sect, to which these two persons belonged, is dominant in Tibet, although in our particular neighborhood there were a large number of monasteries obeying other rules. In them monks and nuns could live a family life together, and the children remained in the monastery. They worked in their fields, but were never appointed to official posts, which were reserved for members of the Reformed Church.

The supremacy of the monastic orders in Tibet is something unique. It can well be compared to a stern dictatorship. The monks mistrust any influence from the outside would that might undermine their authority. They are clever enough not to believe that their power is limitless, but they punish anyone who suggests that it is not. For that reason some of the monks of Kyirong disapproved of our close contact with the villagers. Our behavior, which remained uninfluenced by any of their superstitions, must have given the Tibetans something to think about. We used to go by night into the forests without being molested by demons, we climbed mountains without lighting sacrificial fires, and still nothing happened to us. In some quarters we noticed a certain reserve, which could only be attributed to the influence of the lamas. I think they must have credited us with supernatural powers, for they were convinced that our excursions had some hidden purpose. They kept on asking us why we were always communing with streams and birds. No Tibetan ever takes a step without a particular object, and they felt that when we roamed in the woods or sat by brooks we were not doing so aimlessly.

5

ON THE MOVE

Meanwhile autumn was upon us and the permitted term of our residence coming to an end. It was hard to have to quit this paradise of nature, but we had not succeeded in obtaining a residence permit, and there was no doubt that we would have to leave. Realizing from past experience the importance of a sufficient reserve of provisions, we made a cache twelve miles away on the Dzongka road, where we deposited tsampa, butter, dried meat, sugar, and garlic. As had been the case when we escaped from the camp, we had no transport and had to carry all our stores on our backs.

Heavy snowfalls betokened an early winter and interfered with our calculations. We had already decided what was the maximum weight we could carry, and now had to make up our minds to take another blanket each. The winter was, of course, the most unfavorable season for crossing the high plateaux of Central Asia, but we could not remain in Kyirong. For a time we played with the idea of hiding ourselves somewhere in Nepal and spending the winter there, but we gave it up as the Nepalese frontier guard were known to be highly efficient.

When our depot was ready we set to work to rig up a portable lamp. It was clear that the villagers knew we were up to something, and we were continually spied upon; so in order to prepare our lamp we went one day for a walk in the mountains, where we manufactured a sort of lantern out of Tibetan paper and the binding of a book, inside which we placed a cigarette box filled with butter to keep the flame burning. We needed a light, however faint, as we had determined to travel by night as long as we were in inhabited country. I was now waiting for the repayment of the money I had lent. I expected to get it on the next day and we stood prepared for action.

For tactical reasons it was agreed that Aufschnaiter should go first on the pretext of an excursion. On November 6, 1945, he boldly left the village by daylight with his pack on his back. With him went my long-haired Tibetan dog—a present from a notable of Lhasa. In the meantime I tried to get my money back, but had no luck. My debtor was suspicious and did not want to repay me till Aufschnaiter had returned. It was no wonder that we were suspected of plotting to escape. If we really meant to go to Nepal, there was no need for secrecy. The officials were afraid of getting into trouble with the government if we succeeded in getting into Inner Tibet, and so they egged on the villagers against us. The latter were in constant fear of the local authorities and did what they were told.

A hunt for Aufschnaiter was organized, and I was hauled up and questioned. The authorities were not impressed by my feeble attempts to persuade them that he had gone on one of his usual excursions. As for my money, I had to wait another day and then received only part of it. It would never be repaid in full before Aufschnaiter's return.

I had resolved to break away on the evening of November 8—

by force if need be. I was shadowed wherever I went. There were spies inside and outside the house. I watched till ten o'clock, hoping that they would go to bed, but they showed no signs of doing so. Then I made a scene, pretending to be very angry and saying that the conduct of the people in the house had made it impossible for me to remain there and that I must go and sleep in the forest. As they watched me I started packing. My hostess and her mother rushed in, and when they saw what was happening threw themselves on the ground before me and entreated me with tears not to go. They said that if I did, they would be whipped out of the village and would lose their house and be outlawed. They had not deserved this at my hands. The old mother handed me a white veil in token of her respect for me, and when she saw that my heart was not softened by her appeals, offered me money. I felt sorry for the two women and tried to persuade them that nothing would happen to them if I went away. Unfortunately, their cries and screams had aroused the whole village, and I had to act at once, if it was not already too late.

I can still see the butter-smeared Mongol faces staring into my window with the light of their pine torches shining on them. And now the two mayors arrived panting with a message from the bönpos to say that if I would stay till morning, I could then go wherever I wished. I knew that this was a trick to keep me and did not answer. So they ran off to fetch their chiefs. My hostess clung to me weeping and saying that I had always been like one of her own children and that I ought not to cause her such pain. My nerves were overstrung. Something had to happen. I resolutely shouldered my pack and walked out of the house. I was astonished that the crowd collected round the door did not interfere with me. They said, "He's going, he's going," but no one touched me—they must have noticed that I really meant business. A couple of young men called to one another to stop me, but they got no further than saying it. I walked untouched through the crowd, which gave way before me.

But I was glad when I had passed out of the torchlight into the dark. I hurried along the Nepal road for a bit in order to deceive possible pursuers, then I made a wide detour around the village and by morning had reached our depot. Aufschnaiter was sitting on the side of the road, and my dog jumped up to greet me. We walked on for a bit in search of a good hiding place for the day.

FOR THE LAST TIME for years we camped in a wood. The next night we marched up the valley and soon were far above the tree line. We knew the mountain path well from our excursions, and our feeble lantern did its job. Still, occasionally we did get off the track. We had to be very careful in crossing the narrow wooden bridges over the river. They were glazed over with ice and we had to balance ourselves like tightrope walkers. We made good progress, though each of us was carrying a weight of nearly ninety pounds. By day we always found good secluded spots to rest in, but camping in that temperature was too cold for pleasure.

One fine day we found we could not go on. In front of us was an unclimbable rock face. A path led up to it and lost itself in the wall. What were we to do? We could never get up it with heavy loads on our backs, so we decided to turn back and try to wade through the stream, which here divided into several branches. The cold was intense—fifteen degrees below zero. Earth and stones froze onto our feet when we took off our shoes and stockings to wade across, and it was a painful business pulling them off before putting on our shoes again. And then we were faced by fresh streams. There must have been an exit as the caravans passed that way, but we could not see where. So we decided to pass the night where we were, and the next day to watch from our hiding place to see how the caravans dealt with the situation. Soon after dawn a caravan came along, stopped before the rock face, and then (we could hardly believe our eyes) the heavily laden coolies climbed swiftly up the rocky path like chamois one after the other—a lesson to us hardened mountaineers—while the yaks waded across the stream with their drivers on their backs.

We determined to try again, and after a day that seemed to us endless, night came, and we tackled the difficult ascent. We had the moonlight to see by, which was much more helpful than our little lantern. If we had not seen the coolies negotiating the rocky wall we should have given it up again, but manage it we did.

After two more night marches, we bypassed Dzongka and found ourselves in unknown country. Our next objective was the Brahmaputra River, which provided the most serious question mark in our itinerary. How were we to cross it? We hoped that it was already frozen over. We had only a vague notion of the road that led to the river, but hoped that it would not offer serious obstacles. The great thing was to go ahead as fast as possible and to avoid all places in which we might run into officials. Shortly after passing Dzongka, we camped in a cave where we found thousands of small clay idols. The place must formerly have been a hermitage. The next night we climbed steeply, hoping to get over the pass in one march. But we had overrated our strength; breathless and exhausted by marching in the thin air at an altitude of over 16,000 feet, we had to stop in an ice-cold camp. We were again approaching the Himalayan watershed. The view from the top of the Chakhyungla Pass was disappointing; we had the satisfaction of thinking that we were probably the first Europeans to cross it, but the weather was far too cold to feel pleasure or pride in anything.

In this snowy deserted waste, we ventured to travel by day. We made good progress, and after spending the night freezing in camp, we were rewarded the next morning by a magnificent view of a great deep-blue lake, Pelgu Tso, lying below us. The plateau on which we were was ringed by a gleaming chain of glaciers; we felt proud of knowing the names of two of the peaks, Gosainthan (26,000 feet) and Lapchi Kang. Both were yet unconquered, which one can say of most of the Himalayan peaks. Our fingers were stiff with cold, but we got out our sketchbook and in a few strokes drew the outlines of these mountains. Aufschnaiter took the bearings of the most important peaks with our compass and wrote down the figures, which one day might be of use. We went down through this dreamlike winter landscape to the shore of the lake, where we found a ruined caravansary, and had once more to spend the night in the snow.

As a matter of fact, we were surprised how well we could stand the high altitude and what speed we made, considering our heavy loads. But our poor dog was miserable. He was half-starved. At night he lay across our feet and helped to warm us, and we needed it, for there must have been twenty-two degrees of frost.

How happy we were to find a trace of life the next day! A flock of sheep came slowly toward us, followed by some shepherds muffled in thick cloaks. They pointed out where the next habitations lay, and the same evening we reached the village of Trakchen, which lay a little off the caravan route. It was high time for us to be with human beings again as our provisions had run out. Even if we were arrested! . . .

This little settlement certainly deserved to be called a village. It contained about forty houses with a monastery built above them on the hillside, a better-looking place than Gartok, standing several hundred feet higher. We had indeed discovered here the highest inhabited place in Asia and perhaps in the whole world.

The natives took us for Indians and sold us provisions freely. We were received hospitably in a house, and did we enjoy the luxury of being warm after long marches through snow and ice! We rested here a day and a night, eating well and feeding our dog. We avoided meeting the local authorities as the bönpo had locked up his residence and ignored us. Perhaps he was avoiding responsibility.

Willy-nilly we had to buy another sheepskin as our clothes were not made for the Tibetan winter. And after long and enjoyable bargaining we bought a yak. This was the fourth in our line of Armins, and he was no different from the others except that perhaps he was naughtier.

From here we went on to cross the Yagula Pass, meeting no one on the way. After three days we came to cultivated land belonging to the large village of Menkhap Me. We again introduced ourselves as Indians, and bought straw for our yak and tsampa for ourselves. The people here lead a very hard life. Their barley and lentil fields are strewn with stones and need a great deal of labor to produce a poor crop. But they are cheerful and friendly people, and in the evenings we sat with them and drank beer. On the slopes around the village there are some little monasteries, which the villagers, in spite of the hard lives they lead, keep going with their usual spirit of piety and self-sacrifice. On every side we found ruins of surprising dimensions, bearing witness that this region had seen better times. We could not ascertain if the decline had been due to wars or a change of climate.

We had been marching for an hour when we came out into the huge plain of Tingri. Behind—and we caught our breath—stood the highest mountain in the world, Mount Everest. Full of wonder, enthusiasm, and awe, we looked at the mighty peak and thought of the many expeditions in which brave men had lost their lives vainly trying to win the summit. We made a few sketches of the mountain, which certainly had never been viewed by a European from where we stood.

It was hard to turn from this marvelous spectacle, but we had to move on to our next objective, the 18,000-foot pass of Körala, which lay to the north. Before starting to climb, we spent the night in a little hamlet called Khargyu, at the foot of the pass. This time we could not pass ourselves off as Indians so easily, because the villagers had seen many Europeans. Nearby was the village of Tingri, where all the British Everest expeditions used to hire their bearers. The inhabitants seemed to be appraising us and asked us first if we had been to see the bönpo at Sutso. We then realized that the big house we had seen at that place must have been the official residence. We had noticed the house right enough, as it stood on a hill and commanded a view of the whole district. Luckily, we had got by without being observed.

Now we had to be cautious. We did not pursue the subject but repeated our story of being on a pilgrimage. The villagers appeared to be satisfied and told us about the road we should have to follow, which from their account was a good one.

Late in the afternoon, we reached the top of the pass. At last we would be going downhill again. We had finished with wearisome ascents for the time being and glad we were of it. Our yak, however, thought otherwise. He broke away and ran back uphill toward the pass. After endless difficulty we managed to catch him, but we could not get him to move and were obliged to camp in a most inhospitable spot where we could not light a fire—and so we supped on dry tsampa meal and raw meat. Our only consolation was the distant view of Mount Everest in the sunset glow.

The next day Armin again began to "create." We tied a rope around his horns and led him over the pass, but he continued to misbehave. We had had enough of Armin IV and determined to exchange him at the next opportunity for another animal.

Our chance came soon. At the next village I made what I thought was a good bargain and exchanged him for a shaky-looking nag. We were overjoyed and went on our way in high spirits.

On the same day we reached a broad valley through which

rushed a stream of green water carrying small ice floes with it. It was the Tsangpo (Brahmaputra). That disposed of our dream of finding the river frozen and getting across on the ice. But we did not lose heart. On the opposite bank we saw monasteries and a number of houses and reckoned there must be some means of getting across the river. We thought of a ferry, and as we were searching for one, I found the piers of a hanging rope bridge. When we came to it we concluded that the bridge was all right for us to cross but no good for our horse. Animals have to swim, although the coolies manage sometimes to carry their donkeys across the swaying rope bridges on their backs. We tried to drive our horse into the water, but he simply would not budge. By this time we were quite accustomed to having trouble with our animals, so I sadly made up my mind to go back to the village and try to effect a reexchange. It cost me money and hard words to get back Armin, but I got him. He showed no sign of pleasure or of sorrow at seeing me again.

It was dark by the time I brought him back to the bridge. By that time it was too late to get him across, so I tethered him to a stake nearby. Aufschnaiter had in the meantime found us a lodging, and we passed a pleasant, warm night under cover. The villagers were accustomed to passing traders and took little notice of us.

The next morning I forgave Armin all his misdeeds. When we had managed to persuade him to go into the water, he showed himself to be a splendid swimmer. He was often submerged by the rushing water and was carried some way downstream, but that did not disturb him. He swam steadily on, and when he had come to the other side we admired the gallant way in which he breasted the steep bank and shook the water out of his long coat. We spent the rest of the day in the village which was called Chung Rivoche—a very interesting place with a famous monastery. This building, which contained a number of temples with Chinese inscriptions on their doors, rose sheer from the rocky walls that flanked the river. One of the most remarks able things about this monastery was an outsize *chorten* (a form of totem), perhaps seventy feet high, which bore witness to the sanctity of the place. Around it were grouped a great number of prayer wheels—I counted up to eight hundred—which continually revolved "with their drums containing strips of paper inscribed with prayers entreating the blessing of the gods. It is important that they should be continuously in movement, and I noticed a monk going around and greasing their axles. No devout person passes by the wheels without giving them a turn. Little old men and women often sit by these giant drums for the whole day, turning them with devotion and praying heaven to grant them and those who support them rebirth in a higher state. Others carry little handwheels with them when they go on pilgrimages. These prayer wheels and the childlike mentality that they express are as typical of Tibet as the cairns and prayer flags we had found on all the mountain passes.

As we were very pleased with our quarters and fascinated by all the interesting things we saw here, we decided to remain for another night. It was worth it, as we had a very interesting visitor, a Tibetan who had lived for twenty-two years in a Christian mission in India and had now returned, homesick for Tibet. Like us he had wandered alone over the passes through the winter snow, but when he could he had attached himself to caravans. He showed us English illustrated papers and in them we saw for the first time pictures of bombed cities and read about the end of the war. These were for us shattering moments and we were eager to hear more. In spite of the discouraging news he gave us, we were glad to meet someone who brought us a breath of air from the outside world— our world. What he told us strengthened our resolve to continue our journey into Central Asia. We would have been only too glad to take him with us as a traveling companion but could offer him neither protection nor comfort. We bought from him a few pencils and some paper so that we could continue writing up our diaries, then said good-bye to him and set out alone.

Our route now led us away from the Brahmaputra. We followed it over another pass, and in two days reached Sangsang Gevu and so joined once more the caravan road from Gartok to Lhasa, from which we had branched off a year ago on our way to Kyirong. The bönpo's representative at Sangsang Gevu asked us many questions but treated us kindly. We felt that the gentlemanly way in which the two officials at Tradün had dealt with us had become known in the surrounding country as far Sangsang and had set an example to other authorities. Fortunately, this officer had no idea that we were here contrary to instructions.

It was a blessing that he did not put additional difficulty in our way, as we already had worries and to spare. We had to make a decision one way or the other. We had only eighty rupees left and one gold piece. The rest had gone in the purchase of provisions and in buying a fifth yak to replace our latest Armin. We found prices higher as we approached the towns, and it was clearly impossible for us to think of getting through to the Chinese frontier with no more than the money we had. We still had thousands of miles to cover before we came to China. But our money would be enough to get us to Lhasa. There it was again—the lure of the "Forbidden City." And the possibility of getting acquainted with the object of our dreams was now almost within our grasp. Anyhow, we could not control our desire to go there, and this new objective seemed to us worth any sacrifice.

While we were in the POW camp, we had greedily read every book we could get that dealt with Lhasa. There were few of these, and all of them had been written by Englishmen. We had learned that in 1904 a British punitive expedition consisting of a small force had marched as far as the capital, and that in the last twenty years several Europeans have visited it. Since that time the world possesses only superficial knowledge of Lhasa, and no goal is more attractive to the explorer than the Dalai Lama's home. And we, so short a distance away, should we not seek to get there? For what other purpose had we overcome every sort of difficulty by cunning and stratagem, exerted ourselves physically to the limit of our endurance, and learned to speak the language of the country? The more we thought about it, the stronger was our resolve, and "On to Lhasa" became our motto. Our experience had shown us that high officials were much easier to deal with than subordinates. We felt that we should be all right once we got to Lhasa. I kept thinking of a brilliant example we might follow, that of Father Johann Grueber, who smuggled himself into Lhasa in a caravan three hundred years ago and was hospitably entertained there.

So there was no doubt about our goal, but we were not so sure how to reach it. We were of course attracted by the much-frequented highroad with its roadhouses. Going by it, we should reach Lhasa in a few weeks. But we risked discovery and arrest. Even if we bypassed Shigatse, the second largest city of Tibet, we should find several other administrative centers on the way, each of which might mar our chances. The risk this way was too great. So we decided to travel through the northern plains, which they call Changthang. This district is inhabited solely by nomads with whom we could safely associate. Then, we thought, we could approach Lhasa from the northwest. No one expects foreigners to come from that direction, and it would be easier for us to slip into the town. Sven Hedin made a similar plan forty years ago, but it failed owing to the obstinacy of some local officials. His failure to reach Lhasa may have seemed a great misfortune to him personally, but it enabled him to explore regions hitherto completely unknown. There were no maps or accounts of the route that we meant to follow: we simply had to push on into the unknown, always aiming for the northeast. We should probably meet nomads here and there on our way and get them to put us wise about directions and distances.

While in Sangsang we naturally said nothing about our plans but gave out that we wished to go to the salt deposits in the north. People were horrified at the idea and tried hard to dissuade us. The country was so inhospitable that only lunatics would wish to go there. But our deception had the desired result of removing any suspicion that we might be bound for Lhasa. Our plan, as a matter of fact, involved considerable dangers, and the icy blizzards we encountered in Sangsang gave us an idea of what to expect.

Nevertheless, we set out on December 2, 1945. While at Sangsang we had made friends with some Sherpas. These people are Tibetans who live mostly in Nepal and have made a name for themselves as guides and bearers in the Himalayas. They are nicknamed "the tigers of the Himalayas." They gave us valuable advice regarding our preparations and helped us to find a new yak, which was a real service to us, as we had hitherto invariably been swindled when we bought one of these creatures. We noted with satisfaction that our new yak was a well-behaved beast. He was a powerful bull, black with a few white flecks, and his long flowing coat nearly swept the ground. In his youth his horns had been removed and the operation seemed to have improved his temper without diminishing his strength. He wore the usual nose ring. With a very little encouragement, one could get him to exceed his average speed of two miles an hour. The poor devil had a lot of weight to carry, as we had made it a rule always to have at least eight days' rations with us.

Our first day out from Sangsang passed without difficulties.

Our way led through a gently rising valley. Just as the sun went down and the biting cold began to penetrate our clothing, we saw, as if we had ordered it, a black nomad tent. It was pitched in the shelter of a surrounding stone called a *lhega*. One finds these enclosures scattered over the whole of Tibet, as the nomads are always moving to new pastures, and when they do, they put stone fences around their tents. The lhegas also help to protect their beasts against the cold and the attacks of wolves. As we approached the tent, some dogs made for us, barking. The noise brought a nomad out of the tent. He was not very forthcoming when we asked for a night's shelter, and flatly refused to allow us into his tent, but afterward he brought us some dried yak's dung with which to make a fire. We had to camp in the open, but eventually made ourselves fairly comfortable; we collected a lot of juniper branches with which we managed to keep a good fire going throughout the night.

All the same I could not sleep. I had a feeling in the pit of my stomach reminding me of my sensations before tackling the North Wall of the Eiger. It is certainly a good thing that we did not know what lay before us. Had we had even a faint idea of it, we would certainly have turned back. We were setting out into terra incognita, marked only by blank spaces on the maps, magnetized by the ambition of the explorer.

The next day we reached the top of the pass and were astonished to find that there was no descent and that we had simply come to a high plateau. The view over the unending plain was discouraging. One seemed to be facing infinity, and the huge spaces would certainly take months to cross. As far as we could see, there was no sign of life, and an ice-cold wind blew over the snow.

We spent the following night in abandoned lhegas, finding enough yak's dung to make a fire. In summer, nomads evidently lived here, and caravans passed through the region. The snow plains were then, no doubt, green Alpine pastures—and the thought of them reminded us that we had not chosen the best time of year for our journey.

Then we had a lucky day. We ran into a tent and got a warm reception from an old married couple and their son, who had been camping there for several months. They had had a hard time of it and since the heavy snowfalls eight weeks before had hardly left their tent. Many of their yaks and sheep had died since the deep snow had buried their pasture. The rest stood apathetically near the tent or kicked up the snow with their hoofs in the hope of finding fodder. These heavy falls of snow are rare in Central Asia and do not count among the normal risks of life.

Our hosts seemed glad to see human faces again. This was the first time that we had been invited into a nomad's tent and asked to stay the night. We were taken for Indians and aroused no suspicion. There was plenty of meat as many of the animals had had to be killed. We bought a leg of yak for a *sang* and at once sawed off a huge chunk with a *kukri* in order to make a meal. Our hosts were horrified to hear of the route we proposed to take and strongly advised us to give it up. However, in the course of conversation they did say that we should find other nomad tents on our road, and this information strengthened our determination to carry on.

The next day, soon after setting out, we ran into a deep snowdrift. Walking with our inadequate footwear soon became a torture. The upper crust of snow was treacherous, and we and our yak often broke through. In some places there were streams running under the snow, and we found ourselves wading through ice-cold water, which we could feel but not see, and our shoes and stockings were soon frozen stiff. We had an exhausting day and covered only a few miles. Glad indeed we were to see another nomad tent toward evening. This time the inmates did not invite us to come inside, but they were not unfriendly and pitched a little yak-hair tent for us. I was happy to be able at last to remove my shoes from my smarting feet. Some of my toes showed signs of frostbite, but I rubbed them for a long time and at last the circulation came back.

The difficulties of this day's march and the warning of frost-bite had made us anxious, and Aufschnaiter and I had a long and earnest talk. We could still return, and we thought seriously of do-ing so. We were worried about our yak, which had not eaten prop-erly for days, and we could reckon on our fingers how many days he would last. But we could not think of going on without him. For a long time we argued backward and forward, and eventually came to a compromise solution. We would continue our march for one more day and then decide. Our decision would depend on the snow conditions.

The next day we passed through undulating country till we came to a pass. On crossing it, what was our astonishment but to find no more snow! Providence had decided for us.

We soon ran into a nomad's tent, where we were well received and allowed to graze our yak to his heart's content. This time our hostess was a young woman. She quickly made us cups of butter tea, and for the first time I drank this brew with relish. The warmth ran through our frozen bodies and brought us to life again. Only then did we notice what a picturesque figure our young hostess made. Over her bare skin she wore a sheepskin cloak reaching down to the ground. In her long black pigtail she wore mussel shells, silver coins, and various cheap ornaments imported from abroad. She told us that her two husbands had gone out to drive in the animals. She said they had fifteen hundred sheep and a great many yaks. We were astonished to find polyandry practiced among the nomads. It was only when we were in Lhasa that we came to know all the complicated reasons that led to the simultaneous existence in Tibet of polyandry and polygamy.

The two men, when they came home, greeted us as warmly as their wife had done. An abundant supper was prepared and we even got sour milk to drink. This was a pleasure we had not enjoyed since we used to help the buttermakers in Kyirong. We sat for a long while in comfort by the fire and felt ourselves rewarded for the hardships of the road. We laughed and jested much, and as is usual when the company consists of several men and a single pretty young woman, the latter got her share of teasing.

We started fresh and rested the next day, and were glad to have left the lonely snowy landscape behind us. We saw signs of life here and there. Herds of wild goats showed themselves on the slopes and sometimes came so near that a pistol would have given us a steak for our dinner. Unfortunately, we hadn't one.

It was a pleasant surprise to find more friendly nomads as evening fell. They called in their dogs as we approached and we decided to rest for a day among them and give our yak a chance of grazing on their fertile pastures.

In winter the men living a nomad life have not much to do. They busy themselves with various household chores and for recreation go hunting with their antiquated muzzle loaders. The women collect yak dung and often carry their babies around with them as they work. In the evening the herds are driven in and the cows milked—though it is little they give in winter. As one can imagine, the nomads have the simplest methods of cooking. In winter they eat almost exclusively meat with as much fat as possible. They also eat different kinds of soup—tsampa, the staple diet in agricultural districts, is a rarity here.

The whole life of the nomads is organized so as to make the most of the scanty aids to living which nature provides. At night they sleep on skins spread upon the ground and, slipping out of the sleeves, use their sheepskin cloaks as bedclothes. Before they get up in the morning, they blow up the still live embers of their fire with a bellows and the first thing they do is to make tea. The fire is the heart of the household and is never allowed to go out. As in every peasant's house, one finds an altar in every tent, which usually consists of a simple chest on which is set an amulet or a small statue of the Buddha. There is invariably a picture of the Dalai Lama. A little butter lamp burns on the altar, and in winter the flame is almost invisible owing to the cold and the lack of oxygen.

The greatest event of the year in the life of the nomads is the annual market in Gyanyima to which they drive their flocks and barter some of their sheep for grain. And there they buy household articles, needles, aluminum pots and pans, and brightly colored ornaments for the women.

We were sorry to be on the road once more after a glimpse of domestic life. We would have wished to do something to repay the hospitality of these people. We gave them small presents of colored yarn and paprika—that was all we had.

For a time after this we covered from ten to twenty miles each day, according to whether we found tents on our route or not. Often enough we had to bivouac in the open. At those times it took us all our energy to collect yak dung and find water, and even talking was a waste of strength. We suffered much with our hands, which were always stiff with frost, for we had no gloves and used a pair of socks instead. Once a day we cooked meat and ladled the gravy straight out of the simmering saucepan. One could do that here without fear of scalding one's tongue as the boiling point was so low. We cooked at night, and warmed up anything that was left over before we started in the morning. We marched through the whole day without halting.

I could write a chapter on the miseries of our nights, when we lay close together often unable to sleep because of the cold and the countless lice that tormented us. The reader must imagine what we suffered.

On December 13, we reached Labrang Trowa, a "settlement" consisting of a single house. The family to which the house belonged used it only for camping and lived in their tent which they had pitched nearby. When we asked them why, they replied that the tent was far warmer. We gathered from their conversation that we had landed in an official's residence. The bönpo was away, but his brother acted for him. The latter began to ask us questions, but soon seemed to be satisfied with our tale of being pilgrims. For the first time we admitted that we wished to go to Lhasa, for at this point we were at a safe distance from the caravan route. Our man shook his head in horror and tried to make us understand that the quickest and best way to Lhasa was by way of Shigatse. I had my answer ready. We had chosen the hard way in order that our pilgrimage might have greater merit. He was impressed by this explanation and gladly gave us good advice.

He said we had a choice of two courses. The first was to follow a route which was very difficult. It would take us over many passes and tracts of uninhabited country. The second was easier but it meant going through the middle of the Khampas' country. There it was again, the name "Khampa," spoken in a mysterious tone, which we had already heard from so many nomads. "Khampa" must mean an inhabitant of the eastern province of Tibet, which is called Kham. But you never heard the name mentioned without an undertone of fear and warning. At last we realized that the word was synonymous with "robber."

We, unfortunately, made light of the warning and chose the easier route.

We spent two nights with the bönpo's family—not unfortunately as guests in their tent, as the proud Tibetans did not deem us poor Indians worthy of such an honor. But the bönpo's brother was a very impressive fellow. He was seriousminded and sparing in his speech, but when he said anything it made sense. He shared his brother's wife and lived on his flocks. The family seemed to be well-off, and they lived in a considerably larger tent than those of most nomads. We were able to replenish our stores, and money was accepted for our purchases as a matter of course.

6

THE
WORST TREK
OF ALL

We had been some time on the way when a man came toward us wearing clothes that struck us as unusual. He spoke a dialect different from that of the local nomads. He asked us curiously whence? and whither? and we told him our pilgrimage story. He left us unmolested and went on his way. It was clear to us that we had made the acquaintance of our first Khampa.

A few hours later we saw in the distance two men on small ponies, wearing the same sort of clothes. We slowly began to feel uncomfortable and went on without waiting for them. Long after dark we came across a tent. Here we were lucky, as it was inhabited by a pleasant nomad family, who hospitably invited us to come in and gave us a special fireplace for ourselves.

In the evening we got to talking about the robbers. They were, it seems, a regular plague. Our host had lived long enough in the district to make an epic about them. He proudly showed us a Mannlicher rifle for which he had paid a fortune to a Khampa— five hundred sheep, no less. But the robber bands in the neighborhood considered this payment as a sort of tribute and had left him in peace ever since.

He told us something about the life of the robbers. They live in groups in three or four tents, which serve as headquarters for their campaigns. These are conducted as follows: heavily armed with rifles and swords they force their way into a nomad's tent and insist on hospitable entertainment on the most lavish scale available. The nomad in terror brings out everything he has. The Khampas fill their bellies and their pockets and taking a few cattle with them, for good measure, disappear into the wide-open spaces. They repeat the performance at another tent every day till the whole region has been skinned. Then they move their headquarters and begin again somewhere else. The nomads, who have no arms, resign themselves to their fate, and the government is powerless to protect them in these remote regions. However, if once in a while a district officer gets the better of these footpads in a skirmish, he is not the loser by it for he has a right to all the booty. Savage punishment is meted out to the evildoers, who normally have their arms hacked off. But this does not cure the Khampas of their lawlessness. Stories were told of the cruelty with which they sometimes put their victims to death. They go so far as to slaughter pilgrims and wandering monks and nuns. A disturbing conversation for us! What would we not have given to be able to buy our host's Mannlicher! But we had no money and not even the most primitive weapons. The tent pegs we carried did not impress even the sheepdogs.

The next morning we went on our way, not without misgivings, which increased when we saw a man with a gun, who seemed to be stalking us from the hillside. Nevertheless, we kept straight on our course, and the man eventually disappeared. In the evening we found more tents—first a single one and then a cluster of others.

We called to the people in the first tent. A family of nomads came out. They refused with expressions of horror to admit us and pointed distractedly to the other tents. There was nothing to do but to go on. We were no little surprised to receive a friendly welcome at the next tent. Everyone came out. They fingered our things and helped us to unload—a thing which no nomads had ever done—and suddenly it dawned on us that they were Khampas. We had walked like mice into the trap. The inhabitants of the tent were two men, a woman, and a half-grown youngster. We had to put a good face on a poor situation. At least we were on our guard and hoped that politeness, foresight, and diplomacy would help us to find a way out of the mess.

We had hardly sat down by the fire when the tent began to fill with visitors from the neighboring tents, come to see the strangers. We had our hands full trying to keep our baggage together. The people were as pressing and inquisitive as gypsies. When they had heard that we were pilgrims, they urgently recommended us to take one of the men, a particularly good guide, with us on our journey to Lhasa. He wanted us to go by a road somewhat to the south of our route and, according to him, much easier to travel. We exchanged glances. The man was short and powerful, and carried a long sword in his belt. Not a type to inspire confidence. However, we accepted his offer and agreed on his pay. There was nothing else to do, for if we got on the wrong side of them they might butcher us out of hand.

The visitors from the other tents gradually drifted away, and we prepared to go to bed. One of our two hosts insisted on using my rucksack as a pillow, and I had the utmost difficulty keeping it by me. They probably thought that it contained a pistol. If they did, that suited us and I hoped to increase their suspicion by my behavior. At last he stopped bothering me. We remained awake and on our guard all through the night. That was not very difficult, though we were very weary, because the woman muttered prayers without ceasing. It occurred to me that she was praying in advance for forgiveness for the crime her husband intended to commit against us the next day. We were glad when day broke. At first everything seemed peaceful. I exchanged a pocket mirror for some yak's brains, which we cooked for breakfast. Then we began to get ready to go. Our hosts followed our movements with glowering faces and looked as if they wanted to attack me when I handed our packs out of the tent to Aufschnaiter. However, we shook them off and loaded our yak. We looked out for our guide, but to our relief he was nowhere to be seen. The Khampa family advised us urgently to keep to the southern road, as the nomads from that region were making up a pilgrim caravan to Lhasa. We promised to do so and started off in all haste.

We had gone a few hundred yards when I noticed that my dog was not there. He usually came running after us without being called. As we looked around we saw three men coming after us. They soon caught up with us and told us that they, too, were on the way to the tents of the nomad pilgrims and pointed to a distant pillar of smoke. That looked to us very suspicious as we had never seen such smoke pillars over the nomad tents. When we asked about the dog, they said that he had stayed behind in the tent. One of us could go and fetch him. Now we saw their plan. Our lives were at stake. They had kept the dog back in order to have a chance of separating Aufschnaiter and me, as they lacked the courage to attack us both at the same time. And probably they had companions waiting where the smoke was rising. If we went there, we would be heavily outnumbered, and they could dispose of us with ease. No one would ever know anything about our disappearance. We were now very sorry not to have listened to the well-meant warnings of the nomads.

As though we suspected nothing we went on a short way in the same direction, talking rapidly to each other. The two men were now on either side of us, while the boy walked behind. Stealing a glance to right and left, we estimated our chances if it came to a fight. The two men wore double sheepskin cloaks, as the robbers do, to protect them against knife thrusts, and long swords were stuck in their belts. Their faces had an expression of lamblike innocence.

Something had to happen. Aufschnaiter thought we ought first to change our direction, so as not to walk blindly into a trap. No sooner said than done. Still speaking, we abruptly turned away.

The Khampas stopped for a moment in surprise, but in a moment rejoined us and barred our way, asking us, in none too friendly tones, where we were going. "To fetch the dog," we answered curtly. Our manner of speaking seemed to intimidate them. They saw that we were prepared to go to any length, so they let us go and after staring after us for a while they hurriedly went on their way, probably to inform their accomplices.

When we got near the tents, the woman came to meet us, leading the dog on a leash. After a friendly greeting, we went on, but this time we followed the road by which we had come to the robber camp. There was now no question of going forward—we had to retrace our steps. Unarmed as we were, to continue would have meant certain death. After a forced march, we arrived in the evening at the home of the friendly family with whom we had stayed two nights before. They were not surprised to hear of our experiences and told us that the Khampas' encampment was called Gyak Bongra, a name which inspired fear throughout the countryside. After this adventure it was a blessing to be able to spend a peaceful night with friendly people.

The next morning we worked out our new travel plan. There was nothing for it but to take the hard road, which led through uninhabited country. We bought more meat from the nomads, as we should probably be a week before seeing a soul.

To avoid going back to Labrang Trowa, we took a short cut entailing a laborious and steep ascent but leading, as we hoped, to the route we meant to follow. Halfway up the steep slope we turned to look at the view and saw, to our horror, two men following us in the distance. No doubt they were Khampas. They had probably visited the nomads and been told which direction we had taken.

What were we to do? We said nothing, but later confessed to each other that we had silently made up our minds to sell our lives as dearly as possible. We tried at first to speed up our pace, but we could not go faster than our yak, who seemed to us to be moving at a snail's pace. We kept on looking back, but could not be sure whether our pursuers were coming up on us or not. We fully realized how heavily handicapped we were by our lack of arms. We had only tent pegs and stones to defend ourselves with against their sharp swords. To have a chance we must depend on our wits. . . . So we marched on for an hour that seemed endless, panting with exertion and constantly turning around. Then we saw that the two men had sat down. We hurried on toward the top of the ridge, looking as we went for a place which would, if need be, serve as good fighting ground. The two men got up, seemed to be taking counsel together, and then we saw them turn around and go back. We breathed again and drove our yak on so that we might soon be out of sight over the far side of the mountain.

When we reached the crest of the ridge, we understood why our two pursuers had preferred to turn back. Before us lay the loneliest landscape I had ever seen. A sea of snowy mountain heights stretched onward endlessly. In the far distance were the Transhimalayas, and like a gap in a row of teeth was the pass which we calculated would lead us to the road we aimed at. First put on the map by Sven Hedin, this pass—the Selala—leads to Shigatse. Being uncertain whether the Khampas had really given up the pursuit, we went on marching even after nightfall. Luckily, the moon was high and, with the snow, gave us plenty of light. We could see even the distant ranges.

I SHALL NEVER FORGET that night march. I had never been through an experience that placed such a strain on the body and the spirit. Our escape from the Khampas was due to the desolation of the region, the nature of which brought us new obstacles to surmount. It was a good thing that I had long ago thrown away my thermometer. Here it would certainly have marked −30 degrees as that was the lowest it could record. But that was certainly more than the reality. Sven Hedin registered −40 degrees hereabouts at this season of the year.

We loped on for hours over the virgin snow, and as we went our minds traveled afar on their own journeys. I was tormented by visions of a warm, comfortable room, delicious hot food, and steaming hot drinks. Curiously enough it was the evocation of a commonplace buffet at Graz, known to me in my student days, which nearly drove me crazy. Aufschnaiter's thoughts lay in another direction. He harbored dark plans of revenge against the robbers and swore to come back with a magazine of arms. Woe to all the Khampas!

At last we broke off our march, unloaded our yak, and crawled under cover. We had taken out our bag of tsampa and some raw meat as we were ravenously hungry, but as soon as we put a spoonful of dry meal into our mouths the metal stuck to our lips and would not come away. We had to tear it loose, amid curses and oaths. With appetites blunted by this painful experience, we huddled up together under our blankets and fell, despite the piercing cold, into the leaden sleep of exhaustion.

The next day we toiled on painfully, trudging along in the footprints of our gallant yak and hardly looking up. In the afternoon we suddenly thought we were seeing the fata morgana, for, far away on the horizon, yet very clearly outlined, appeared three caravans of yaks moving through the snowy scene. They were moving very slowly forward, and then they seemed to come to a stop—but they did not vanish. So it was no mirage. The sight gave us new courage. We summoned up all our strength, drove our yak on, and after three hours' march reached the spot where the caravans were camped. There were some fifteen persons in the caravan—men and women—and when we arrived their tents were already pitched. They were astonished to see us but greeted us kindly and brought us in to get warm by the fire. We found out that they were returning from a combined pilgrimage and trading voyage to Mount Kailas to their homes by Lake Namtsho. They had been warned by the district officials about the brigands and so had chosen to follow this difficult route in order to avoid the region infested by the Khampas. They were bringing home fifty yaks and a couple of hundred sheep. The rest of their herds had been bartered for goods, and they would have been a rich prize for the robbers. That was why the three groups had joined together, and they now invited us to come along with them. Reinforcements could be useful if they met the Khampas.

What a pleasure it was to be once more sitting by a fire and ladling down hot soup. We felt that this meeting had been ordained by providence. We did not forget our brave Armin, for we knew how much we owed him, and we asked the caravan leader to let us load our baggage on one of their free yaks, for which we would pay a day's hire. So our beast was able to enjoy a little rest.

Day after day we wandered on with the caravans and pitched our little mountaineer's tent alongside theirs. We suffered very much from the difficulty of pitching our tents during the hurricanes that often blew in these regions. Unlike the heavy yak-hair tents, which could resist the wind, our light canvas hut would not stand up in rough weather, and we sometimes had to bivouac in the open air. We swore that if we ever again came on an expedition to Tibet we should have with us three yaks, a driver, a nomad's tent, and a rifle!

We thought ourselves very lucky to be allowed to join the caravans. The only thing that disturbed us was the extreme slowness of our progress. Compared with our previous marches, we seemed to be gently strolling along. The nomads start early, and after covering three or four miles, pitch their tents again and send their animals out to graze. Before nightfall they bring them in and fold them near the tents, where they are safe from wolves and can ruminate in peace.

Only now did we perceive how we had imposed on our poor Armin! He must have thought us as mad as the Tibetans did when we spent our days climbing the mountains round Kyirong. During our long periods of rest, we devoted much time to filling in our diaries, which we had recently neglected. We also began systematically to collect information about the road to Lhasa from the people in the caravan. We questioned them separately and gradually gathered a definite sequence of place names. That was of great value to us as it would enable us later to ask the nomads the way from one place to another. We had long agreed that we could not go on spending our life taking short walks. We must leave the caravan in the near future. We took leave of our friends on Christmas Eve and started off again alone. We felt fresh and rested, and covered more than fourteen miles on the first day. Late in the evening we came to a wide plain on which were some isolated tents. Their inmates seemed to be very much on their guard, for as we approached, a couple of wild-looking men, heavily armed, came up to us. They shouted at us rudely and told us to go to the devil. We did not budge, but put up our hands to show we were not armed and explained to them that we were harmless pilgrims. In spite of our rest days with the caravan, we must have presented a pitiful appearance. After a short discussion, the owner of the larger tent asked us in to spend the night. We warmed ourselves by the fire and were given butter tea and a rare delicacy—a piece of white bread each. It was stale and hard as stone, but this little present on Christmas Eve in the wilds of Tibet meant more to us than a well-cooked Christmas dinner had ever done at home.

Our host treated us roughly at first. When we told him by what route we aimed at reaching Lhasa, he said dryly that if we had not been killed up to now, we certainly would be in the next few days. The country was full of Khampas. Without arms we would be easy prey for them. He said this in a fatalistic tone, as one utters a self-evident truth. We felt very disheartened and asked for his advice. He recommended we take the road to Shigatse, which we could reach in a week. We would not hear of that. He thought for a while and then advised us to apply to the district officer of this region, whose tent was only a few miles distant. The officer would be able to give us an escort if we absolutely insisted on going through the robbers' country.

That evening we had so much to discuss that we hardly gave a thought to Christmas in our own homes. At last we agreed to take a chance and visit the bönpo. It took us only a few hours to reach his tent, and we found it a good omen that he greeted us in a friendly way and placed a tent at our disposal. He then called his colleague and we all four sat down in conference. This time we discarded our story about being Indian pilgrims. We gave ourselves out as Europeans and demanded protection against the bandits. Naturally, we were traveling with the permission of the government and I coolly handed him the old travel permit, which the garpon had formerly given us in Gartok. (This document had a story. We three had tossed up to decide who should keep it, and Kopp had won. But when he left us, I had had an inspiration and bought it from him. And now its hour had come.) The two officials examined the seal and were clearly impressed by the document. They were now convinced that we had a right to be in Tibet. The only question they asked was where the third member of the party was. We explained that he had been taken sick and had traveled back to India via Tradün. This satisfied the bönpos, who promised us an escort; they would be relieved at different stages by fresh men, and would conduct us as far as the northern main road.

That was a real Christmas greeting for us! And now at last we felt like keeping the Feast. We had stored up a little rice at Kyirong especially for the occasion. This we prepared and invited the two bönpos to come and share it. They came bringing all sorts of good things with them, and we passed a happy, friendly evening together.

On the following day a nomad accompanied us to the next encampment and "delivered" us there. It was something like a relay race with us as the baton. Our guide went back after handing us over. With our next guide we made wonderful progress and we realized how useful it was to have a companion who really knew the way, even though he did not provide absolute security against robbers.

Our permanent companions were the wind and the cold. To us it seemed as if the whole world was a blizzard with a temperature of –30 degrees Centigrade. We suffered much from being insufficiently clothed, and I was lucky to be able to obtain an old sheepskin cloak from a tent dweller. It was tight for me and lacked half a sleeve, but it cost me only two rupees. Our shoes were in a wretched state and could not last much longer; and as for gloves, we hadn't any. Aufschnaiter had had frostbite in the hands, and I had trouble with my feet. We endured our sufferings with dull resignation, and it needed a lot of energy to accomplish our daily quota of miles. How happy we would have been to rest for a few days in a warm nomad's tent. Even the life of the nomads, hard and poverty-stricken as it was, often seemed to us seductively luxurious. But we dared not delay if we wanted to get through to Lhasa before our provisions ran out. And then? Well, we preferred not to speculate.

We often saw, happily in the far distance, men on horseback, whom we knew to be Khampas from the unusual type of dogs that accompanied them. These creatures are less hairy than ordinary Tibetan dogs, lean, swift as the wind, and indescribably ugly. We thanked God we had no occasion to meet them and their masters at close quarters.

On this stage of our travels we discovered a frozen lake that, on later search, we could find on no map. Aufschnaiter sketched it into our map at once. The local inhabitants call it Yöchabtso, which means "water of sacrifice." It lies at the foot of a chain of glaciers. Before we came to the main road, we met some armed footpads carrying modern European rifles against which no courage could have helped us. They, however, let us alone—no doubt because we looked so wretched and down-at-heel. There are times when visible poverty has its advantages.

After five days' march we reached the famous Tasam road. We had always imagined this to be a regular highway that, once reached, would put an end to all the miseries of our march. Imagine our disappointment when we could not find even the trace of a track! The country was in no way different from that through which we had been wandering for weeks. There were, it is true, a few empty tents at which caravans could halt, but no other signs of an organized route.

For the last stage we had been accompanied by a couple of sturdy women, who now handed us over to the Tasam road after a touching farewell. We quartered ourselves in one of the empty tents and lit a fire, after which we took stock of our position. We really had some grounds for satisfaction. The most difficult part of our journey lay behind us, and we were now on a frequented route, which led straight to Lhasa, fifteen days' march ahead. We ought to have been happy in the knowledge that we were so near our goal. But, as a matter of fact, our terrific exertions had got us down to such an extent that we were no longer capable of enjoyment. What with frostbite, and lack of money and food, we felt nothing but anxiety. We worried most of all about our animals. My faithful dog was reduced to skin and bones. We had hardly enough food to keep ourselves alive and could spare very little for him. His feet were in such a dreadful state that he could not keep up with us, and often we had to wait for hours in our camp before he arrived. The plight of the yak was little better. He had not had enough grass to eat for weeks and was fearfully emaciated. It is true that we had left the snow behind us after leaving Lake Yöchabtso, but the grass was scanty and dry, and there was little time for grazing.

All the same we had to go forward next day; and the fact that we were now on a caravan route, and had no longer to think of ourselves as Marco Polos in the unknown gave a spur to our morale.

Our first day on the Tasam route differed very little from our worst stage in uninhabited country. We did not meet a soul. A raging storm, driving snow, and swathes of mist made our journey a hell. Fortunately the wind was at our backs and drove us onward. If it had been in our faces, we could not have moved a step forward. All four of us were glad when we saw the roadside tents in the evening. I made the following note in my diary that night: December 3, 1945. Heavy snowstorm with mist—first mist we have met in Tibet. Temperature: about −30 degrees. The most exhausting day of our journey up to date. The yak's load kept slipping off, and we nearly got frozen hands adjusting it. Lost the way once and had to go back two miles. Towards evening reached the route-station of Nyatsang. Eight tents. One tent occupied by road officer and his family. Well received.

SO THIS WAS our second New Year's Eve in Tibet. Thinking about what we had achieved in all this time made one despondent. We were still "illegal" travelers—two down-at-heel, half-starved vagabonds forced to dodge the officials, still bound for a visionary goal that we seemed unable to reach—the Forbidden City. On such a night, one's thoughts turn in sentimental retrospect to home and family. But such dreams could not distract us from the stern reality of the struggle to keep alive, which needed all our physical and spiritual strength. For us an evening in a warm tent was more important than if, in the safety of our homes, we had been given a racing car as a New Year's gift.

So we kept St. Sylvester's day in our own fashion. We wanted to stay here somewhat longer in order to thaw ourselves out and to give our beasts a day of rest. Our old travel paper did its job here too, and the road official was friendly and put his servants at our disposal, sending us water and fuel.

We took it easy and slept late. As we were breakfasting some-what before noon, there was a stir before the tents. The cook of a bönpo, wearing a foxskin hat, had arrived to announce the coming of his master and make preparations for him. He ran around and threw his weight about properly.

The arrival of a high official might be of importance for us, but we had been long enough in Asia to know that "high" official status is a relative conception. For the moment we did not excite our-selves. But things turned out well. The bönpo soon arrived on horseback surrounded by a swarm of servants. He was a merchant in the service of the government and was at present engaged in bringing several hundred loads of sugar and cotton to Lhasa.

Hearing about us, he naturally wanted to ask questions. Putting on a virtuous expression I handed him our travel paper, which had the usual good effect. No longer acting the stern official, he invited us to travel with his convoy. That sounded well, so we gave up our rest day and began to pack our baggage, as the caravan was to move on in the afternoon. One of the drivers shook his head as he looked at Armin, a veritable skeleton, and finally offered for a small sum to load our baggage on one of the Tasam yaks and let our beast run loose with us. We gladly agreed. Then off we started in haste. We had to go on with the caravan on foot, while the bönpo and his servants, who had changed horses at the stage, started later. They caught us up before long.

It had been a sacrifice to give up our rest day and set out on a twelve-mile march. My poor dog was too exhausted to accompany us, so I left him behind in the settlement, which was better for him than dying on the road.

Marching with the caravan, we covered long distances every day. We profited by the patronage of the bönpo and were everywhere well received. It was only at Lhölam that the road official looked askance at us. He would not even give us fuel and insisted on our showing our permit to go to Lhasa. Unfortunately we could not oblige him. However, we had a roof over our heads and were to be glad of it, because soon after our arrival all sorts of suspicious-looking characters began to gather around the tents. We recognized them at once for Khampas, but we were too tired to bother about them and left the rest of our party to deal with the situation. We at least had nothing worth stealing. Some of them tried to get into our tent, but we shouted at them, and they went away.

The next morning we missed our yak. We had tethered him the night before and thought he might be grazing somewhere, but Aufschnaiter and I could find no sign of him. The ruffians who had been there the night before had also vanished, and the connection was obvious. The loss of our yak was a serious blow to us, and we burst into the tent of the Tasam official and in my rage I threw the packsaddle and coverings at his feet, telling him that he was responsible for the loss of our beast. We had become very much attached to Armin V, the only yak who had served us well, but we had no time to mourn his loss. We had to catch up with the caravan, which had gone ahead some hours before with our baggage.

We had already been marching for some days toward a huge chain of mountains. We knew they were the Nyenchenthangla range. There was only one way through them and that was the pass that led direct to Lhasa. On our way to the mountains, we passed through low hills. The country was completely deserted, and we did not see even wild asses. The weather had improved greatly, and the visibility was so good, that, at a distance of six miles, our next stopping place appeared to be just in front of us.

The next halt was at a place called Tokar. From here we began the ascent into the mountains, and the next regular station was five days away. We did not dare to think how we could hold out till then. In any case, we did what we could to keep up our strength and bought a lot of meat to keep us going.

The days seemed endless and the nights even longer. We traveled through an improbably beautiful landscape and came to one of the largest of the world's lakes—Nam Tsho or Tengri Nor. But we hardly looked at it, though we had for long looked forward to seeing this mighty inland sea. The once-longed-for sight could not shake us out of our apathy. The climb through the rarefied air had left us breathless, and the prospect of an ascent to nearly 20,000 feet was paralyzing. From time to time we looked with wonder at the still higher peaks visible from our route. At last we reached the summit of our pass, Guring La. Before us this pass had only once been crossed by a European. This was Littledale, an Englishman, who came over it in 1895. Sven Hedin had estimated it at nearly 20,000 feet and described it as the highest of the passes in the Trans-himalaya region. I think I am right in saying that it is the world's highest pass traversable all the year round.

HERE WE AGAIN FOUND the typical cairns, and fluttering over them the brightest-colored prayer flags I had yet seen. Near them was a row of stone tables with prayers inscribed on them—an imperishable expression of the joy felt by thousands of pilgrims when, after their long and weary march, they saw the pass opening to them the road to the holiest of cities.

Here, too, we met an astonishing throng of pilgrims returning to their distant homes. How often has this road echoed to the words *"Om mani padme hum,"* the time-honored formula of prayer that all Buddhists use and the pilgrims murmur ceaselessly, hoping, among other things, that it will protect them against what they believe is poison gas and we know to be lack of oxygen. They would do better to keep their mouths closed! From time to time we saw on the slopes below us skeletons of animals, bearing witness to the dangerous nature of the road. Our driver told us that almost every winter pilgrims lost their lives in snowstorms in this mountain crossing. We thanked God for the good weather that had favored us during our climb of seven thousand feet.

The first part of our descent led over a glacier. I had fresh cause to wonder at the extraordinary sure-footedness of the yaks in finding their way across the ice. As we stumbled along I couldn't help thinking how much easier it would be to glide over these smooth, uncreviced surfaces on skis. I suppose Aufschnaiter and I were the only people who had even talked about skiing on the Pilgrims' Road to Lhasa.

While we were marching along, a young couple caught up to

us. They had come a long distance and, like us, were bound for Lhasa. They were glad to join the caravan, and we fell into conversation with them. Their story was a remarkable one.

This pretty young woman with her rosy cheeks and thick black pigtails had lived happy and contented with her three husbands— three brothers they were—for whom she kept house in a nomad tent in the Changthang. One evening a young stranger arrived and asked for lodging. From that moment everything was different. It must have been a case of this famous "love at first sight." The young people understood each other without saying anything and the next morning went off together. They made nothing of a flight over the wintry plain. Now they were happy to have arrived here, and meant to begin a new life in Lhasa.

I remember this young woman as a gleam of sunshine in those hard, heavy days. Once as we were resting she took out her wallet and smilingly handed each of us a dried apricot. This modest gift was as precious to us as the white bread the nomad had given us on Christmas night.

In the course of our journey, I realized how strong and enduring Tibetan women are. This very young woman kept up with us easily and carried her pack as well as a man. She had not to worry about her future. In Lhasa she would hire herself out as a daily servant and with her robust country-girl's health easily earn her living.

We marched for three successive days without coming to tents. Then we saw in the distance a great column of smoke rising into the sky. We wondered if it came from a chimney or a burning house, but when we got near we saw it was the steam rising from hot springs. We were soon gazing at a scene of great natural beauty. A number of springs bubbled out of the ground, and in the middle of the cloud of steam shot up a splendid little geyser fifteen feet high. After poetry, prose! Our next thought was to have a bath. Our young couple disapproved, but we did not let that deter us. The water was boiling when it came out of the ground, but it was quickly cooled to a bearable temperature by the frosty air. We hurriedly turned one of the pools into a comfortable bathtub. What a joy it was! Since we had left the hot springs at Kyirong we had not been able to wash or bathe, and our hair and beards were frozen stiff. In the brook which flowed out of the hot springs there were a lot of good-sized fish. We hungrily debated how to catch them—we could boil them easily enough in the spring—but we found no way, and so, much refreshed, we hurried on to catch up with the caravan.

We spent the night with the yak drivers in their tent. There I had for the first time in my life a bad attack of sciatica. I had always regarded this painful complaint as a disorder of old age and had never dreamed I should make acquaintance with it so soon. I probably contracted it as a result of sleeping every night on the ground.

One morning I could not get up. Besides suffering frightful pain, I was chilled by the thought that I would not be able to go on. I clenched my teeth and hoisted myself to my feet and took a few steps. The movement helped, but from that time on I suffered much every day during the first few miles of our march.

In the evening of the fourth day after crossing the pass, we reached Samsar, where there was a road station. At last we were in an inhabited place with built houses, monasteries, and a castle. This is one of the most important road junctions in Tibet. Five routes meet here, and there is a lively caravan traffic. The road-houses are crowded, and animals are changed in the relay stables. Our bönpo had already been here for two days, but though on a government mission he had to wait five days for fresh yaks. He procured us a room, fuel, and a servant. For the moment the traffic was, so to speak, intense and we had to make up our minds for a long wait, for we could not go on alone.

We used our leisure to go on a day's excursion to some hot springs that we had seen steaming in the distance. These turned out to be a unique natural phenomenon. We came to a regular lake whose black bubbling waters flowed off into a clear brook. Of course we decided to bathe, and walked into the water at a point where it was pleasantly warm. As we walked upstream toward the lake, it grew hotter and hotter. Aufschnaiter gave up first, but I kept on, hoping that the heat would be good for my sciatica. I wallowed in the hot water. I had brought with me my last piece of soap from Kyirong, and put it on the bank beside me, looking forward to a thorough soaping as the climax of my bath. Unluckily, I had not noticed that a crow was observing me with interest. He suddenly swooped and carried off my treasure. I sprang onto the bank with an oath, but in a moment was back in the hot water, my teeth chattering with cold. In Tibet the crows are as thievish as magpies are with us.

On our way back we saw for the first time a Tibetan regiment—five hundred soldiers on maneuvers. The population is not very enthusiastic about these military exercises, as the soldiers have the right to requisition what they want. They camp in their own tents, which are pitched in very orderly fashion, and there is therefore no billeting, but the local people have to supply them with transport and even riding horses.

When we came back to our lodging a surprise was awaiting us. They had given us as roommate a man wearing fetters on his ankles and able to take only very short steps. He told us smilingly, and as if it was a perfectly normal thing, that he was a murderer and a robber and had been condemned first to receive two hundred lashes and afterward to wear fetters for the rest of his life. This made my flesh creep. Were we already classed with murderers? However, we soon learned that in Tibet a convicted criminal is not necessarily looked down on. Our man had no social disadvantages:

he joined in conversation with everybody and lived on alms. And he didn't live badly.

It had got around that we were Europeans, and curious persons were always coming to see us. Among these was a nice young monk, who was bringing some goods to the monastery of Drebung and had to be off the next day. When he heard that we only had one load of baggage and were very keen to continue our journey, he offered us a free yak in his caravan. He asked no questions about our travel permit. As we had previously reckoned, the nearer we came to the capital, the less trouble we had—the argument being that foreigners who had already traveled so far into Tibet must obviously possess a permit. Nevertheless, we thought it wise not to stay too long in any one place, so as not to invite curiosity.

We accepted the monk's offer at once and bade farewell to our bönpo with many expressions of gratitude. We started in pitch darkness, not long after midnight. After crossing the district of Yangpachen, we entered a valley that debouched into the plain of Lhasa.

So near to Lhasa! The name had always given us a thrill. On our painful marches and during icy nights, we had clung to it and drawn new strength from it. No pilgrim from the most distant province could ever have yearned for the Holy City more than we did. We had already got much nearer to Lhasa than Sven Hedin. He had made two attempts to get through from the region through which we had come, but had always been held up in Changthang by the escarpment of Nyenchenthangla. We two poor wanderers were naturally less conspicuous than his caravan, and we had our knowledge of Tibetan to help us, in addition to the stratagems we had been compelled to use; so we had some things in our favor.

In the early morning we arrived at the next locality, Dechen, where we were to spend the day. We did not like the idea. There were two district officers in residence, and we did not expect them to be taken in by any travel document.

Our friend the monk had not yet arrived. He had been able to allow himself a proper night's sleep, as he traveled on horseback, and no doubt he started about the time when we arrived at Dechen.

We cautiously started looking for a lodging and had a wonderful "break." We made the acquaintance of a young lieutenant, who very obligingly offered us his room, as he had to leave about midday. He had been collecting in the neighborhood the money contributions payable in lieu of military service. We ventured to ask him whether he could not take our baggage in his convoy. Of course we would pay for it. He agreed at once, and a few hours later we were marching with light hearts out of the village behind the caravan.

Our satisfaction was premature. As we passed the last houses someone called to us, and when we turned around we found ourselves facing a distinguished-looking gentleman in rich silk garments. Unmistakably the bönpo. He asked politely but in an authoritative tone where we had come from and where we were going. Only presence of mind could save us. Bowing and scraping we said we were going on a short walk and had left our papers behind. On our return we would give ourselves the pleasure of waiting on his lordship. The trick succeeded, and we cleared off.

We found ourselves marching into spring scenery. The pasture lands grew greener as we went on. Birds twittered in the plantations, and we felt too warm in our sheepskin cloaks, though it was only mid-January.

Lhasa was only three days away. All day Aufschnaiter and I tramped on alone and caught up with the lieutenant and his little caravan only in the evening. In this region all sorts of animals were used for transport—donkeys, horses, cows, and bullocks. One saw yaks only in the caravans, as the peasants had not enough pasture to feed herds of them. Everywhere we saw the villagers irrigating their fields. The spring gales would come later, and if the soil were too dry it would all be blown away in dust. It often took generations before constant watering made the soil fertile. Here there is very little snow to protect the winter seed, and the peasants cannot grow more than one crop. The altitude has naturally a great influence on agriculture. At 16,000 feet only barley will thrive, and the peasants are half-nomads. In some regions the barley ripens in sixty days. The Tölung valley through which we were now passing is 12,000 feet above sea level, and here they grow roots, potatoes, and mustard.

We spent the last night before coming to Lhasa in a peasant's house. It was nothing like so attractive as the stylish wooden houses in Kyirong. In these parts, wood is rare. With the exception of small tables and wooden bedsteads, there is practically no furniture. The houses, built of mud bricks, have no windows; light comes in only through the door or the smoke hole in the ceiling.

Our hosts belonged to a well-to-do peasant family. As is usual in a feudally organized country, the peasant manages the property for his landlord and must produce so much for the latter before making any profit for himself. In our household there were three sons, two of whom worked on the property while the third was preparing to become a monk. The family kept cows, horses, a few fowls, and pigs—the first I had seen in Tibet. These are not fed but live on offal and whatever they can root up in the fields.

We passed a restless night thinking of the next day, which would decide our future. Now came the great question: even if we managed to smuggle ourselves into the town, would we be able to stay there? We had no money left. How, then, were we going to live? And our appearance! We looked more like brigands from the Changthang than Europeans. Over our stained woolen trousers and torn shirts we wore greasy sheepskin cloaks, which showed, even at a distance, how we had knocked about in them. Aufschnaiter wore the remains of a pair of Indian Army boots on his feet, and my shoes were in fragments. Both of us were more barefoot than shod. No, our appearance was certainly not in our favor. Our beards were perhaps our most striking feature. Like all Mongols, the Tibetans have almost no hair on their faces or bodies, whereas we had long, tangled, luxuriant beards. For this reason we were often taken for Kazaks, a Central Asian tribe whose members migrated in swarms during the war from Soviet Russia to Tibet. They marched in with their families and flocks and plundered right and left, and the Tibetan army was eager to drive them on into India. The Kazaks are often fair-skinned and blue-eyed and their beards grow normally. It is not surprising that we were mistaken for them, and met with a cold reception from so many nomads.

There was nothing to be done about our appearance. We could not spruce ourselves up before going into Lhasa. Even if we had had money, where could we buy clothes?

Since leaving Nangtse—the name of the last village—we had been left to our own devices. The lieutenant had ridden on into Lhasa, and we had to bargain with our host about transport for our baggage. He lent us a cow and a servant, and when we had paid we had a rupee and a half left, and a gold piece sewn up in a piece of cloth. We had decided that if we could not find any transport, we would just leave our stuff behind. Barring our diaries, notes, and maps, we had nothing of value. Nothing was going to keep us back.

7

THE
FORBIDDEN
CITY

I t was January 15, 1946, when we set out on our last march.
From Tölung we came into the broad valley of Kyichu. We
turned a corner and saw, gleaming in the distance, the golden roofs
of the Potala, the winter residence of the Dalai Lama and the most
famous landmark of Lhasa. This moment compensated us for
much. We felt inclined to go down on our knees like the pilgrims
and touch the ground with our foreheads. Since leaving Kyirong
we had covered over six hundred miles with the vision of this fabulous city ever in our mind's eye. We had marched for seventy
days and rested during only five. That meant a daily average of almost ten miles. Forty-five days of our journey had been spent in
crossing the Changthang—days full of hardship and unceasing
struggle against cold, hunger, and danger. Now all that was forgotten as we gazed at the golden pinnacles—six miles more and we
had reached our goal.

We sat down near the cairns that the pilgrims put up to mark
their first sight of the Holy City. Our driver, meanwhile, performed his devotions. Going on, we soon came to Shingdongka,
the last village before Lhasa. The cowman refused to come any

farther, but nothing could discourage us now. We went to find the bönpo and coolly informed him that we were the advance party of a powerful foreign personage on his way to Lhasa and that we had to reach the city as quickly as possible in order to find quarters for our master. The bönpo swallowed our tale and gave us an ass and a driver. Years later this story used still to set people laughing at parties in Lhasa, even in the houses of ministers. The fact is the Tibetans are very proud of their organization for keeping foreigners out of the country, and they found the manner in which we had broken through the barriers not only deserving of attention but highly humorous. That was all to our advantage, for the Tibetans are a laughter-loving folk.

During the last six miles of the road, we mixed with a stream of pilgrims and caravans. From time to time we passed stalls displaying all sorts of delicacies—sweets, white bread, and whatnot—which almost brought the tears to our eyes. But we had no money. Our last rupee belonged to our driver.

We soon began to recognize the landmarks of the town about which we had read so often. Over there must be Chagpori, the hill on which stands one of the two famous schools of medicine. And here in front of us was Drebung, the greatest monastery in the world, which houses ten thousand monks and is a city in itself, with its multitude of stone houses and hundreds of gilded pinnacles pointing upward above the shrines. Somewhat lower down lay the terraces of Nechung, another monastery, which has for centuries been the home of the greatest mystery of Tibet. Here is made manifest the presence of a protective deity, whose secret oracle guides the destines of Tibet and is consulted by the government before any important decision is taken. We had still five miles to go and every few steps there was something fresh to look at. We passed through broad, well-tended meadows surmounted by willows where the Dalai Lama pastures his horses.

For nearly an hour a long stone wall flanked our road, and we were told that the summer palace of the God-King lay behind it. Next we passed the British Legation, situated just outside the town, half-hidden by willow trees. Our driver turned to go toward it, thinking it must be our destination, and we had some trouble in persuading him to go straight on. In fact, for a moment we hesitated about going there ourselves, but the memory of the internment camp was still present in our minds, and we thought that, after all, we were in Tibet and that it was the Tibetans we should ask for hospitality.

Nobody stopped us or bothered about us. We could not understand it, but finally realized that no one, not even a European, was suspect, because no one had ever come to Lhasa without a pass.

As we approached, the Potala towered ever higher before us. As yet, we could see nothing of the town itself, which lay behind the hills on which the palace and the school of medicine stood. Then we saw a great gate crowned with three chortens, which spans the gap between the two hills and forms the entrance to the city. Our excitement was intense. Now we should know our fate for certain. Almost every book about Lhasa says that sentries are posted here to guard the Holy City. We approached with beating hearts. But there was nothing. No soldiers, no control post—only a few beggars holding out their hands for alms. We mingled with a group of people and walked unhindered through the gateway into the town. Our driver told us that the group of houses on our left was only a sort of suburb, and so we went on through an unbuilt area coming ever nearer to the middle of the town. We spoke no word, and to this day I can find no terms to express how overwhelming were our sensations. Our minds, exhausted by hardships, could not absorb the shock of so many and such powerful impressions.

WE WERE SOON in front of the turquoise-roofed bridge and saw for the first time the spires of the Cathedral of Lhasa. The sun set and bathed the scene in an unearthly light. Shivering with cold, we had to find a lodging, but in Lhasa it is not so simple to walk into a house as into a tent in the Changthang. We should probably be at once reported to the authorities. But we had to try. In the first house we found a dumb servant, who would not listen to us. Next door there was only a maid who screamed for help till her mistress came and begged us to go somewhere else. She said she would be driven out of the quarter if she received us. We did not believe that the government could be as strict as all that, but we did not want to cause her unpleasantness and so went out again. We walked through some narrow streets and found ourselves already at the other side of the town. There we came to a house much larger and finer looking than any we had yet seen, with stables in the courtyard. We hurried in to find ourselves confronted by servants, who abused us and told us to go away. We were not to be moved and unloaded our donkey. Our driver had already been pressing us to let him go home. He had noticed that everything was not in order. We gave him his money, and he went off with a sigh of relief.

The servants were in despair when they saw that we had come to stay. They begged and implored us to go and pointed out that they would get into fearful trouble when their master returned. We, too, felt far from comfortable at the idea of exacting hospitality by force, but we did not move. More and more people were attracted by the din, and the scene reminded me of my departure from Kyirong. We remained deaf to all protestations. Dead-tired and half-starved we sat on the ground by our bundles, indifferent to what might befall us. We wanted only to sit, to rest, to sleep.

The angry cries of the crowd suddenly ceased. They had seen our swollen and blistered feet, and, openhearted simple folk as they were, they felt pity for us. A woman began it. She was the one who had implored us to leave her house. Now she brought us butter tea. And they brought us all sorts of things—tsampa, provisions, and fuel. The people wanted to atone for their inhospitable reception. We fell hungrily on the food and for the moment forgot everything else.

Suddenly we heard ourselves addressed in perfect English. We looked up, and though there was not much light to see by, we recognized that the richly clad Tibetan who had spoken to us must be a person of the highest standing. Astonished and happy we asked him if he was not, perchance, one of the four young nobles who had been sent to school at Rugby. He said he was not but that he had passed many years in India. We told him shortly what had happened to us, saying we were Germans, and begging to be taken in. He thought for a moment and then said that he could not admit us to his house without the approval of the town magistrate, but he would go to that official and ask for permission.

When he had gone, the other people told us that he was an important official and was in charge of the electricity works. We did not dare to set too much store by what he had said, but nevertheless began to settle down for the night. Meanwhile, we sat by the fire and talked to the people, who kept coming and going. Then a servant came to us and asked us to follow him saying that Mr. Thangme, the "Master of Electricity," invited us into his house. They called him respectfully "Kungö," equivalent to "Highness," and we followed suit.

Thangme and his young wife received us very cordially. Their five children stood around and looked at us openmouthed. Their father had good news for us. The magistrate had allowed him to take us in for one night, but future arrangements would have to be decided by the cabinet. We did not worry our heads about the future. After all, we were in Lhasa and were the guests of a noble family. A nice, comfortable room was already prepared for us with a small iron stove, which warmed us well. It was seven years since we had seen a stove! The fuel used was juniper wood, which smelled very good and was a real luxury, for it needed weeks of travel on the backs of yaks to bring it into Lhasa. We hardly dared, in our ragged garments, to sit on our clean, carpet-covered beds. They brought us a splendid Chinese supper, and as we ate they all stood around and talked to us without ceasing. What we must have been through! They could hardly believe that we had crossed the Changthang in winter and climbed over the Nyenchenthangla range. Our knowledge of Tibetan astonished them. But how ugly and shabby we seemed to ourselves in these civilized surroundings. Our possessions, indispensable to our journey, suddenly lost all their attraction, and we felt we would be glad to be rid of them.

Dead-tired and confused in mind, we went at last to bed, but we could not go to sleep. We had spent too many nights on the hard ground with nothing but our sheepskin cloaks and a torn blanket to cover us. Now we had soft beds and a well-warmed room, but our bodies could not quickly accustom themselves to the change and our thoughts revolved like mill wheels in our heads. All we had gone through crowded into our minds—the internment camp and the adventures and hardships of the twenty-one months since our escape. And we thought of our comrades and the unbroken monotony of their lives, for though the war had long been over the prisoners were still in captivity. But, for that matter were *we* now free?

Before we were properly awake, we found a servant with sweet tea and cakes standing by our beds. Then they brought us hot water and we attacked our long beards with our razors. After shaving we looked more respectable but our long hair was a grave problem. A Muslim barber was called in to get busy on our manes. The result was somewhat exotic, but provoked lively admiration. Tibetans have no trouble with their coiffure. They have either pigtails or shaven heads.

We did not see Thangme till noon, when he came home much relieved after a visit to the foreign minister. He brought us good news and told us we would not be handed over to the English. For the time being we might remain in Lhasa but were politely requested to stay indoors until the regent, who was in a retreat in Taglung Tra, decided about our future. We were given to understand that this was a precautionary measure made advisable by previous incidents in which fanatical monks had been involved. The government was willing to feed and clothe us.

We were highly delighted. A few days' rest was just what we needed. We attacked a mountain of old newspapers with enthusiasm, though the news we gathered was not precisely exhilarating. The whole world was still simmering, and our country was going through hard times.

On the same day, we received a visit from an official sent by the town magistrate. He was accompanied by six policemen, who looked dirty and untrustworthy. But our visitor was most polite and asked leave to inspect our baggage. We were astonished that he should be doing his job with such exactness. He had with him a report from Kyirong which he compared with the dates of our itinerary. We ventured to ask him if all the officials through whose districts we had passed would really be punished. "The whole matter will come before the cabinet," he said thoughtfully, "and the officials must expect to be punished." This upset us very much, and to his amusement we told him how we had dodged the district officers and how often we had deceived them. It was our turn to laugh when he then announced to us that the evening before he had been expecting a German invasion of Lhasa. It seems that everyone with whom we had spoken had rushed off to report to the magistrate. They had the impression that German troops were marching into the city!

In any case, we were the talk of the town. Everyone wanted to see us and to hear the story of our adventures with his own ears, and as we were not allowed out, people came to visit us. Mrs. Thangme had her hands full and prepared her best tea service to receive guests. We were initiated into the ceremonial of tea parties. Respect for guests is shown by the value and beauty of the tea service. The table stand consists of a metal mat, often of gold or silver, on which stands the Chinese teacup. I often saw marvelous Chinese tea sets many hundreds of years old.

Every day important guests came to Thangme's house. He himself was a noble of the fifth class, and since etiquette is very closely observed here, he had hitherto received the visits only of persons of equal or inferior rank. But now it was the most highly placed personages who wanted to see us. Foremost among them was the son of the celebrated Minister Tsarong and his wife. We had already read much about his father. Born in humble circumstances, he became the favorite of the thirteenth Dalai Lama, rose to a highly honorable position, and acquired a great fortune by his industry and intelligence. Forty years ago the Dalai Lama was obliged to flee before the Chinese into India, and Tsarong then rendered his master valuable service. He was for many years a cabinet minister and as first favorite of the Lama had virtually the powers of a regent. Subsequently, a new favorite named Khünpela dislodged Tsarong from his position, of authority. He was, however, able to retain his rank and dignities. Tsarong was now in the third order of nobility and was Master of the Mint.

His son was twenty-six years old. He had been brought up in India and spoke fluent English. Conscious of his own importance he wore a golden amulet in his pigtail, as the son of a minister had the right to do.

When this young noble came to call, servants handed tea and soon the conversation became lively. The minister's son was an incredibly versatile young man with a special interest in technical matters. He asked us about the latest discoveries, and told us that he had put together his own radio receiving set and fixed a wind-driven generator on the roof of his house.

We were in the middle of a technical discussion in English when his wife interrupted us laughingly and said she wanted to ask us some questions. Yangchenla, as she was called, was one of the beauties of Lhasa; she was well dressed and very soignée, and clearly acquainted with the use of powder, rouge, and lipstick. She was not at all shy, as was obvious from the lively manner in which she questioned us in Tibetan about our journey. Now and again she broke into our explanations with swift gestures and bursts of laughter. She was particularly amused by our account of how we had imposed on the officials with our expired travel permit. She seemed to be astonished at our fluency in Tibetan, but we noticed that neither she nor even the most staid of our visitors could forbear from laughing at us from time to time. Later our friends told us that we spoke the commonest kind of peasant dialect that one could imagine. It was rather like a backwoodsman from the remotest Alpine valley talking his own lingo in a Viennese drawing room. Our visitors were immensely amused but much too polite to correct us.

By the time this young couple left us we had made friends with them. They had brought with them some very welcome gifts—linen, pullovers, and cigarettes, and they begged us to tell them frankly when we wanted anything. The minister's son promised to help us and later delivered a message from his father inviting us to go and stay with him if the government gave us their approbation. That all sounded very consoling.

More visitors came trooping in. Our next was a general of the Tibetan Army, who was desperately anxious to learn everything possible about Rommel. He spoke with enthusiasm of the German general and said that with his smattering of English he had read everything available about him in the newspapers. In this respect Lhasa is not at all isolated. Newspapers come in from all over the world via India. The Indian daily papers arrive regularly a week after publication. There are even a few persons in the town who take *Life*.

The procession of visitors continued. Among them were highly placed monks, who courteously brought us gifts. Some of them became my good friends later on. Then there was a representative of the Chinese Legation and after him an official belonging to the British Agency in Sikkim.

We were particularly honored by the visit of the Commander in Chief of the Tibetan Army, General Künsangtse, who insisted on seeing us before leaving for China and India on a friendly mission. He was the younger brother of the foreign minister and an unusually well-informed man. It took a load off our minds when he assured us that our request for permission to stay in Tibet would certainly be approved.

We gradually began to feel at home. Our relations with Thangme and his wife developed into a cordial friendship. We were mothered and well-fed, and everyone was pleased to see that we had such good appetites. However, doubtless as a reaction from hardship and overstrain, we suffered from all sorts of minor complaints. Aufschnaiter had an attack of fever, and my sciatica gave me a lot of trouble. Thangme sent for the doctor of the Chinese Legation, who had studied in Berlin and Bordeaux. He examined us in approved European style and prescribed various medicines.

IT IS PROBABLE that no other country in the world would welcome two poor fugitives as Tibet welcomed us. Our parcel of clothes, the gift of the government, had arrived with apologies for delay caused by the fact that we were taller than the average Tibetan and there were no ready-made clothes to fit us. So our suits and shoes were made to measure. We were as pleased as children. At last we were able to throw away our lousy old rags. Our new suits, though not up to the highest sartorial standards, were decent and tidy and quite good enough for us.

In the intervals between our numerous visits, we worked at our notebooks and diaries. And we soon made friends with the Thangmes' children, who usually had already gone off to school before we got up. In the evening they showed us their homework, which interested me very much as I was taking some trouble to learn the written language. Aufschnaiter had long been studying this and during our wanderings had taught me something, but it took me years to learn to write Tibetan more or less fluently. The individual letters present no difficulty, but their arrangement into syllables is no easy task. Many of the characters are taken from the ancient Indian scripts, and Tibetan writing looks more like Hindi than Chinese. Fine, durable parchmentlike paper is used and Chinese ink. There are in Tibet several high-class mills, where the paper is made from juniper wood. In addition, thousands of loads of paper are imported yearly from Nepal and Bhutan, where the stuff is manufactured in the same way as in Tibet. I have often watched the process of papermaking on the banks of the Kyichu River. The chief drawback of Tibetan paper is that the surface is not smooth enough, which makes writing difficult. Children are usually given wooden tablets for their exercises and use watered ink and bamboo pens. The writing can afterward be wiped out with a wet cloth. Thangme's children often had to rub out their exercises twenty times before getting them right.

Soon we were treated like members of the family. Mrs. Thangme talked over her problems with us, and was delighted when we paid her compliments on her good looks and good taste. Once she invited us to come into her room and look at her jewels. These she kept in a great chest in which her treasures were stored either in small jewel cases or in fine silk wrappings. Her treasures were worth looking at. She had a glorious tiara of corals, turquoise, and pearls, and many rings as well as diamond earrings and some little Tibetan amulet lockets, which are hung round the neck by a coral chain. Many women never take these lockets off. The amulet they contain acts as a talisman which, they believe, protects them from evil.

Our hostess was flattered by our admiration of her treasures. She told us that every man was obliged to present his wife with the jewels corresponding to his rank. Promotion in rank entailed promotion in jewelry! But to be merely rich was not enough, for wealth did not confer the right to wear costly jewels. Of course, the men grumble about their wives' pretensions, for here, as in the West, every woman seeks to outshine her rivals. Mrs. Thangme, whose jewels must have been worth several thousand pounds, told us that she never went out unaccompanied by a servant, as attacks by thieves on society women were common.

EIGHT DAYS PASSED, during which we had dutifully kept indoors. It was a great surprise to us when one day servants came bringing an invitation to visit the home of the Dalai Lama's parents, and telling us to come at once. As we felt ourselves bound by our promise not to leave the house, we consulted our host. He was horrified that we should have any misgivings; such an invitation overrode everything else. A summons from the Dalai Lama or the regent had precedence over all other considerations. No one would dare to detain us or later to call us to account. On the contrary, hesitation to comply would be a serious offense.

We were glad to learn his opinion, but then began to be nervous about the reason for our summons. Was it a good omen for our future? Anyhow we hurriedly prepared ourselves for the visit, dressing ourselves in our new clothes and Tibetan boots for the first time. We looked quite presentable. Thangme then gave us each a pair of white silk scarves and impressed on us that we must present them when we were received in audience. We had already witnessed this custom in Kyirong and had noticed that it was observed by quite simple people. When paying visits or presenting a petition to a person of higher standing, or at the great festivals, one is supposed to give presents of scarves. These scarves are found in all sort of qualities and the kind of scarf offered should be consistent with the rank of the giver.

The house of the parents of the Dalai Lama was not far away. We soon found ourselves standing before a great gate, near which the gatekeeper was already on the lookout for us. When we approached he bowed respectfully. We were led through a large garden full of vegetable plots and clusters of splendid willows till we came to the palace. We were taken up to the first floor: a door was opened and we found ourselves in the presence of the mother of the God-King, to whom we bowed in reverence. She was sitting on a small throne in a large, bright room surrounded by servants. She looked the picture of aristocratic dignity. The humble awe which the Tibetans feel for the "Holy Mother" is something strange to us, but we found the moment a solemn one.

The Holy Mother smiled at us and was visibly pleased when we handed her the scarves with deep obeisances, stretching out our arms to the fullest extent as Thangme had instructed us. She took them from us and handed them at once to the servants. Then with a beaming countenance she shook our hands, contrary to Tibetan custom. At that moment in came the father of the Dalai Lama, a dignified elderly man. We bowed low again and handed him scarves with due ceremony, after which he shook our hands most unaffectedly. Now and then Europeans came to the house, and the host and hostess were to some degree familiar with European customs and not a little proud of the fact.

Then we all sat down to tea. The tea we drank had a strange flavor, and was made differently from the usual Tibetan brew. We asked about it, and the question broke the ice, for it led our hosts to tell us about their former home. They had lived at Amdo as simple peasants until their son was recognized as the Incarnation of the Dalai Lama. Amdo is in China, in the province of Chinghai, but its inhabitants are almost all Tibetan. They had brought their tea with them to Lhasa and now made it, not as the Tibetans do with butter, but adding milk and salt. They brought something else from their old home—the dialect they spoke. They both used a patois similar to that of the central provinces, but not the same. The fourteen-year-old brother of the Dalai Lama interpreted for them. He had come as a child to Lhasa and had quickly learned to speak pure Tibetan. He now spoke the Amdo dialect only with his parents.

While we were conversing with them, we took occasion to observe our hosts. Each of them made a very good impression. Their humble origin expressed itself in an attractive simplicity, but their bearing and demeanor were aristocratic. It was a big step from a small peasant's house in a distant province to a dukedom in the capital. They now owned the palace they lived in and large properties in the country. But they seemed to have survived the sudden revolution in their lives without deterioration.

The boy whom we met, Lobsang Samten, was lively and wide awake. He was full of curiosity about us and asked us all manner of questions about our experiences. He told us that his "divine" younger brother had charged him to report on us exactly. We felt pleasantly excited by the news that the Dalai Lama was interested in us, and would have liked to learn more of him. We were told that the name Dalai Lama is not used in Tibet at all. It is a Mongolian expression meaning "Broad Ocean." Normally the Dalai Lama is referred to as the "Gyalpo Rimpoche," which means "Treasured King." His parents and brothers use another title in speaking of him. They call him "Kundün," which simply means "Presence."

The Holy Parents had, in all, six children. The eldest son, long before the discovery of the Dalai Lama, had been recognized as an Incarnation of Buddha and invested with the dignity of a lama in the monastery of Tagtsel. He too was styled Rimpoche, the form of address applied to all lamas. The second son, Gyalo Thündrup, was at school in China. Our young acquaintance Lobsang was destined for a monastic life. The Dalai Lama himself was now eleven years old. Besides his brothers he had two sisters. Subsequently the Holy Mother gave birth to another Incarnation, Ngari Rimpoche. As the mother of three Incarnations she held the record for the Buddhist world.*

Our visit led to cordial relations with this adaptable, clever woman, which were to continue until she fled before the invasion of the Reds to India. Our friendship had nothing to do with the transcendental worship that the Holy Mother received from others. But though I have a fairly skeptical attitude toward metaphysical matters, I could not but recognize the power of personality and faith with which she was invested.

---

*For the "recognition" of the Dalai Lama see Chapter 16.

It gradually became clear to us what a distinction this invitation was. One must not forget that, with the exception of his family and a few personal servants holding the rank of abbot, no one has the right to address the God-King. Nevertheless, in his isolation from the world he had deigned to take an interest in our fate. When we rose to leave, we were asked if we needed anything. We thanked our hosts, but preferred modestly to ask for nothing, in spite of which a line of servants marched up with sacks of meal and tsampa, a load of butter, and some beautiful soft woolen blankets. "By the personal desire of the Kundün," said the Holy Mother, smiling, and pressed into our hands a hundred-sang note. This was done so naturally and as if it was a matter of course that we felt no shame about accepting.

After many expressions of thanks and deep obeisances, we left the room in some embarrassment. As a final proof of friendliness, Lobsang, on behalf of his parents, laid the scarves once more on our necks as we bowed to him. He then took us into the garden and showed us the grounds and the stables, where we saw some splendid horses from Siling and Ili, the pride of his father. In the course of conversation, he let drop the suggestion that I might give him lessons in some branches of Western knowledge. That coincided with my own secret wishes. I had often thought that I could manage to keep myself by giving lessons to the children of noble families.

Loaded with gifts and escorted by servants, we returned to Thangme's house. We were in high spirits and felt that now our fortunes were on the mend. Our hosts awaited us with impatient excitement. We had to tell them everything that had happened, and our next visitors were informed in detail of the honor that had been done to us. Our stocks rose considerably!

The next day, when the brothers of the Dalai Lama came to visit us, our hostess at first concealed herself out of reverence and appeared only when the whole household had been mustered to greet them. The young lama, Rimpoche, now five and twenty years old, had actually come from his monastery to see us. He laid his hand in blessing on each member of the household. He was the first Incarnated Lama whom we came to know. People are accustomed to think of all Tibetan monks as lamas. In fact this name is only given to Incarnations, and a few other monks distinguished by their ascetic lives or the miracles they have performed. All lames have the right to give their blessing and are revered as saints.

8

CALM WATERS

Ten days after our arrival, we received word from the foreign ministry that we could move about freely. At the same time, we were supplied with the splendid full-length cloaks of lambskin for which we had lately been measured. For each of these, sixty skins were used. On the same day, we went for a walk in the town and in our Tibetan cloaks attracted no attention. We wanted to see everything. The inner town is composed of nothing but stores. Shops extend in unbroken lines and the dealers overflow into the street. There are no shop windows in our sense of the word. One finds numbers of general stores containing a large range of goods from needles to rubber boots, and near them smart shops selling draperies and silks. Provision stores contain, as well as local produce, American corned beef, Australian butter, and English whisky. There is nothing one cannot buy, or at least order. One even finds the Elizabeth Arden specialities, and there is a keen demand for them. American overshoes, dating from the last war, are displayed between joints of yak meat and chunks of butter. You can order, too, sewing machines, radio sets, and gramophones, and hunt up Bing Crosby's latest records for your next party. The gaily dressed crowds of shoppers laugh and haggle and shout. They find a special pleasure in bargaining, which to be enjoyed must be long drawn out. Here you can see a nomad exchanging yak hair for snuff, and nearby a society lady with a swarm of servants wallowing for hours in a mountain of silks and brocades. The nomad women are no less particular in selecting Indian cotton lengths for their prayer flags.

The common people generally wear the *nambu*, a sash made of pure home-woven wool, which is practically untearable. This sash or belt is about eight inches in width. Bales of material used for these nambus are displayed in the stores. The wool is either pure white or dyed mauve with a blend of indigo and rhubarb. The white nambu is hardly worn except by donkey drivers, as absence of colors is reckoned a sign of poverty. Since tape measures are not used here, they measure cloth by the length of one's arm. Thanks to my long limbs I have always profited by this custom.

Then we found an enormous store full of European felt hats, which are the dernier cri in Lhasa. A smart felt hat over Tibetan dress certainly looks odd, but Tibetans value broadbrimmed European hats as a protection against the sun. Sunburnt faces are not an attraction here. Native Tibetan hats go much better with Tibetan dress and look more attractive in the street, and, in fact, the government was trying at that time to stem the influx of European fashions, not with any idea of interfering with individual liberty, but in order to preserve the beautiful native style of dress.

The Tibetans are also addicted to umbrellas and sunshades, which you can find in all sizes, qualities, and colors. The monks are the best customers for these articles since, except at solemn festivals, they go bareheaded.

When we got home we found the Secretary of the British Legation waiting for us. He was a personal friend of Thangme, and his call was by no means an official visit. He said that he had heard

much of us and was greatly interested in our journey and our experiences. He had himself been British trade representative in
Gartok and knew something of the country through which we had
traveled. We found him an opportune visitor as we very much
wanted to send news to our families at home, who must have long
given us up for lost. Only the British representative had direct
communication with the outside world, as Tibet does not belong
to the World Postal Union and its postal arrangements are somewhat complicated.

Our visitor encouraged us to apply personally for assistance in
this matter and so the next day we set out for the legation, which
we had already noticed on our way into the town. Servants in
red livery showed us first into the garden, where we found Reginald Fox, the wireless operator, taking his morning stroll.* Fox
had lived for many years in Lhasa and was married to a Tibetan
lady. They had four enchanting children with fair hair and large,
black almond eyes. The two eldest were at a boarding school in
India.

Fox was the only man in Lhasa who possessed a reliable motor,
and in addition to his duties at the legation he was regularly occupied in charging all the radio batteries in the town. He could communicate by wireless telephone with India and was much
appreciated in Lhasa for his ability and thoroughness.

Meanwhile, the servants had announced us, and we were conducted to the first floor of the building. The Chief of the British
Legation greeted us cordially and invited us to a good English
breakfast, which had been prepared on the veranda. How long it
seemed since we had last sat on comfortable chairs and seen table
decorations, flowers in vases, and books in a real European setting.
We let our eyes wander in silence around the room. It seemed,

*He died in the spring of 1953, in Kalimpong (India).

somehow, as though we had come home. Our host understood what we were thinking. When he saw us looking at his books, he kindly offered to let us use his library. Soon we began to talk freely. The question that worried us most, namely whether he still regarded us as prisoners of war, was tactfully avoided. At last we asked him bluntly whether our comrades were still behind the barbed wire. He could not say but promised to obtain information from India. He then spoke frankly of our situation and told us that he had been informed in detail of our escape and subsequent journey, and inferred that he had learned from the Tibetan government that we would soon go back to India. This prospect, we said, did not appeal to us, so he asked us if we would be interested to find work in Sikkim. We made no secret of our wish to stay on in Tibet, but said that if that was not possible we would gladly consider his offer.

The importance of the question we were discussing did not spoil our appetites, and with encouragement from our host we did more than justice to the good food we were offered. When we had finished, we thought the time had come to submit our request to be allowed to send word to our families. Our host promised to arrange for a message to go through the Red Cross. We were later allowed to send letters now and then through the legation, but for the most part we had to use the complicated Tibetan post, sending our letters to the frontiers in double envelopes, the outside one bearing a Tibetan stamp. At the frontier we arranged for a man to remove the outer envelope, put an Indian stamp on the inner one, and post it on. With luck it took only a fortnight for a letter to get to Europe. In Tibet the post is carried by runners who work in relays of four miles each. Along all the highroads are huts in which relays wait ready to relieve the runners as they arrive. Postal runners carry a spear with bells attached as a sign of their office. The spear can, if necessary, be used as a weapon, and the bells serve to frighten off wild animals at night. Stamps are printed in five different denominations and are on sale in the post offices.

OUR VISIT to the British Legation had done much to relieve our minds. We had been welcomed there and had reason to hope that the English now realized we were harmless.

On our way back, we were stopped by some servants who told us that their master desired us to visit him. When we asked who their master was, we learned that he was a high monastic official in the government service, one of the four Trünyi Chemo, in whose hands authority over all the monks in Tibet is concentrated.

We were taken to a large, stately mansion, scrupulously clean and well kept. One really could have eaten off the stone floors. The servants were all monks. We were greeted by a kindly, elderly gentleman and offered tea and cakes. After the usual courtesies we fell into conversation and soon became aware of the reason why our host was interested in us. He stated frankly that Tibet was a backward country and that men like us could be made good use of. Unfortunately, everyone did not hold the same opinion. However, he would see what he could do and would say a good word for us. Meanwhile, he asked us what our professions had been in our own country and what subjects we had studied. He was particularly interested in the fact that Aufschnaiter was an agricultural engineer. No one in Tibet was an expert in this branch, and what scope there was in this great country!

The next day we paid official visits to each of the four cabinet ministers. Responsible only to the regent, these men represent the supreme authority in Tibet. Three of them are civil dignitaries and the fourth a monastic official. They all belong to the highest families and live in great style.

We wondered with whom we should begin. We ought to have

started with the minister-monk, but we decided to bypass the protocol and call on the youngest minister first, Surkhang by name. He was thirty-two years old and was considered more progressive than his colleagues. We hoped for counsel and understanding from a young man.

He welcomed us with frank cordiality, and we were immediately on good terms. He was astonishingly well informed about events in the outside world. He entertained us at a princely dinner, and when we took our leave we felt that we had known each other for years.

The next minister we visited was Kabshöpa, a corpulent and somewhat self-important gentleman, who treated us with a certain condescension. He made us sit down on two chairs in front of his comfortable throne and then overwhelmed us with a flood of eloquent phrases. He punctuated his most effective passages by clearing his throat noisily, at which a servant hurried forward and offered him a golden spittoon. Spitting is not a breach of etiquette in Tibet, and small spittoons are placed on every table, but it was new to us to see one presented to the spitter by a servant.

At this first meeting it was hard for us to know what to make of Kabshöpa. He held forth, and we passively submitted to his eloquence, at the right time replying courteously to his politenesses. We drank the ceremonial cup of tea in exemplary fashion. As he had not realized that we spoke Tibetan, his nephew was asked to interpret. This young man's knowledge of English had secured him a post in the foreign ministry, and we often had dealings with him later. He was a typical example of the younger generation. He had studied in India and was full of plans for reforming Tibet, though he had not yet ventured to stand up for his theories in the presence of the conservative monks. Once when we were alone he caused me to remark that Aufschnaiter and I should have come to

Lhasa a few years later, for if he and some of the other young aristocrats had been ministers, there would have been work for us in plenty.

The minister-monk who lived on the Lingkhor, the five-mile-long Pilgrims' Road that goes around Lhasa, received us with less formality. He was no longer young and had a nice little white beard of which he was very proud, for beards in Tibet are a rarity. In a general way he seemed very detached, and in contrast with the other ministers avoided expressing any definite opinions. His name was Rampa, and he was one of the few official monks who belonged to the aristocracy. The way in which the political situation was developing must have been causing him secret anxiety. He was much interested in our views on Russia's policy and told us that in the old scriptures it was prophesied that a great power from the north would overrun Tibet, destroy religion, and make itself master of the whole world.

Finally we called on Pünkhang, the oldest of the four ministers. He was a little man compelled by shortsightedness to wear thick-lensed spectacles. This was something quite unusual in Tibet, where spectacles are disapproved of as "un-Tibetan." No official was allowed to use them and even wearing them in the house was discouraged. Our minister had received special permission from the Dalai Lama to wear them in the office. At important ceremonies his poor sight rendered him quite helpless. Pünkhang's wife was present when he received us. He was, it is true, of higher rank than she, but it required no great penetration to see that it was madame who wore the trousers. After the first words of greeting Pünkhang spoke hardly a sentence, whereas his lady drenched us with a shower of questions.

Later he showed us his domestic chapel. He was a scion of one of the families that had produced a Dalai Lama and prided himself on it. He showed us a figure of the Holy One in his dim and dusty chapel.

In course of time I came to know Pünkhang's sons. The eldest of them was Governor of Gyantse and was married to a princess of Sikkim, who was, however, Tibetan by descent. She was more interesting than her husband and was, to boot, one of the most beautiful women I have ever seen. She possessed the indescribable charm of Asian women and the stamp of age-old oriental culture. At the same time she was clever, well educated, and thoroughly modern, and had been taught in one of the best schools in India. She was the first woman in Tibet to refuse to marry her husband's brothers, because this did not conform with her principles. In conversation she was the equal of the most intelligent woman you would be likely to meet in a European salon. She was interested in politics, culture, and all that was happening in the world. She often talked about equal rights for women . . . but Tibet has a long way to go before reaching that point.

When we said good-bye to Pünkhang, we begged him to support our request to be allowed to reside in Tibet. He of course offered to do all in his power to help us, but we had been long enough in Asia to know that nobody ever bluntly refused anything.

In order to assure our position from all sides, we tried to get on good terms with the Chinese Legation. The chargé d'affaires received us with the politeness for which his people are famous, and when we asked about the possibility of being admitted to China and finding an occupation there, he promised to submit our question to his government.

In these ways we did what we could to get support in all quarters and to convince people of our harmlessness. It happened quite often that strangers addressed us while we were out for walks and asked us very peculiar questions. One day a Chinese took a snapshot of us. A camera in Lhasa was something very unusual, and the incident gave us food for thought. We had already heard that there were a number of people in Lhasa supplying information to foreign countries. Perhaps we, too, were believed to be agents of a foreign power. Only the English knew how innocent we were, for they knew where we had come from, and were in a position to test the truth of our statements. Other people, not so well informed about us, might think all sorts of things. In fact, we had no political ambitions. All we asked for was shelter and work to do till the time came when we could return to Europe.

Meanwhile spring had come, bringing beautiful warm weather, though it was only early February. Lhasa lies south of Cairo, and in high altitudes the sun's rays seem perceptibly stronger. We felt very well, but longed for regular occupation. Daily invitations and visits and banquets that lasted for hours were our lot, as we were passed from hand to hand like a couple of animal prodigies. We were soon sick of this idle life and hankered for work and sport. Beyond a small ground for basketball Lhasa made no provision for games. The young Tibetans and Chinese who played basketball were very glad when we offered to play with them. There were also hot shower baths in the square, but a single shower bath cost ten rupees—an enormous price when one thinks that a sheep costs no more.

Some years before, we heard, there had been a football ground in the town. Eleven teams were formed and cup-tie matches organized. One day during a match a hailstorm occurred and did a lot of damage, as a result of which football was forbidden. Perhaps the regent disapproved of the sport and most likely it was thought to be a threat to the influence of the Church, for the people were enthusiastic about the game and many monks from Sera and

Drebung were to be found watching the matches. Anyhow, the hailstorm was interpreted as a sign that the gods disapproved of this frivolous sport, and football was abolished.

In connection with this story, we asked our friends if there really were lamas who could hold up hailstorms or call down showers of rain, for this belief is firmly held in Tibet. In all the fields there are small stone towers containing shells deposited as offerings, in which incense is burned when a storm occurs. Many villages actually have regular weathermakers. These are monks with a reputation for special skill in managing the weather. For the purposes of their magic, they blow on conchs, which make a vibrating sound. In many of our mountain villages, the church bells are rung when a storm is approaching, and the effect of these conchs can be compared to the effect of the vibration of the bells. But, of course, Tibetans do not recognize any physical explanation—for them all is magic and spells and the sport of the gods.

We heard a nice story dating from the time of the thirteenth Dalai Lama. He, of course, had his court weathermaker, who was the most famous wizard ever known. His special job was to protect the God-King's summer garden when a storm approached. One fine day a heavy hailstorm came and beat down all the flowers and ruined the ripening fruit. The weathermaker was summoned into the presence of the Living Buddha, who sat grumbling on his throne and ordered the trembling magician at once to perform a miracle, otherwise he would be dismissed and punished. The man prostrated himself and asked for a sieve—just an ordinary sieve. He then asked the Holy One whether he would be satisfied if the water poured into the sieve did not flow through it. The Dalai Lama nodded, and lo and behold! the water that was passed into the sieve remained in it. The magician's reputation was saved and he was allowed to retain his well-paid post.

ALL THIS TIME we were racking our brains to find some means of earning our living if we stayed on in Lhasa. For the moment we were treated most generously, receiving parcels of tsampa, meal, butter, and tea. A pleasant surprise was Kabshöpa's nephew handing us five hundred rupees as a present from the foreign ministry. In our letter of thanks, we said we were prepared to work for the government if they would guarantee us food and lodging.

For the past three weeks, we had been enjoying Thangme's hospitality. Now the wealthy Tsarong invited us to stay with him, and we gratefully accepted. Thangme had four children and needed our room. He had taken us in as poor vagabonds off the street and had shown himself a true friend. We have never forgotten his kindness. At the New Year, he was the first to receive white scarves from us, and later on when I had a house of my own, he was a regular guest at my Christmas parties.

In Tsarong's house we were given a large room with European furniture, a table, easy chairs, beds, and fine carpets. Next door we had a little room to wash in. We also found something which we had missed very much up to now, a closet for the relief of nature. In this respect the habits of Tibetans are casual to the last degree and any place seems to be regarded as a suitable latrine.

Tsarong could afford to have a number of cooks. His chef had been for years in the best hotel in Calcutta and understood European cooking. His roast meats were wonderful, and he was in addition outstanding as a pastry cook and confectioner. Another of the cooks had been sent to China and had come back with a repertoire of Chinese dishes. Tsarong liked to astonish his guests with unknown delicacies. We were surprised to find that in the best houses women were never employed as cooks—only as kitchen maids.

Tibetan mealtimes are not quite the same as ours. In the early morning one drinks butter tea and indeed very often throughout the day. I have heard of people drinking two hundred cups in a single day, though I daresay that is an exaggeration. There are two main meals in the day, one at 10 A.M. and the other after sunset. The first of these, consisting of a dish of tsampa and some trimmings, we took together in our own room. For the evening meal we were generally invited to join our host. The whole family sat around a large table. Many courses were served, and this meal was the central point of the day, at which everyone in the house was assembled and the day's happenings discussed.

After supper we all sat in the living room, which with its numerous rugs, chests, and figures seemed overcrowded. Here we smoked cigarettes and drank beer. We also had occasion to admire our host's latest acquisitions, for he was always buying something new. He had a wonderful radio set, which gave one all the stations in the world. The reception was excellent, as on the "Roof of the World" there is no atmospheric disturbance. Then there were the latest records to play, a motion-camera to be inspected, a new apparatus for enlarging photographs to be examined, and one evening he unpacked a theodolite! Tsarong was perfectly familiar with all these instruments. I suppose he had more hobbies than anyone in the town. We could not have wished for a better home than in his house. He collected stamps and kept up a correspondence with people in all parts of the world—his son who was a linguist helped him in this—and he possessed a well-chosen library including a fine collection of Western books, many of which were gifts, for every European who came to Lhasa stayed in his house, and most of them left books as a souvenir of their visit.

Tsarong was an extraordinary man. He had constantly endeavored to introduce reforms, and whenever the government was busy with an important problem, he was called in to advise. He was responsible for the only iron bridge in the country. This he had constructed and assembled in India. It was then taken to pieces and carried piece by piece into Tibet by yaks and coolies. Tsarong was a self-made man of the most modern brand, and his ability would have made him an outstanding personality even in Western countries.

His son George—he had kept his Indian school name—followed in his father's footsteps. At our first meeting, we had been impressed by his knowledge and the variety of his interests. At this time photography was his passion, and the pictures he took were worth seeing. One evening he astonished us by showing a color film that he had made himself. It was so successful and so noiseless that at first one might have imagined oneself in a first-class moving-picture theater. However, hitches occurred later on with the motor and the spool, which Aufschnaiter and I helped to put right.

Our supper with Tsarong, and the books that we borrowed from him and the British Legation provided us with our only form of evening entertainment. There were no moving pictures or theaters in Lhasa and no hotels or public houses. Social life was entirely confined to private houses.

We spent our days collecting impressions as we were afraid lest we might have to leave before we had seen everything. We had no absolute grounds for misgiving, but we felt that we could not really count on our friends for support in a crisis, generous as they had been. We had several times heard a story that sounded like a warning. An English teacher had been asked by the government to start a European type of school in Lhasa and had been offered a long contract. After six months he packed up his traps and went away. The reactionary monks had made his task impossible.

WE CONTINUED to pay daily visits—so many people had called on us—and thus acquired a good knowledge of the home life of distinguished Tibetans. There was one point in which we could compare the people of Lhasa favorably with the inhabitants of our own cities. They always had time.

Tibet has not yet been infested by the worst disease of modern life, the everlasting rush. No one overworks here. Officials have an easy life. They turn up at the office late in the morning and leave for their homes early in the afternoon. If an official has guests or any other reason for not coming, he just sends a servant to a colleague and asks him to officiate for him.

Women know nothing about equal rights and are quite happy as they are. They spend hours making up their faces, restringing their pearl necklaces, choosing new material for dresses, and thinking how to outshine Mrs. So-and-so at the next party. They do not have to bother about housekeeping, which is all done by the servants. But to show that she is mistress the lady of the house always carries a large bunch of keys around with her. In Lhasa every trifling object is locked up and double-locked.

Then there is mah-jongg. At one time this game was a universal passion. People were simply fascinated by it and played it day and night, forgetting everything else—official duties, housekeeping, the family. The stakes were often very high and everyone played—even the servants, who sometimes contrived to lose in a few hours what they had taken years to save. Finally the government found it too much of a good thing. They forbade the game, bought up all the mah-jongg sets, and condemned secret offenders to heavy fines and hard labor. And they brought it off! I would never have believed it, but though everyone moaned and hankered to play again, they respected the prohibition. After mah-jongg had been stopped, it became gradually evident how everything else had been neglected during the epidemic. On Saturdays—the day of rest—people now played chess or halma, or occupied themselves harmlessly with word games and puzzles.

ON FEBRUARY 16, we had been just a month in Lhasa. Our fate was still undecided; we had no work and we worried about our future. On that very day, Kabshöpa came to us looking solemn, as befitted an envoy from the foreign ministry. We knew from his expression that he had bad news for us. He told us that the government did not approve of our continued residence in Tibet and that we must proceed forthwith to India. We had always envisaged this possibility in our own minds but were disconcerted by the reality. We began to protest, but Kabshöpa shrugged his shoulders and said we must do that in higher quarters.

Our next reaction to this mournful news was to collect all the maps of Eastern Tibet we could find in Lhasa. In the evening we set to work to plot a route and make plans. We were determined on one thing—no more barbed wire for us! We would rather flee and try our luck in China. We had some money and were well equipped. It would not be difficult to lay in a stock of provisions. But I had to think of my sciatica, which was not getting better. Aufschnaiter had already got the doctor of the British Legation to visit me. He had prescribed some powders and given me injections, but they had done no good. Was this confounded complaint going to wreck our plans? I felt like despairing.

Next day, disheartened as I was, I hobbled over to the house of the Dalai Lama's parents. We thought their intervention would help us. The Holy Mother and Lobsang Samten promised to tell the whole story to the young God-King and felt sure that he would say a good word for us. This he actually did, and though the young Dalai Lama had not as yet any executive powers, his good will was certainly of use to us. In the meantime, Aufschnaiter went from one acquaintance to another with the object of setting all the wheels in motion. And in order to omit no precaution, we composed a petition in English in which we set forth all the arguments in favor of our being allowed to remain in Tibet.

Fate seemed to be conspiring against us, for my sciatica suddenly became so bad that I could not move. I suffered great pain and had to remain in bed, while Aufschnaiter ran around the town till his feet were sore. These were anxious days.

On February 21, some soldiers appeared at our door. They called on us to pack our things, as they had been ordered to escort us to India. We were to start early the next morning. That seemed to be the end of all things, but how was I to travel? I could not walk as far as even the window, as I tried to demonstrate to the lieutenant. He put on a helpless expression. Like all soldiers he had to obey orders and was not qualified to receive explanations. Pulling myself together, I asked him to tell his superior that I could not leave Lhasa unless I was carried. The soldiers retired.

We at once applied to Tsarong for advice and help, but he had nothing fresh to tell us. He said that one could not resist an order from the government. Alone in our room, we cursed my sciatica. If I had been fit, nothing would have prevented us from escaping, and we should have got away that very night. We preferred hardship and danger to the most comfortable quarters behind barbed wire. It would not be so easy to move me tomorrow, and I bitterly decided to adopt an attitude of passive resistance.

But the next morning, nothing happened—no soldiers came, and there was no news. We anxiously sent for Kabshöpa, who came in person and seemed embarrassed. Aufschnaiter explained how ill I was and began to discuss our problem. "Would it not be possible," he said, with a serious expression, "to arrive at a compromise?"

We had, meanwhile, come to suspect that perhaps the British were at the bottom of this business and had asked Tibet to hand us over.

We realized that Tibet was a small country and it was to her interest to be on good terms with her neighbors. What was the point of risking a misunderstanding with England for so small a matter as a couple of German POWs? So Aufschnaiter proposed that the English doctor, at that moment acting as chargé d'affaires at the legation, should be requested to give a certificate as to my condition. Kabshöpa accepted the suggestion with such alacrity that we stole a glance at one another and felt sure that our suspicion was justified.

The doctor visited me in the course of the day and informed me that the decision about the date of our departure had been left in his hands by the government. He gave me injections that did no good. I got more comfort from a present from Tsarong in the shape of some thermogene wool.

I now set myself to overcome my illness, which, I was determined, should no longer thwart our plans. Exerting all my strength of will, I forced myself to do exercises every day. A lama had recommended me to roll a stick backward and forward with the soles of my feet. This I did for hours every day, sitting in a chair. The exercise was exceedingly painful, but it gradually improved my condition and eventually I was able to go out into the garden and warm myself, like an old man, in the spring sunshine.

WE WERE NOW in full spring. March had come and on the fourth of the month began the New Year Festival—the greatest of all Tibetan feasts, which lasts for three weeks. Alas! I could not take part in it. In the distance I heard drums and trombones and saw by the excitement that reigned in the house how important it all was. Tsarong and his son came every day to see me and show off their splendid new robes of silk and brocade. Aufschnaiter, of course, went everywhere, and told me all about it in the evening.

This year was the "Fire-Hound-Year." On March 4 (or a date near to this, as the Tibetan New Year is flexible—similar to our Easter), the city magistrate hands over his authority to the monks—symbolizing the restoration by the secular power of its office to religion, to whom it originally belonged. This is the beginning of a strict and formidable regime. To start with, the whole place is tidied up, and during this season Lhasa is renowned for its cleanliness—which is not a normal condition. At the same time, a sort of civil peace is proclaimed. All quarrels cease. Public offices are closed, but the bargaining of street traders is livelier than ever, except during the festal processions. Crimes and offenses, including gambling, are punished with especial severity. The monks are relentless judges and are accustomed to inflict fearful floggings, which occasionally cause the death of the victim. (Although it is true that in such cases the regent intervenes and deals with the persons responsible.)

In the midst of the celebrations, we seemed to have been forgotten, and we took care not to attract notice. The government probably was satisfied with the English doctor's ruling that I was not yet fit to travel. We were gaining valuable time. The great thing was for me to get well, and then perhaps we could realize our flight to China.

Day after day I used to sun myself in the garden, enjoying the increasing heat, so my astonishment was all the greater when one morning I woke up to find all the spring greenery deep in snow. It is very seldom that snow falls so late in the year at Lhasa, which lies so deep in the heart of Asia that atmospheric depressions seldom reach it. Even in winter the snow does not lie for long. On this occasion it was soon melted. It had done some good, because by converting the sand and dust into mud it had mitigated the discomforts of the subsequent sandstorm.

These storms recur regularly every spring and continue for a period of about two months. They usually reach the town in the early afternoon. One sees them approaching with terrific rapidity in a huge black cloud. The Potala Palace disappears and at once everyone rushes for home. Street life stops, the windows rattle, and the animals in the fields resignedly turn their tails to the wind and wait patiently till they can start grazing once more. The countless street dogs huddle together in corners. (They are not usually so peaceful. One day Aufschnaiter came home with a torn cloak— he had been attacked by dogs, which had killed and devoured a dying horse; the pack had tasted blood.)

The period of dust storms is the most unpleasant time of the year. Even sitting in one's room, one gets sand between one's teeth as there are no double windows in Lhasa. The only positive comfort one can get out of these spring storms is in the knowledge that winter has really ended. All the gardeners know that they have no more frost to fear. At this season the meadows along the canals get their first breath of green and Buddha's hair begins to bloom. That is what they call the famous weeping willow at the gate of the cathedral. The slender, hanging branches with the fine yellow blooms give a meaning to this poetic name in the springtime.

When I was able to hobble around again, I was anxious to make myself useful in some way or other. Tsarong had planted hundreds of young fruit trees in his garden. They were all grown from seed and had up to now borne no fruit. Together with George (my host's son), I now set to work to graft them systematically. That gave the household something new to laugh at. In Tibet grafting is practically unknown and there is no word for it. They called it "marrying" and found it all very amusing.

Tibetans are a happy little people full of childish humor. They are grateful for any opportunity to laugh. If anyone stumbles or slips they enjoy themselves for hours. Pleasure in the misfortunes of others is almost universal, but somehow it is not ill meant. They make a mock of everything and everybody. As they have no newspapers they indulge their criticism of untoward events or objectionable persons by means of songs and satire. Boys and girls walk through the Parkhor in the evening singing the latest verses. Even the highest personages must put up with being pulled to pieces. Sometimes the government proscribes a particular song, but no one is ever punished for singing it. It is no longer sung in public, but is heard all the more in private.

The Parkhor is most thronged at the New Year. This street runs in a circle around the cathedral and most of the life of the city is concentrated in it. Many of the big business houses are here, and here all religious and military processions begin and end. Toward evening, especially on public holidays, pious citizens swarm over the Parkhor mumbling their prayers, and many of the faithful cover the whole distance in successive prostrations. But not only piety is represented in the Parkhor. You find also pretty women showing off their newest frocks and flirting a little with the young bloods of the nobility. Ladies of easy virtue are also there professionally.

In a word, the Parkhor is a center of business, sociability, and frivolity.

BY THE FIFTEENTH of the first Tibetan month, I was so much better that I, too, could attend the festivities. The fifteenth is one of the great days. There is a magnificent procession in which the Dalai Lama takes part. Tsarong had promised us a window in one of his houses looking onto the Parkhor. Our places were on the ground floor as no one is allowed to be at a higher elevation than the heads of the grandees, who march with measured tread along the street. No houses in Lhasa may be more than two stories high as it is considered a form of blasphemy to compete with the Cathedral or the Potala. This rule is strictly observed and the wooden shanties—easily taken to pieces—which some of the nobles put up on the flat roofs of their houses in the warm weather disappear like magic when the Dalai Lama or the regent takes part in a procession.

While the brightly colored crowd flowed through the streets, we sat at our window with Mrs. Tsarong. Our hostess was a friendly old lady, who had always mothered us. We were very glad of her company in surroundings very strange to us, and her familiar friendly tones explained to us the novel sights that met our eyes.

We saw strange, framelike objects rising from the ground, sometimes to a height of thirty or more feet. She told us that these were for the butter figures. Soon after sunset these works of art, made of butter by the monks, are brought along. There are departments in the monasteries where particularly gifted monks, true artists in their own line, knead and model figures out of butter of different colors. This work, which requires inexhaustible patience, is often in the finest filigree. There is competition in the production of these masterpieces of a single night, as the government gives a prize for the best one. For many years past the monastery of Gyü has been the winner. Soon the whole street front of the Parkhor was hidden behind these gaily colored butter pyramids. In front of them was an endless mass of people, and we wondered if we should be able to see anything. It was beginning to grow dark when the Lhasa regiments marched up to the sound of trumpets and drums. They lined the street and pressed the spectators back against the houses, leaving the roadway free.

Night fell swiftly, but soon the scene was brightly illuminated with a swarm of lights. There were thousands of flickering butter lamps and among them a few petroleum pressure lamps with their fearful glaring light. The moon came up over the roofs to throw more light on the proceedings. The months are lunar in Tibet, so it was full moon on the fifteenth. Everything was ready: the stage was set and the great festival could now begin. The voices of the crowd were hushed in anticipation. The great moment had come.

The cathedral doors opened, and the young God-King stepped slowly out, supported to right and left by two abbots. The people bowed in awe. According to strict ceremonial they should prostrate themselves, but today there was no room. As he approached they bowed, as a field of corn bends before the wind. No one dared to look up. With measured steps the Dalai Lama began his solemn circuit of the Parkhor. From time to time he stopped before the figures of butter and gazed at them. He was followed by a brilliant retinue of all the high dignitaries and nobles. After them followed the officials in order of precedence. In the procession we recognized our friend Tsarong, who followed close behind the Dalai Lama. Like all the nobles, he carried in his hand a smoldering stick of incense.

The awed crowd kept silent. Only the music of the monks could be heard—the oboes, tubas, kettledrums, and *chinels*. It was like a vision of another world, a strangely unreal happening. In the yellow light of the flickering lamps, the great figures of molded butter seemed to come to life. We fancied we saw strange flowers tossing their heads in the breeze and heard the rustling of the robes of gods. The faces of these portentous figures were distorted in a demonic grimace. Then the God-King raised his hand in blessing.

Now the Living Buddha was approaching. He passed quite close to our window. The women stiffened in a deep obeisance and hardly dared to breathe. The crowd was frozen. Deeply moved, we hid ourselves behind the women as if to protect ourselves from being drawn into the magic circle of this Power.

We kept saying to ourselves, "It is only a child." A child, indeed, but the heart of the concentrated faith of thousands, the essence of their prayers, longings, hopes. Whether it is Lhasa or

Rome—all are united by one wish: to find God and to serve Him. I closed my eyes and hearkened to the murmured prayers and the solemn music and sweet incense rising to the evening sky.

Soon the Dalai Lama had completed his tour around the Parkhor and vanished into the Tsug Lag Khang. The soldiers marched away to the music of their bands.

As if awakened from a hypnotic sleep, the tens of thousands of spectators passed from order into chaos. The transition was overwhelmingly sudden. The crowds broke into shouts and wild gesticulation. A moment ago they were weeping and praying or sunk in ecstatic meditation, and now they are a throng of madmen. The monk-guards begin to function. They are huge fellows with padded shoulders and blackened faces to make them more terrible. They lay about them with their whips, but the crowds press frantically around the statues of butter, which are now in danger of being overturned. Even those who have been bludgeoned come back into the fray. One would think they were possessed by demons. Are they really the same people who just now were bowing humbly before a child?

The next morning the streets were empty. The butter figures had been carried away, and no trace remained of the reverence or the ecstasy of the night before. Market stalls had taken the place of the stands that had carried the statues. The brightly colored figures of the saints had melted and would be used as fuel for lamps—or would be made up into magic medicines.

9

ASYLUM GRANTED

Many people came to visit us. Tibetans journeyed from far and wide to Lhasa to attend the New Year Festival, among them people whom we had got to know on our journey. It was not hard for them to find us, as we were still much talked of, and every child knew where we lived. Some brought us presents of dried meat, which is much appreciated in Lhasa. We learned, moreover, from these people that the officials through whose districts we had passed had been severely censured by the government. It depressed us to feel that persons who had received us in such a friendly manner had suffered such unpleasantness on our account. But it seemed that they bore us no grudge. We met a bönpo whom we had bamboozled with our old travel permit, and he only laughed and seemed glad to see us again.

The New Year's celebrations did not pass off this year without a mishap. An accident that attracted much attention occurred on the Parkhor.

Every year they put up high flagstaffs made of heavy tree trunks fitted into one another. These are brought from distant places, and it is quite a task to carry them to Lhasa. It is managed in a very primitive way, and my indignation was aroused when I saw, for the first time, a procession coming in. It reminded me of the Volga boatmen. About twenty men drag each trunk, which is attached to them by a rope round their waists. They sing a monotonous air as they trudge along, keeping step with one another. They sweat and pant, but their foreman, who leads the singing, gives them no pause for rest. This forced labor is in part a substitute for taxation. The carriers are picked up at villages on the road and dismissed when they come to the next settlement. The monotonous airs to which they drag their burden are said to distract their minds from the severity of their task. I should have thought they would do better to save their breath. The sort of fatalistic resignation with which they lent themselves to this backbreaking toil always used to infuriate me. As a product of our modern age, I could not understand why the people of Tibet were so rigidly opposed to any form of progress. There obviously must be some better means of transporting these heavy burdens than by manhandling them. The Chinese invented and used the wheel thousands of years ago. But the Tibetans will have none of it, though its use would give an immense impulse to transport and commerce, and would raise the whole standard of living throughout the country.

When, later, I was engaged in irrigation works, I made various finds that strengthened my belief that the Tibetans had known and used the wheel many centuries ago. We uncovered hundreds of great blocks of stones as big as wardrobes. These could not have been carried save by mechanical means from the remote quarries where they had been hewn. When my workmen wanted to carry such a block from one place to another, they had first to hew it into eight pieces.

I became more and more convinced that Tibet's great days belonged to the past. There is a stone obelisk dating from A. D. 763

that bears witness to my theory. It records the fact that in that year the Tibetan armies marched to the gates of the Chinese capital and there dictated to the Chinese terms of peace, which included an annual tribute of fifty thousand bales of silk.

And then there is the Potala Palace, which must date from Tibet's days of greatness. No one today would think of erecting such a building. I once asked a stonemason who was working for me why such buildings were no longer put up. He answered indignantly that the Potala was the handiwork of the gods. Men never could have achieved anything like it. Good spirits and supernatural beings had worked by night on this wonderful building. I found in this view another instance of the indifference to progress and ambition that characterized the attitude of the men who dragged the tree trunks.

To return to my story. When the tree trunks are brought into Lhasa, they are bound together with strips of yak's hide to form a thick mast nearly seventy feet high. Then a huge flag bearing printed prayers and extending from the top to the bottom of the pole is nailed onto it. On this occasion the trunks were probably too heavy for the yak-skin straps, for the whole mast broke into its component parts, which crushed three watchers to death and injured several others. The whole of Tibet took this for an evil omen, and people prophesied a black future for the country. Catastrophes such as earthquakes and floods were foretold. Men spoke of war and looked meaningly toward China. Everyone, even those who had had an English education, was a prey to superstition.

Nevertheless, they did not carry the men wounded in this accident to their lamas, but to the British Legation, where there was a hospital with a number of beds for Tibetans. The English doctor had plenty of work. Every morning there was a queue of clients waiting before his door, and in the afternoon he visited his patients in the town. The monks tolerated in silence this intrusion into their territory. They could hardly do otherwise, because it was impossible to ignore the doctor's success.

The policy of the government toward medicine is a dark chapter in the history of modern Tibet. The doctors of the British legations were the only qualified medical men in a population of three and a half million. Doctors would find a rich field of activity in Tibet, but the government would never consent to allow foreigners to practice. The whole power was in the hands of the monks, who criticized even government officials when they called in the English doctor.

IT WAS A HOPEFUL OMEN for our future when Aufschnaiter was summoned by a high monastic official and commissioned to build an irrigation canal. We were speechless with joy! This was our first step toward a settled existence in Lhasa, and it was the monks who had put us on the road.

Aufschnaiter began at once to work on his measurements. I wanted to help him as he had no trained assistant, so I walked out to his work place on the Lingkhor. An indescribable scene awaited us. There squatted hundreds, nay thousands, of monks wearing their red cowls and busy doing something for which privacy is generally regarded as essential. I did not envy Aufschnaiter his place of work. We went obstinately on with our job, looking neither to the right nor to the left, but vowed to ourselves to move as soon as possible from the neighborhood.

Aufschnaiter made good headway and in a fortnight was ready to start digging. A hundred and fifty workers were placed at his disposal, and we began to feel that we were important contractors. But we had yet to learn the methods of work practiced in this country.

In the meantime I had also found a job myself. I was still an invalid, and Tsarong's garden was the best place for a man in my condition; but I kept wondering what I could do to make it more beautiful. Then I had an inspiration. I would make a fountain.

I took measurements and made drawings and soon had prepared a beautiful plan. Tsarong was enthusiastic. He chose the servants who were to help me, and I sat comfortably in the sunshine and directed my gang. Underground pipes were soon laid and a pool dug. Tsarong insisted on taking a hand personally in the cementing. Since the erection of the famous iron bridge he had been an authority on reinforced concrete. Then we had to build a cistern on the roof of the house to supply the fountain with water. It was pretty hard work pumping the water up into the cistern, but I made a virtue of necessity and used the hand pump for training my muscles.

At last the great moment arrived and for the first time a jet of water, as high as the house, sprang from my fountain. We were all as happy as children. This was the only fountain in Tibet and from now on it was the pièce de résistance at Tsarong's garden parties.

New impressions and an unwonted activity almost made us forget our cares. One day Thangme brought us a newspaper in Tibetan and showed us an article about ourselves, which related in a very friendly spirit how we had burst our way through the mountain barriers and reached Lhasa, and how we were now begging for the protection of this pious, neutral country. We thought that these friendly lines could have a favorable influence on public opinion and hoped they might lend some support to our petition. It is true that the journal in question would have been of little account in Europe. It appeared once a month and was published at Kalimpong, in India. Its circulation did not exceed five hundred copies, but it was read rather extensively in Lhasa in certain circles, and individual numbers were sent to Tibetologues throughout the world.

THE NEW YEAR CELEBRATIONS were not yet at an end, though the most important ceremonies had been performed. Now came the athletic gathering on the Parkhor in front of the Tsug Lag Khang. As an old athlete, I was particularly interested, and every day at sunrise found me at the games, which started early in the morning. We had been lucky enough to secure places at a window on the second floor of the Chinese Legation, from which we watched, well concealed behind a curtain. That was our only way of getting around the order forbidding anyone to sit above the ground floor in the presence of the regent, who sat, enthroned behind a muslin curtain, on the first floor of the Tsug Lag Khang. The four cabinet ministers watched through the windows.

The first events were wrestling bouts. I could not make up my mind whether the wrestlers' methods were more like the Greco-Roman or the catch-as-catch-can style. They obviously had their own rules. Here a fall is given when any part of the body except the feet touches the ground. There are no lists of competitors nor any preliminary announcements. A felt mat is spread out, and men come out of the crowd and take each other on. The combatants wear only a loin cloth and shiver in the cold morning air. They are all well-grown, muscular fellows. They jig around with wild gestures under the noses of their opponents and assume an air of swaggering courage. But they have no notion of the art of wrestling and would be easily vanquished by a real wrestler. The bouts are soon over, and a new pair comes on the scene. One never seems to see a keen struggle for victory. Winners get no special distinction, but winners and losers both receive white scarves. They bow to the bönpo, who hands them the scarves with a benevolent smile, and prostrate themselves three times in honor of the regent; after which they rejoin the crowd the best of friends.

Next came a weight-lifting competition. The weight is a heavy, smooth stone, which must have seen hundreds of New Year festivals. It has to be lifted and carried around the flagstaff. Very few people can perform this feat. There is much laughter when a competitor swaggers up to the stone with an air of overweening confidence and then finds that he can hardly lift it off the ground, or when it slips out of his hands, threatening to squash his toes in its fall.

Then suddenly one hears the far-off thud of galloping horses. Weight lifting comes to an end. The horse races are starting. Here come the beasts in a thick cloud of dust. In these races there is no staked-out course. The riderless horses take their own line, often through the crowd, whom the monk-soldiers have been trying to drive out of the way with their cudgels. These races, like some of the other events, are hard to understand. The unridden beasts start off in a mass some miles outside the town and burst through the excited public, who unwillingly withdraw to the side of the track in order to let them go by on their way to the winning post. Only horses bred in Tibet are allowed to enter, and each horse carries the owner's name on a cloth on his back. There is keen competition between the stables, but when the Dalai Lama or a minister has a horse running, it is obvious that he has got to come in first. When it looks as if an outsider is likely to beat an "official" horse, grooms run out and stop him before he gets to the post. The races are followed with tremendous excitement. The crowd and the servants of owners howl and cry to encourage the runners, while the noble lords who own the animals try to look dignified. The whole field storms madly past toward the winning post, which lies a little way to the back of the town.

The cloud of dust kicked up by the hoofs of the horses had

scarcely time to settle before the first of the foot runners came panting up. And what a rabble they were! Anyone can take part in a foot race, from old men to small boys. Here they come—with bleeding, blistered feet, out of breath and with distorted faces. One can see that they have never been in training in their lives. Many drop out long before completing the five-mile course, having gained nothing by their efforts except the laughter of the bystanders.

The last of the runners are still limping in when the next event is started. This time it is a mounted race with the riders wearing historic costumes. They are greeted with cries of enthusiasm and use their whips wildly to get the last ounce out of their beasts. The crowd wave their arms and shout, a horse bucks and his rider flies in an arc into the midst of the spectators. Nobody minds. This is the last athletic event of the meeting, and afterward the prize winners come forward, each carrying a wooden square showing in what order he reached the post. There are about a hundred runners and almost the same number of riders in the two events. They receive colored or white scarves from the judges, but there is no applause from the spectators.

To close the proceedings, a gymkhana is held in a huge field outside Lhasa. We hurried along with the crowd and were very glad to be invited by one of the nobles into his tent. These festival tents offer a wonderful picture. They are pitched in serried ranks, and each is furnished in a manner corresponding to the station of its owner. Many of them are draped with silks and brocades and decorated with gorgeous ornaments. Add to them the rich robes of the men and women, and you have a real symphony in color. Civil officials of the fourth rank and upward wear glossy yellow silk robes with large plate-shaped hats with brims of blue-fox fur. (These furs come from Hamburg! Tibetans find their own foxes are not good enough.)

Competition in smartness of dress is not confined to the women. The men take their part. Their Asiatic love of finery puts them in contact with many parts of the world. Thus blue foxes come from Hamburg, cultured pearls from Japan, turquoise from Persia via Bombay, corals from Italy, and amber from Berlin and Königsberg. I have often written letters for rich noblemen to addresses all over the world ordering this or that article de luxe. Pomp and decoration are here a necessity. They have to be displayed to advantage in clothes and furnishings. The common people enjoy no luxury themselves but appreciate it in their betters.

The great festivals are really an occasion for displaying pomp and power, and the high dignitaries know that they owe it to the people to make a good show. When, on the last day of the feast, the four cabinet ministers exchange their costly headdresses for the red-fringed hats of their servants in order to show for a moment their equality with the people, the enthusiasm and admiration of the public know no bounds.

The gymkhana, or horse show, is the most popular of all spectacles. It is probably a survival of former great military parades. In the past the feudal lords had at certain times to march their troops past their overlord and thus show their readiness for war, but this significance has long disappeared. Nevertheless, there are many features of these games that recall the warlike days of Mongol influence, when marvelous feats of horsemanship were the order of the day.

We had occasion to admire some incredibly skillful performances by Tibetan horsemen. Every noble family enters a certain number of participants for these games, and, of course, there is the utmost keenness to choose the best men so that the team may do well in the final classification. Competitors have to show off their skill in riding and shooting. When I saw what they could do, I simply could not get over it! They stood upright in the saddle and while their horses were galloping past a hanging target, swung up their matchlocks and shot into the bull's-eye. Before they had reached the next target, twenty yards away, they had exchanged their muskets for bows and arrows. Shouts of joy acclaimed the mounted archer who hit the mark. It is incredible how adroit the Tibetans are at changing from one weapon to another.

At these festivities the Tibetan government displays typical hospitality, even toward foreigners. Splendid tents of honor are put up for all the foreign legations, and servants and liaison officers see to it that the guests have everything they want.

I noticed an unusual number of Chinese on the sports ground. They are easily distinguishable from the Tibetans though they belong to the same racial family. The Tibetans are not markedly slit-eyed; they have pleasant, refined faces and red cheeks. The rich Chinese costumes of the past have in many cases given way to European suits, and many Chinese, in this respect more progressive than the Tibetans, wear spectacles. Most of the Chinese in Lhasa are merchants who maintain prosperous trade relations with their own country. They enjoy living in Tibet, and many settle down permanently in Lhasa. One reason for this is that most Chinese are passionate opium smokers, and there is no explicit prohibition of opium smoking in Tibet. Sometimes a Tibetan, seduced by the example of the Chinese, takes to the opium pipe. If he does, he is likely to be punished. There is no danger that opium smoking may become a national vice. The vigilance of the authorities is far too keen. They already consider tobacco smoking to be a vice and control it very closely and, though one can buy any sort of cigarette in Lhasa, there is no smoking in offices, in the streets, or at public ceremonies. When the monks take control in the Fire-Hound-Year they even forbid the sale of cigarettes.

That is why all Tibetans are snuff takers. The laity and the monks use their own preparation of snuff, which they find stimulating. Everyone is proud of his own mixture, and when two Tibetans meet, the first thing they do is to take out their snuffboxes and exchange a pinch of snuff. Snuffboxes, too, are a subject for pride. One finds them in all materials from yak horn to jade. The hardened snuff taker spreads his dose on his thumbnail, sniffs it up, and then blows a cloud of dust out of his mouth, and never dreams of sneezing. If anyone burst out into a fearful sneeze, it was always I, and the company never failed to laugh.

There are also Nepalese in Lhasa, richly clad and stout of body. One can see, even at a distance, that they are prosperous. By virtue of an old treaty, they are exempt from taxation, and they have the means to exploit this favored situation thoroughly. The finest businesses in the Parkhor belong to them. They are expert dealers, with a sixth sense for a good bargain. Most of them leave their families at home and go back to them from time to time, unlike the Chinese, who are apt to marry Tibetan women, to whom they make model husbands.

At official festivities the representatives of Nepal outdo even the gaily clad Tibetans in brilliance of dress, and the red tunics of the Gurkhas, who form their bodyguard, are conspicuous from afar. These Gurkhas have acquired a certain reputation in Lhasa. They alone venture to contravene the prohibition against fishing. When the government hears of such breaches of the law, it sends a solemn protest to the Nepalese Legation. This gives rise to a nice little comedy. The guilty persons must, of course, be punished, as the legation sets much store on good relations with the Tibetan government. But as a matter of fact, more important persons than mere soldiers are often involved—indeed many high-class Tibetans enjoy a plate of fish when they can get it. The poor culprits receive a terrible reprimand and are sentenced to be whipped, but the chastisement is not meant to hurt.

No one would dare to go fishing in Lhasa. In the whole of Tibet there is only one place where fishing is allowed, and that is where the Tsangpo River runs through a sandy desert. Here there are no crops and no pasture for animals: in fact, there is nothing to eat but fish, and so the law has been relaxed. The people of this region are looked down upon, like the slaughterers and blacksmiths.

In point of numbers the Muslims form an appreciable part of the population of Lhasa. They have a mosque of their own and enjoy full freedom to practice their religion. (One of the best characteristics of the Tibetan people is their complete tolerance of other creeds. Their monastic theocracy has never sought the conversion of infidels.) Most of the Muslims have immigrated from India and have intermingled with the Tibetans. Their religious zeal led them at first to demand that their Tibetan wives should be converted, but here the Tibetan government stepped in and made it a condition that native women could marry Muslims only if they kept to their own faith.

At the gymkhana it is possible to pick out examples of all the population groups. One sees Ladhakis, Bhutanese, Mongolians, Sikkimese, Kazaks, and representatives of all the neighboring tribes, among whom one finds Hui-Huis—Chinese Muslims from the province of Kuku-Nor. These people own the slaughterhouses situated in a special quarter outside the Lingkhor. Buddhists look askance at them because they take the life of animals, but they are allowed to have their own place of worship.

At the end of the festival the nobles and notables march back to the town in a glittering procession. The common people stand by the roadside and admire the splendor of their demigods. They have had their fill of excitement and drama, and the faithful will feast for long on the memory of these tremendous ceremonies at which the God-King showed himself to them. Workaday life begins again. Shops are opened, and bargains driven as keenly as ever. Dice players appear at street corners, and the dogs, who during the "Lenten" fast have migrated to the outskirts of the Lingkhor, come back to the town.

Our life continued peacefully. Summer approached. My sciatica got better, and nothing was said about our expulsion. I was receiving regular treatment from the English doctor, but on fine days I was able to work in the garden. And I had a lot to do, for when it was known that I was responsible for Tsarong's fountain and various other rearrangements in his grounds, notables came, one after another, and asked me to do the same for them.

Aufschnaiter was very busy making his canal. From early morning till evening, he was at his workplace, for work stopped only on feast days. It was a fortunate thing that he had been employed by the monks, for though the lay nobles play an important part in the administration of the country, a small group of monks has the last word in everything. For this reason I felt no little satisfaction when one day I was summoned to the garden of the Tsedrung.

The monks of this foundation are officials who form a sort of monastic order. Brought up to be strictly loyal to their own community, they have become far more powerful than the secular officials. They provide the immediate entourage of the Dalai Lama, and all the personal servants of the young God-King belong to this order. His chamberlains, his tutor, and his personal guardians are all Tsedrung monks of high standing. Moreover, the Dalai Lama attends the meetings which they are obliged to hold daily, to discuss the interests of their community.

The officials of this order are, without exception, strictly trained. Their school is situated in the east wing of the Potala, and their teachers come, according to tradition, from the famous cloister of Möndroling, which specializes in Tibetan calligraphy and grammar. Anybody can enter the school, but adoption into the order is very difficult. A rule dating from many centuries prescribes that the members of the Tsedrung shall not exceed 175.

When the student has reached his eighteenth year and has passed his examinations, he can enter the order with powerful patronage. Beginning at the bottom, he may, if sufficiently capable, attain to the third class in the order. Monks of the Tsedrung wear, in addition to the usual red cowls, garments distinctive of their rank. Most of the students in the Tsedrung school come from the people, and they provide a useful counterpoise to the influence of the hereditary nobles. They have a wide field of activity as there are no government offices in which there is not at least one monastic official to every layman. This system of dual control is considered an insurance against the exercise of dictatorial power, which is one of the standing dangers of feudalism.

It was the High Chamberlain who had sent for me. He proposed that I should rearrange the garden of the Tsedrung. That was a great chance for me. I was told that additions were to be made to the Dalai Lama's garden as well, and if my work was found satisfactory, I might be employed there. I set to work at once with the utmost zeal. They placed a number of men under my orders, and we soon got things moving. I now had no time for the private lessons in English and mathematics that I was giving to some young nobles.

Suddenly, just as I was beginning to feel sure of our position in view of the powerful protection we now enjoyed, I had a fearful shock. One morning we received a visit from Mr. Kyibub, a high official at the foreign ministry and the last of the four Tibetans who had been educated at Rugby many years ago. He was clearly upset by his mission. After many apologies and expressions of regret, he told us that the English doctor had now certified that I was fit to travel and that the government expected us to depart at once. In confirmation he showed us the certificate, which stated that although I was not completely cured, I could travel without endangering my life.

This was a stunning and unexpected blow to Aufschnaiter and me. We pulled ourselves together and endeavored politely and calmly to present our side of the question. We explained that my illness might recur at any moment. What would I do if, in the middle of an arduous journey, I found I could not move a step farther? Moreover, the hot season in India had just begun. No one who had been living for so long in the healthy highland air of Tibet could endure the transition without prejudice to his health. And what was to happen to the tasks with which we had been charged by the highest authorities, and which we felt bound to carry to completion? We promised to submit another petition to the government.

From this day forth we heard never a word more about an order of expulsion, though for a while we lived in daily expectation of it.

In the meantime, we had come to feel at home in Lhasa, and the people had got used to us. We received no more visits from curious people—only from friends. The British Legation seemed convinced that we were not dangerous, for though Delhi had asked for our surrender, the point was not pressed. The Tibetan authorities assured us that we were not considered undesirable.

We were now earning so much that we were no longer dependent on Tsarong's hospitality. We made many friends during the course of our work, and time passed very quickly. The only thing for which we hankered was letters from home. We had now been over two years without news. Still, we comforted ourselves with the thought that our life was very tolerable and that we had many reasons for satisfaction. We had a good roof over our heads and were no longer struggling to exist. We did not miss the appliances of Western civilization. Europe with its life of turmoil seemed far away. Often as we sat and listened to the radio bringing reports from our country we shook our heads at the depressing news. There seemed no inducement to go home.

10

LIFE IN LHASA—I

All my previous experiences were put in the shade by the first official party I attended at the home of the parents of the Dalai Lama. It was by chance that I was there. I was working in the garden, where I had some new plots to lay out, when the Holy Mother sent for me and told me to leave my work for the day and join her guests. With some embarrassment I joined the brilliant throng in the reception room. Some thirty nobles were gathered there, all in their finest robes, and the scene was one of dignified splendor. The reception was to celebrate the birth of our hostess's youngest son, born three days before. I haltingly stammered my congratulations and offered a white scarf that I had managed to borrow. The Holy Mother smiled graciously. It was wonderful to see her walking unconcernedly about the room and entertaining her guests. The women here recover from their confinements with miraculous speed, and make very little fuss about childbirth. No doctors are called in, but the women help one another. Every woman is proud to have a lot of healthy children. The mother invariably nurses her own children and sometimes goes on suckling them for three or four years.

When a child is born in a noble family, the infant at once gets a special nursemaid, who must never leave it day or night. Great celebrations follow the birth of a child, but there is nothing like our baptismal ceremony, and there are no godfathers. Before giving the infant its name (or rather names, as every child has several), the parents consult a lama, who decides what the infant shall be called only after studying the astrological aspects of the case. If the child subsequently suffers a serious illness, it is usual to give him fresh names. One of my grown-up friends once changed his name after an attack of dysentery, to my perpetual confusion.

At the celebration of the birth of the Dalai Lama's little brother, we were entertained to a Lucullan feast, at which we sat on cushions at little tables in due order of precedence. For two consecutive hours the servants served course after course—I counted forty, but that was not the end. To eat through such a dinner required special training. I must be excused from mentioning all the delicacies that were offered to us, but I remember that they included all sorts of Indian spiced dishes and ended up with soup of noodles. For drinks we had, among other things, beer, whisky, and port. By the end of the repast, many of the guests were tipsy, but that is no disgrace in Tibet; it contributes to the general merriment.

The party broke up soon after the banquet. Horses and servants provided by the host waited outside to take the guests home. Invitations to other parties were launched indiscriminately, and it needed a discerning ear to distinguish between those that were meant seriously and those that were just a form of politeness.

Aufschnaiter and I were often invited to this house, and I was soon on terms of cordial friendship with Lobsang Samten. This attractive youth was just entering upon his career as a monk. As the brother of the Dalai Lama he had brilliant prospects. One day he was to play a great part as the intermediary between his brother and the government. But the burden of a great position was already beginning to weigh him down. He could not choose his acquaintances freely. Whatever he did and wherever he went, all sorts of inferences were drawn. When he called on a high functionary on some official occasion, his entry into the room caused an awestruck silence and everyone, even cabinet ministers, rose from their seats to show respect to the brother of the God-King. All this might have turned a young man's head, but Lobsang Samten never lost his modest demeanor.

He often talked to me about his young brother who lived a lonely life in the Potala. I had already noticed that all the guests at parties hid themselves when the figure of the Dalai Lama appeared walking on the flat roof of the palace. Lobsang gave me a rather touching explanation of this. The young God-King possessed a number of excellent telescopes and field glasses, and it amused him to watch the life and doings of his subjects in the town. For him the Potala was a golden prison. He spent many hours daily praying and studying in the dark palace rooms. He had little free time and few pleasures. When the guests at a merry party felt themselves being looked at, they vanished as soon as possible from the field of vision. They did not want to sadden the heart of the young ruler, who could never hope to enjoy such distractions.

Lobsang Samten was his only friend and confidant, and had access to him at all times. He served as the link between him and the outer world and had to tell his brother everything that was going on. I learned from Lobsang that he was much interested in our activities and that he had often watched me through his telescope as I worked in the garden. He also told me that his brother was much looking forward to moving into his summer residence at Norbulingka. The fine weather had come, and he felt himself cramped in the Potala and longed to be able to take exercise out of doors.

Now the season of sandstorms was over, and the peach trees were in blossom. On the neighboring peaks, the last remnants of the snow shone blindly white in the warm sunshine, giving that peculiar charm to the springtime that I remembered in our mountain scenery at home. One day the summer season was officially declared to have begun, and summer clothes might be worn. One had no right to leave off one's furs when one wanted to. Every year, after considerations of the omens, a day was fixed on which the nobles and monks put on summer dress. The weather might have already been very warm, or snowstorms might follow. That did not matter. Summer dress must be worn from that date only. The same thing happens in autumn, when winter dress is officially resumed. I continually used to hear complaints that the changeover had come too soon or too late and that people were stifling or half-frozen.

The change of clothing is accompanied by a ceremony that lasts for hours. Servants bring new clothes bound up in bundles on their backs. The monks have an easier passage. They merely change their fur-brimmed hats for plate-shaped papier-mâché headdress. The whole appearance of the town is changed when everyone suddenly appears in new clothes.

There is, however, one other occasion for a change of costume, and that is when the whole official world accompanies the Dalai Lama in a gorgeous procession to the Summer Garden. Aufschnaiter and I looked forward to watching it. We felt that we might get a close-up view of the Living Buddha.

IT WAS a glorious summer day, and the whole town moved out through the western gate along the two-mile stretch that separates the Potala and the Norbulingka palaces. It was quite a job finding room to walk without being trodden on.

I was sorry I had no camera to take pictures of the variegated crowds. Of course, only a color film would do it justice. This was a day of rejoicing for everyone, the opening day of summer, and I was glad for the boy who was going to exchange his gloomy prison for a lovely summer garden. He had little enough sunshine in his life.

Splendid and imposing as the Potala Palace is externally, it is miserably dark and uncomfortable as a dwelling place. It is probable that all the God-Kings were glad to get away from it as soon as possible, for the Summer Garden residence of Norbulingka was planned as long ago as the reign of the seventh Dalai Lama, but completed only by the thirteenth.

The latter monarch was a great reformer and at the same time a man of modern ideas. He actually imported for his own use three automobiles. These were taken to pieces at the frontier and carried by coolies and yaks over the mountains to the capital, where an Indian-trained mechanic reassembled them. This man was then appointed as chauffeur to His Majesty. He often used to talk to me sadly about his three cars, which now stood idle, but not unguarded, in a shed. They were two Austins and a Dodge. For a short while, they had been the sensation of Tibet, and now they mourned for their dead lord and rusted in honorable decay. The story of how the thirteenth Dalai Lama used his automobiles to escape from his winter prison still provokes laughter. In the autumn he used to return with pomp and circumstance to the Potala, but as soon as the crowds were out of the way, he would get into one of the cars and drive back to Norbulingka.

We heard the blare of trumpets and trombones. The procession approached. The murmurs of the crowd were hushed, and a reverent silence reigned, for the head of the column was in sight. A host of serving monks formed the vanguard. With them they carried the God-King's personal effects done up in bundles, each bundle wrapped in a yellow silk cloth. Yellow is the color of the

Reformed Lamaistic Church, which is also known as the Yellow Church. An old legend tells why this color was chosen.

Tsong Kapa, the great reformer of Buddhism in Tibet, was standing on the day of his entry into the monastery of Sakya at the tail of a line of novices. When it was his turn to be robed, the supply of red hats had run out. In order that he should not be hatless, someone grabbed the first hat that came to hand and put it on his head. It chanced to be a yellow one. Tsong Kapa never gave up wearing it, and so yellow came to be adopted as the color of the Reformed Church. The Dalai Lama always used to wear a yellow silk cap at receptions and ceremonies, and all the objects in regular use by him were of this color. The use of yellow was a privilege which he alone possessed.

Soon we saw the God-King's favorite birds being carried by in their cages. Now and then a parrot called out a welcoming word in Tibetan, which the faithful crowd received with rapturous sighs as a personal message from their God. At an interval behind the servants came monks with banners decorated with texts. Next came a band of mounted musicians wearing brightly colored, old-fashioned garb and playing old-fashioned instruments, from which they produced curious, whimpering sounds. After them followed an army of monks from the Tsedrung, also on horseback and marshaled in order of rank. Behind them, grooms led the favorite horses of the Dalai Lama, splendidly caparisoned. Their bridles were yellow and their bits and saddles of pure gold.

Then came a flock of high dignitaries and senior members of the God-King's household, the latter all monks with the rank of abbot. These are the only persons, except his parents and brothers and sisters, who have the right of speech with the Dalai Lama. Alongside them marched the tall figures of the bodyguard—huge fellows chosen for their size and strength. I was told that none of them is under six feet six inches in height, and one of them measures eight feet. Their padded shoulders make them look even more formidable, and they carry long whips in their hands. The only sound to be heard came from them as in deep bass voices they called on the crowd to make way and take off their hats. This was obviously part of the ceremonial, as the people were already standing in dead silence with bowed heads and folded hands by the roadside.

Then followed the Commander in Chief of the army. He held his sword at the salute. Compared with the silks and brocades of the other dignitaries, his khaki uniform looked strikingly modest. However, as he was free to choose the trimmings of his dress, his badge of rank and epaulettes were of pure gold. On his head he wore a sun helmet.

And now approached the yellow, silk-lined palanquin of the Living Buddha, gleaming like gold in the sunlight. The bearers were six-and-thirty men in green silk cloaks, wearing red plate-shaped caps. A monk was holding a huge iridescent sunshade made of peacock's feathers over the palanquin. The whole scene was a feast for the eyes—a picture revived from a long-forgotten fairy tale of the Orient.

Around us, all heads were bowed in deep obeisance, and no one dared to raise his eyes. Aufschnaiter and I must have been noticeable with our heads only slightly bent. We absolutely had to see the Dalai Lama. And there he was—bowing to us with a smile behind the glass front of his sedan chair. His finely cut features were full of charm and dignity, but his smile was that of a boy, and we guessed that he, too, was curious to see us.

The procession had passed its peak. Now came the secular authorities. The four cabinet ministers rode on splendid horses on either side of the sovereign. Behind them came another magnificent chair, carried by fewer bearers, in which sat the Regent, Tagtra Gyeltsab Rimpoche, styled "the Tiger Rock," an old gentleman of seventy-three. He looked sternly before him and gave no smile of greeting. He seemed not to see the people. Strict and severe in the performance of his duties, he has as many enemies as friends. After him rode the representatives of the Three Pillars of the State, the abbots of Sera, Drebung, and Ganden. Then came the nobles in due order of rank, each group wearing the costume appropriate to its status. The junior orders wore absurd little caps that just covered their topknots and were fastened with a ribbon under their chins.

Deep in contemplation of the spectacle, I suddenly heard the sound of familiar music. Yes—no mistake about it, the British National Anthem! The band of the bodyguard had taken up its station halfway along the route, and the royal chair must just have come up to them. So, to honor the God-King, they played "God Save the Queen." I have generally heard it better played, but it has never caused me such bewilderment. I learned later that the bandmaster had been trained in the Indian Army. He had noticed that this air played an important part at all ceremonies, so he brought the music back with him. It has been set to Tibetan words, but I have never heard them sung. The brass band finished the anthem creditably with the exception of a few wrong notes by the trumpets due to the rarefied air, and then the pipers of the police band played a selection of Scottish airs.

Tibetan music knows no harmonies, but its melodies are pleasing to our ears. In the same piece they pass easily from the gloomy to the gay, and changes of rhythm are frequent.

The procession vanished behind the gates of the Summer Palace, and the crowds dispersed, mostly to spend the rest of the day in the open air. The nomads, sweating in their warm sheepskin cloaks, strike their tents and move off to their highland homes in the Changthang. No Tibetan is anxious to go on a pilgrimage to India in summer, and no nomads come willingly to Lhasa in the warm weather. The capital is only 12,000 feet above sea level, and the nomads, most of whom live at 15,000 feet, find the warmth oppressive.

We walked home deeply impressed by all that we had seen. We could not have witnessed a better example of the distribution of authority in Tibet than in the procession that had moved by before us—with the Dalai Lama and the regent as the high peaks, and the different grades tapered downward to front and rear. It was significant of their power in the state that the monks marched in front.

Religion is the heart of the fabric of the State. Pilgrims from the remotest parts of the Changthang undergo countless hardships in order to come once a year and witness this brilliant manifestation of their religious faith, and they feed on the memory during their hard and lonely lives. The daily life of Tibetans is ordered by religious belief. Pious texts are constantly on their lips; prayer wheels turn without ceasing; prayer flags wave on the roofs of houses and the summits of the mountain passes; the rain, the wind, all the phenomena of nature, the lonely peaks of the snow-clad mountains, bear witness to the universal presence of the gods whose anger is manifested by the hailstorm, and whose benevolence is displayed by the fruitfulness and fertility of the land. The life of the people is regulated by the divine will, whose interpreters the lamas are. Before anything is undertaken, we must test the omens. The gods must be unceasingly entreated, placated, or thanked. Prayer lamps burned everywhere, in the house of the noble and in the tent of the nomad—the same faith has kindled them. Earthly existence is of little worth in Tibet, and death has no terrors. Men know that they will be born again and hope for a higher form of existence in the next life, earned by pious conduct in this one. The Church is the highest court of appeal, and the simplest monk is respected by the people and addressed by the title of Kusho, as if he were a member of the nobility. In every family at least one of the sons is dedicated to the cloister in token of reverence for the Church and to give the child a good start in life.

In all these years I have never met anyone who expressed the slightest doubt about the truth of Buddha's teaching. There are, it is true, many sects, but they differ only in externals. One cannot close one's heart to the religious fervor that radiates from everyone. After a short time in the country, it was no longer possible for one thoughtlessly to kill a fly, and I have never in the presence of a Tibetan squashed an insect that bothered me. The attitude of the people in these matters is really touching. If at a picnic an ant crawls up one's clothes, it is gently picked up and set down. It is a catastrophe when a fly falls into a cup of tea. It must at all costs be saved from drowning as it may be the reincarnation of one's dead grandmother. In winter they break the ice in the pools to save the fishes before they freeze to death, and in summer they rescue them before the pools dry up. These creatures are kept in pails or tins until they can be restored to their home waters. Meanwhile, their rescuers have done something for the good of their own souls. The more life one can save the happier one is.

I shall never forget an experience I had with my friend Wangdüla. We went one day to the only Chinese restaurant and there saw a goose running around the courtyard, apparently on its way to the cooking pot. Wangdüla quickly took a bank note of considerable value from his pocket and bought the goose from the restaurant keeper. He then had his servant carry the goose home, and for years afterward I used to see the lucky creature waddling about his place.

Typical of this attitude toward all living creatures was a rescript issued in all parts of the country to persons engaged in building operations—this was during the three years that the young Dalai Lama spent in meditation. It was pointed out that worms and insects might easily be killed during the work of building, and the utmost care to avoid this was enjoined on all. Later on, when I was in charge of earthworks, I saw with my own eyes how the coolies used to go through each spadeful of earth and take out anything living.

It follows from this principle that there is no capital punishment in Tibet. Murder is regarded as the most heinous of crimes, but the murderer is only flogged and has iron fetters forged onto his ankles. It is true that the floggings are in fact less humane than the death penalty as it is carried out in Western lands. The victim often dies an agonizing death after the penalty has been inflicted, but the religious principle has not been infringed. Criminals condemned to a life in chains are either shut up in the state prison at Shö or sent to a district governor who is responsible for their custody. Their fate is certainly preferable to that of the convicts in the prisons who are permitted to leave their gaol only on the birth- and death-day of the Buddha, when they may beg for alms in the Lingkhor, chained to fellow prisoners.

Theft and various minor offenses are punished with public whipping. A board on which his offense is written is slung around the neck of the offender, and he has to stand for a few days in a sort of pillory. Here again, charitable people come and give him food and drink. When highwaymen or robbers are caught, they are usually condemned to have a hand or a foot cut off. I was horrified to see in what manner wounds so inflicted were sterilized. The limb is plunged into boiling butter and held there. Even that does not deter evildoers. A governor told me of criminals who held out their hands for punishment with an impudent gesture and after a few weeks resumed their life of crime. In Lhasa such savage forms of punishment have now been discontinued.

The penalties for political offenses are very strict. People still speak of the monks of Tengyeling, who forty years ago sought to come to terms with the Chinese. Their monastery was demolished and their names blotted out.

There is no organized system of law courts in Tibet. The investigation of offenses is entrusted to two or three persons of noble rank, but corruption is unfortunately very prevalent; in fact, very few nobles have a high reputation for integrity. The sums received as bribes are regarded by many as part of the perquisites of the feudal system. If a defendant considers that he has been unjustly condemned, he is allowed to appeal to the Dalai Lama. If he is thus proved innocent, he receives a free pardon, and if not his penalty is doubled.

In Lhasa the city magistrate officiates permanently as judge, except during the twenty-one days following the New Year, when all authority is exercised by the monks. The magistrate is assisted by a couple of assessors, and they are kept very busy, for, in addition to the pilgrims, many bad characters come to the capital.

AFTER THE DALAI LAMA had moved to his summer residence the weather became very warm, but not unpleasantly so. At this season the day temperature never exceeds 85 degrees Fahrenheit, and the nights are cool. The air is very dry, and rain falls seldom. Soon everybody is praying for rain. There are a number of springs around Lhasa, but almost every year they dry up. When that happens the people have to fetch their water from the river Kyichu, which runs down clear and cold from the glaciers.

When the springs have ceased to flow and the barley fields are dry and withered, the government decrees that every citizen must water the streets till the order is withdrawn. At once the whole town gets busy, and everyone hurries to the river with jugs and buckets and carries the water back to the city. The nobles send their servants to fetch the water, but when they have brought it, they take a hand in pouring it on the streets and on their neighbors.

There is a regular water carnival in which all participate without distinction of rank or station. Streams of water flow from the windows and roofs onto the heads of the passersby, and it is bad form to take offense if one is wet through. The children have the time of their lives. For my part, being tall and conspicuous, I got more than my share of soaking. Everyone thought that the "German Henrigla" was fair game.

While the water fight is going on in the street, the Oracle of Gadong, the most famous rainmaker in Tibet, is summoned to the garden of the Dalai Lama. Here are gathered together the highest officers of the government, and the Grand Lama himself presides over the ceremony. The rainmaker, a monk, soon falls into a trance. His limbs begin to move convulsively, and he gives utterance to strange groans. At that moment, one of the monastic officials begs the oracle to vouchsafe rain and thereby save the harvest. The movements of the rainmaker become more and more ecstatic, and high-pitched words escape him. A clerk takes down the message and hands it to the cabinet ministers. Meanwhile, the body of the entranced medium, now no longer possessed by the divinity, sinks unconscious to the ground and is carried out.

After this performance everyone in Lhasa excitedly waits for the rain. And rain it does. Whether one believes in miracles or looks for a logical explanation, the fact is that soon after this drama is enacted, it always does rain. The Tibetans do not doubt that the protecting deity enters the medium's body while he is in a trance, and hears and grants the prayers of the people.

This explanation naturally did not satisfy me, and I tried to find a more scientific solution. I wondered if perhaps the intensive watering of the streets had caused evaporation, or if the monsoon rains had spilled over into the highlands of Tibet. The British Legation had set up a meteorological station and measured the rainfall scientifically. It amounted to an average of about fourteen inches a year and mostly occurred at this season. Aufschnaiter later installed a water gauge on the Kyichu and recorded the first rise in the river level on almost the same day every year. Had he followed the rainmaker's methods he could have instituted as a successful oracle.

In former times the rainfall in Lhasa must have been much heavier. There used to be great forests, which must have made for rainier and cooler weather. The deforestation of centuries had done its work in the provinces. Lhasa itself, with its meadows and groves of willows and poplars, was a green oasis in the treeless valley of the Kyichu.

IN LHASA we were constantly invited out and often consulted. Thus we came to know the life of the town from every angle. We had opportunities for studying the details of public administration and family life, viewpoints, manners, and morals. Something new turned up every day, and many mysteries became commonplaces, but not all. One thing had certainly changed in our situation. We were no longer outsiders. We belonged.

The bathing season had come. Old and young, great and small flocked to the gardens by the river and enjoyed themselves swimming and paddling in the shallow water. Smart people organized comfortable picnic parties and put up their own tents. You could see many young women who had studied in India proudly displaying their modern bathing dresses. In the intervals of splashing about in the water the bathers picnicked and played dice, and in the evening every party burned a stick of incense by the riverside in gratitude to the gods for a lovely day.

I was much admired for my prowess as a swimmer. Tibetans do not know much about swimming as the water is too cold for learning. Those who can swim at all can just keep themselves afloat. Now they had an expert among them. I was invited right and left, of course with the idea that I should show off my skill, but my sciatica made swimming a painful pastime, as the water was very cold—never above 50 degrees Fahrenheit. Sometimes I used to dive in order to give my friends pleasure, but not often. Still, there were times when my presence was of service. I managed to save three people from drowning, for there were some dangerous places in the river where obstructions had created whirlpools and undercurrents.

One day I was the guest of Surkhang, the Foreign Minister, and his family, who had put up their tent beside the water. The minister's only son Jigme (meaning "Dreadnought") was there on a holiday from school in India. He had learned how to swim, more or less, at school. I was floating downstream when I suddenly heard cries and saw people gesticulating wildly on the bank and pointing to the water. I hurriedly swam to land and ran to the tent. From there I saw Jigme being whirled round in a swirling eddy. I at once dived in and though the whirlpool caught me, too, I was a strong swimmer and managed to get hold of the unconscious lad and bring him to the bank. As a former instructor, I knew how to revive him, and in a short time he was breathing again to the great joy of his father, who shed tears and overwhelmed me with expressions of gratitude. I had saved a life, and that was accounted a great merit.

As a result of this episode, my relations with the Surkhang family became intimate, and I had an opportunity to study a marital combination that even in Tibet was quite out of the ordinary.

The minister was separated from his first wife. The second, the mother of Jigme, was dead. Surkhang now shared the young wife of a nobleman of lower rank. In the marriage contract, Jigme was brought in as the third husband, because his father did not wish to leave all his fortune to his widow. Similar complications are found in many families. I once came across a case in which a mother was the sister-in-law of her own daughter. In Tibet one finds polygamy and polyandry, but most people are monogamous.

When a man has several wives, his relations with them are different from those that prevail in a Moslem harem. It is common practice for a man to marry several daughters of a house in which there is no son and heir. This arrangement prevents the family fortune from being dispersed. Our host Tsarong had married three sisters and had obtained permission from the Dalai Lama to take their family name.

In spite of the frequently unusual relationships created by these alliances, broken marriages are not commoner in Tibet than with us. This is largely due to the fact that these people are not inclined to let their feelings run away with them. When several brothers share the same wife, the eldest is always the master in the household and the others have rights only when he is away or amusing himself elsewhere. But no one gets short measure as there is a superfluity of women. Many men live a celibate life in monasteries. There is a cloister in every village. The children of irregular alliances have no right to inherit, and all the property goes to the children of the legitimate wife. That is why it is not so important which of the brothers is the father of the child. The great thing is that the property remains in the family.

Tibet knows nothing about the drawbacks of overpopulation. For centuries the number of inhabitants has remained about the same. In addition to the practices of polyandry and monasticism, infant mortality contributes to this state of things. I calculate that the average expectation of life among the Tibetans is only about thirty years. A great number of small children die, and among the whole mass of officials there is only one septuagenarian.

I had read in many books about Tibet that the host is accustomed to offer his wife or daughter to his guest. If I had counted on that, I should have been badly disappointed. Sometimes it happened that a pretty young servant girl was lightheartedly offered to one, but the girls don't give themselves without being courted. Of course, loose girls can be found in all parts of the world, and even in Lhasa there are certain beauties who make love on a professional basis.

In former times marriages were arranged by the parents, but today the young people choose their own partners. They marry very young, the girls at sixteen and the boys at seventeen or eighteen at latest. The aristocracy may marry only in their own class, and this rule is strictly applied. Relatives may not marry each other except after seven generations, in order to avoid inbreeding. The Dalai Lama alone may permit exceptions to these rules. Occasionally, capable men of the people are promoted to the nobility, and that brings a little fresh blood into the small circle of about two hundred families that constitute the aristocracy.

Divorces are rare and have to be approved by the government. Very drastic penalties are inflicted on unfaithful spouses, for example cutting off the nose. But, as a matter of fact, I never heard of a case where this punishment was carried out. They once showed me an old woman without a nose, who was alleged to have been detected in infidelity—but it might just as well have been a case of syphilis.

VENEREAL DISEASE is very common in Tibet. Many cases occur in Lhasa, but not much importance is attached to them. They are generally neglected, and the doctor is called in when it is too late to do much good. The ancient remedy of mercury is known to the monks in the schools of medicine.

What a lot could be done for the future of Tibet if medical and sanitary conditions were improved! Surgery is completely unknown in the country. Aufschnaiter and I used to have a panic at the thought of an attack of appendicitis. Every suspicious pain used to alarm us. It seemed absurd in the twentieth century to die of this illness. The Tibetans know nothing of operations on the human body except the lancing of boils. The use of instruments in confinements is likewise unknown. The only connection Tibetans have with surgery is in the activities of the people who dissect corpses, the Domdens. These often report to the relatives on the cause of death or inform interested students of medicine when they find any interesting feature in a corpse.

The schools of medicine are unfortunately opposed to all progress. The doctrines taught by Buddha and his apostles are an overruling law, which may not be tampered with. There are two schools, the smaller situated on the Chagpori or "Iron Mountain," and the larger down below in the town. Every monastery sends a number of intelligent youngsters to these schools. The course lasts from ten to fifteen years. Learned old monks give instruction to the boys, who sit cross-legged on the ground with their tablets on their knees. Colored illustrations are often displayed on the walls. I was once present when a teacher was explaining by means of illustrations the symptoms of poisoning caused by a certain plant. The pupils were shown pictures of the plant, the symptoms, the antidotes and their reactions—just like the wall pictures in our schools.

Astronomy is an integral part of medical science. The yearly lunar calendar is put together in the schools of medicine after old works have been consulted. Eclipses of the sun and moon are carefully recorded, and monthly and yearly weather forecasts prepared.

In the autumn the whole school goes off to search for herbs in the mountains. The boys enjoy the expedition tremendously, though they are kept very busy. Every day they camp in a fresh place, and at the end of their excursion they drive their heavily laden yaks to Tra Yerpa. This is one of the holiest places in Tibet.

It contains a sort of temple in which the herbs are sorted and laid out to dry. In winter the youngest of these little monks have to grind the dried herbs into powders, which are kept in carefully labeled, airtight leather bags by the abbot in charge of the school. These schools serve at the same time as pharmacies from which anyone can get medicine gratis or for a small present. The Tibetans are really advanced in the knowledge of herbs and their healing properties, and I have often had recourse to them. Their pills did not do my sciatica much good, but I staved off many a cold and fever with their herb teas.

The abbot of the Medical School of Lhasa is at the same time the Dalai Lama's personal physician—an honorable but dangerous charge. When the thirteenth Dalai Lama died at the age of fifty-four, all kind of suspicions were openly voiced, and the abbot of the time could consider himself lucky to have escaped with loss of rank. He might have been sentenced to a flogging.

In the towns and monasteries one can get oneself vaccinated against smallpox, but no other forms of inoculation are practiced, and many lives are lost needlessly in epidemics for want of prophylactic treatment. What saves Tibet is its cool climate and pure mountain air. But for them, the universal dirt and the wretched sanitary conditions would surely engender catastrophic plagues. In season and out we preached the necessity of better sanitation and had thought out a drainage scheme for Lhasa. Superstition is the enemy. We found that the people had more confidence in the laying on of hands and faith healing than in the ministration of the monks of the schools of medicine. The lamas often smear their patients with their holy spittle. Tsampa, butter, and the urine of some saintly man are made into a sort of gruel and administered to the sick. The wooden prayer stamps, which are dipped in holy water and then applied to the painful spot, do no one any harm. Nothing ranks higher as a remedy for illness than objects that have belonged to the Dalai Lama. All the nobles used to show me with pride relics of the thirteenth Dalai Lama carefully sewn up in little silk bags. Tsarong, as his former favorite, possessed many articles of personal use that had belonged to him, and it astonished me that Tsarong and his son, who had been educated in India, were superstitious enough to set store by these relics.

Many men and women live by fortune-telling and casting horoscopes. Characteristic of the streets of Lhasa are the little old women who crouch beside the pilgrims' road and tell the future for a small fee. They ask you the date of your birth, make a small calculation with the help of their rosaries, and you go on your way consoled by the mysterious words. The greatest confidence is placed in the soothsaying powers of lamas and incarnations. One does not do a thing without consulting the omens. No one would think of going on a pilgrimage or taking up a new office before ascertaining on what date it will be lucky to start.

Not long ago there lived in Lhasa a very celebrated lama, whose visits and consultations were booked up for months ahead. He used to travel with his disciples from place to place receiving hospitality. His patients gave him so many presents that he and his group lived very comfortably on them. He had such a reputation that even Mr. Fox, the English radio operator, who for years had been a victim of gout, arranged for the lama to visit him. But poor Fox missed his turn as the old man died before he could come.

The old lama had originally been a simple monk. After studying for twenty years in one of the greatest monasteries, he passed his examinations brilliantly and retired to a hermitage for several years. He lived in one of the lonely cells that one finds scattered over the whole country and in which monks settle down to a period of meditation. Many of them have themselves walled in by their disciples and live on nothing but tsampa and tea. This monk became celebrated for his exemplary life. He never ate food which life had been taken to provide, and abstained even from eggs. He was reputed to need no sleep and never to use a bed. This latter detail I can confirm, as he once lived near me for three days. He was also said to perform miracles. Once his rosary caught fire from the powerful rays that emanated from his own hand. He presented to the town of Lhasa a great gilded statue of Buddha, which he paid for out of the gifts and contributions he had received from his patients and admirers.

There was only one female Incarnation in Tibet. Her name, as interpreted, was "Thunderbolt Sow." I often used to see her at ceremonies in the Parkhor. She was then an insignificant-looking student of about sixteen, wearing a nun's dress. However, she was the holiest woman in Tibet, and the people entreated her to bless them wherever she went. Later on she became abbess in a convent by Lake Yamdrok.

Lhasa was always full of rumors and stories about saintly nuns and lamas, and I would gladly have investigated some of their miracles. But one must not offend against people's beliefs. The Tibetans were happy in their own convictions and had never tried to convert Aufschnaiter or me. We contented ourselves with studying their customs, visiting their temples as spectators, and making presents of white silk scarves as etiquette prescribed.

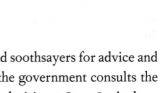

11

LIFE IN LHASA—II

Just as the people apply to lamas and soothsayers for advice and help in the cares of daily life, so the government consults the State Oracle before making important decisions. Once I asked my friend Wangdüla to take me to an official consultation, and so one morning we rode out to the Nechung Monastery. At that time a nineteen-year-old monk was the mouthpiece of the oracle.

He was brought up in simple circumstances but had attracted much attention by his gifts as a medium. His technique was not so striking as that of his predecessor (who had cooperated in the discovery of the present Dalai Lama), but much was expected of him. I have often wondered whether it was by an unheard-of effort of concentration that he was able so quickly to throw himself into a trance before large crowds of people, or whether he used drugs or other expedients. In order to function as an oracle, the monk has to be able to dislodge his spirit from his body, to enable the god of the temple to take possession of it and to speak through his mouth. At that moment, the god is manifested in him. That is the belief of the Tibetans, and Wangdüla was convinced of its truth.

We talked about these things during our five-mile ride to the cloister. Hollow, eerie music greeted us at the gate of the temple. Inside, the spectacle was ghastly. From every wall looked down hideous, grimacing faces, and the air was filled with stifling fumes of incense. The young monk had just been led from his private quarters to the gloomy temple. He wore a round metal mirror on his breast. Attendants robed him in gay silks and led him to his throne. Then everyone drew back from around him. No sound could be heard except the hollow music. He began to concentrate. I watched him closely, never taking my eyes from his face—not the slightest movement of his features escaped me. He looked as if the life were fading out of him. Now he was perfectly motionless, his face a staring mask. Then suddenly, as if he had been struck by lightning, his body curved upward like a bow. The onlookers gasped. The god was in possession. The medium began to tremble; his whole body shook and beads of sweat stood out on his forehead. Servants went to him and placed a huge, fantastic headdress on his head. This was so heavy that it took two men to carry it. The slender body of the monk sank deeper into the cushions of the throne under the weight of his monstrous miter. It is no wonder, I thought, that these mediums die young. The spiritual and physical strain of these séances must be killing.

The trembling became more violent. The medium's heavily laden head wavered from side to side, and his eyes started from their sockets. His face was swollen and covered with patches of hectic red. Hissing sounds pierced through his closed teeth. Suddenly he sprang up. Servants rushed to help him, but he slipped by them and to the moaning of the oboes began to rotate in a strange exotic dance. Save for the music, his groans and teeth gnashings were the only sounds to be heard in the temple. Now he started beating on his gleaming breastplate with a great thumb ring, making a clatter that drowned the dull rolling of the drums. Then he gyrated on one foot, erect under the weight of the giant headdress, which just now two men could hardly carry. The attendants filled his hands with barleycorns, which he threw into the awestruck crowd of onlookers. All bent low before him, and I feared lest I be noted as an intruder. The medium became calmer. Servants held him fast, and a cabinet minister stepped before him and threw a scarf over his head. Then he began to ask questions carefully prepared by the cabinet about the appointment of a governor, the discovery of a new Incarnation, matters involving war and peace. The oracle was asked to decide on all these things. Often the question had to be repeated several times before the medium began to mumble. I tried to pick out intelligible words but made nothing of the sounds. While the minister stood humbly there trying to understand the answers, an old monk took them down with flying pen. He had done this hundreds of times in his life, as he was also secretary to the late oracle. I could not prevent myself from suspecting that perhaps the real oracle was the secretary. The answers he wrote down, though ambiguous, suggested a line to be followed and relieved the cabinet of a heavy load of responsibility. When an oracle goes on giving bad advice, they make short work of the mouthpiece. He is relieved of his office. This always seemed to me illogical. Did the god speak through the medium or did he not?

In spite of the risks, the post of State Oracle is much sought after. It carries with it the office of Dalama, corresponding with the third rank in the orders of nobility, and its holder is Prior of the Cloister of Nechung with all its benefices.

The last questions put by the minister to the oracle remained unanswered. Was the medium exhausted, or was the god out of humor?

I left the temple and stood in the blinding sunlight feeling quite benumbed by what I had seen. My European mentality was baffled at the experience. I subsequently attended many consultations of the oracle, but have never been able to arrive even at an approximate explanation of the riddle.

It was always a curious experience to meet the State Oracle in ordinary life. I could never get quite accustomed to sitting at the same table with him and hearing him noisily gulping his noodle soup. When we met in the street, I used to take off my hat, and he bowed and smiled in return. His face was that of a nice-looking young man, and bore no resemblance to the bloated, red-flecked, grimacing visage of the ecstatic medium.

Another occasion on which the State Oracle plays a great part is that of the so-called Great Procession, when the Dalai Lama is carried into the city to visit the cathedral. This ceremony is called the Great Procession to distinguish it from the procession to the Summer Garden, which I have already described.

On this occasion the whole of Lhasa is afoot; there is hardly standing room anywhere. There is a tent pitched on a piece of open ground, and around it are stationed monkish guards, who as usual are engaged in keeping curious people back with their whips. This tent conceals a great mystery. In it the Dalama of Nechung is preparing to go into a trance. In the meantime the God-King is slowly approaching in his sedan chair with his six-and-thirty bearers. Now the Holy One has halted before the tent out of which the god-possessed monk reels with staggering steps. His face is swollen, hissing tones proceed from his mouth, and the weight of his headdress almost bears him to the ground. Waving the bearers aside, he breaks through the line and puts his shoulders under the shafts and runs for a few steps. He looks as though he were upsetting his Holy Burden, but all is well. The other bearers take the strain, and the Dalama falls to the ground in a faint and is carried off in a litter, which is waiting to receive him. The procession then proceeds on its stately way. I have never been able to understand the exact meaning of this ritual. Perhaps it is meant to symbolize the subjection of the protecting deity to the higher powers of the Living Buddha.

In addition to the State Oracle and the rainmaker, there are in Lhasa at least six mediums, including an old woman who is reckoned to be a manifestation of a protecting goddess. She was prepared, for a small fee, to fall into a trance and allow the goddess to speak. On some days she went through this performance four times!

There are also mediums who, while in a state of trance, can bend long swords into a spiral. Several friends of mine keep such swords lying before their house altars. I have made various attempts to emulate this feat, but could not begin to do it.

The consultation of oracles originated in pre-Buddhistic times when the gods demanded human sacrifices, and I think the ritual has continued almost unchanged since early days. I was always deeply impressed by these uncanny performances, but was glad to think that my own decisions were not subject to the dictation of an oracle.

By the time the autumn came, we had already been several months in Lhasa and were thoroughly acclimatized. This is the best season of the year. The flower gardens, in which I had done so much work, were in full bloom, and the trees had just begun to change color. There was fruit in abundance—peaches, apples, and grapes from the southern provinces. Splendid tomatoes and marrows were displayed in the market, and it was during this season that the gentry gave their great parties at which an unbelievable choice of delicacies was offered to their guests.

It was also the right time of year for excursions, but unfortunately no Tibetan would climb a mountain for pleasure. On special days the monks go on a pilgrimage to some sacred mountain peak, and the nobles send their servants with them to propitiate the gods,

The Forbidden City of Lhasa.
Lhasa lies on a 12,000-foot plateau amid the Himalayas,
at approximately the same latitude as New Orleans.

Two-thousand feet up the sacred peak of Chomo Lari,
the author rests in the thin air.

Masked priests dance in the Tibetan New Year before the Potala.

Jewels and a ton of gold adorn the tomb of the thirteenth Dalai Lama. Spires on the tomb's roof represent baskets holding Buddhist scriptures. Bells are strung to ring out the doctrine, while sculpted figures repel evil spirits.

Vivid religious art on the walls of the Potala.

The Dalai Lama's mother, *right,* and sister.

A three-year-old boy, selected as the incarnation of a high-ranking lama, begins his parade through Lhasa to the monastery he will rule.

The noon hour is signalled by trumpet from atop a temple on Chagpori Hill.

Children learn their alphabet under the eye of a tutor.

The high rank of a cabinet minister's wife is indicated by her adornment.

Tibetan noblewomen in their elaborate headdress.

Attendants carry incense sticks behind the Dalai Lama's instructor, *far right,* and the god-king's elder brother.

Skating, introduced by the author, became known as "walking on knives."

The Dalai Lama's retinue in flight through the gorges of
the Himalayas.

Helmeted monks greet the Living Buddha's caravan.

to whom they burn incense on the summits. The windy mountain heights resound with prayers and new flags are put up, while crows fly around waiting to eat up the offerings of tsampa. It must be added that everyone is happy to be back in town after two or three days in the mountains.

Aufschnaiter and I made a point of climbing all the peaks in the neighborhood. They offered no technical difficulties as an attraction, but the views from them were splendid. To the south we could see the Himalayas, and quite near us towered a 23,000-foot peak of the Nyenchenthangla range, over which we had scrambled eight months before on our way down to Lhasa.

There are no glaciers to be seen from the town. The assumption that one finds snow and ice everywhere in Tibet is not true. We should have loved to go skiing, but even if we could have repeated our experiment with homemade skis, the distances were too great. We should have needed horses, tents, and servants. Sport in uninhabited regions is a costly business.

So we had to content ourselves with climbing expeditions. Our equipment was not exactly professional. We wore army boots and other articles of clothing—surplus stores sold to Tibet by American dealers. They were good enough for our purposes. The Tibetans could not get over their astonishment at the speed with which we completed our tours. Once I had to light a bonfire of incense on a mountaintop for my friends to see from the roofs of their houses. Otherwise no one would have believed that we had really got there. Aufschnaiter and I used to walk in one day as far as our friends' servants did in three. The first Tibetan in whom I managed to create some enthusiasm for mountain walks was my friend Wangdüla, who had very good powers of endurance. Later on other friends accompanied us, and all greatly enjoyed the views and took pleasure in the wonderful mountain flowers that we found.

My favorite expedition was to a little mountain lake a short day's march from Lhasa. The first time I went there was during the rainy season, when it was feared that the waters would overflow and flood the town. According to an ancient legend, this lake is connected by a subterranean channel with an underground lake said to exist beneath the cathedral. Every year the government used to send monks to propitiate the spirits of the lake with prayers and offerings. Pilgrims, too, used to go there and throw rings and coins into the water. By the lake stood a few stone huts in which one could find shelter. I found that the lake did not threaten the safety of the town in the slightest degree. Even if it had overflowed, no harm would have been done. It was a peaceful, idyllic little place. Herds of wild sheep, gazelles, marmots, and foxes sauntered casually by, and high in the blue the *lammergeier* wheeled his flight. To all these creatures man was not an enemy. No one would dare to hunt in the neighborhood of the Holy City. The flora around the lake are of a kind to quicken the pulse of any botanist. Marvelous yellow and blue poppies grow on the shore. They are a specialty of Tibet, which elsewhere you will find only at Kew.

These expeditions did not quite satisfy my appetite for sport. I kept wondering what else I could do, and at last the idea came to me to make a tennis court. I managed to interest a good many people in the idea and prepared a list of prospective members of the Lhasa T. C. I also collected some funds in advance. The list of members was very imposing and had an almost international character. There were Indians, Sikkimese, Nepalese, and of course numbers of the young gentlemen of Lhasa. These had hesitated at first about joining, in view of the attitude of the government toward football. But I was able to allay their fears by pointing out that tennis was a sport that did not attract onlookers or cause contention. Even the Church must realize that it was an innocent

game. Besides, there was already a tennis court at the British Legation.

I then engaged workmen and got them to level a piece of
ground near the river. It was not easy to find the right kind of soil
to surface the court with, but in a month it was all ready. I was very
proud of the job. We had already ordered nets, racquets, and balls
from India, and we organized a small party to start off the Lhasa
Tennis Club.

There was keen competition among the children to become ball
boys. They were fearfully clumsy, having never before had a ball
in their hands. But when we invited members of the British Legation to play with us, the soldiers of the bodyguard of the Nepalese
Mission came and fielded the balls for us. It was killing to see them
running around in their splendid uniforms.

Soon we had collected quite a number of players. Incontestably
the best was Mr. Liu, the secretary of the Chinese Legation; then
came Mr. Richardson, the British Minister, a gaunt Scotsman, slim
and tough in his professional work. He had only one hobby—his
splendid flower and vegetable garden. When one visited him, one
imagined oneself in a garden in fairyland.

Tennis playing provided new occasions for pleasant social in-
tercourse. Parties were arranged, now on our courts and now at
the British Legation, after which we had tea and bridge. I regarded
these meetings as my Sunday social outings and used to look forward to them with pleasure. One had to dress oneself decently and
got the feeling, for the moment, of being back in the milieu from
which one had come. My friend Wangdüla proved his worth in this
field, too. He was a keen tennis player and an excellent partner at
bridge.

Our tennis court had another advantage. We could play on it
the whole year round. But in the season of dust storms, we had to
be careful. Instead of wire netting we had enclosed the court with

high curtains, so when we saw the dust clouds gathering over the Potala, we had to look sharp and get them down before they were blown away by the storm.

In autumn Tibetans practiced their age-old pastime of kite flying. When the rains are over and the clear autumn weather has set in, the bazaars are full of brightly colored kites. The sport begins punctually on the first day of the eighth month. But it is not just a children's game, as it is with us. The opening day is a popular festival, and the nobles are just as keen on the pastime as the common people. The first kite goes up over the Potala, and very soon the sky is full of them. Children and grownups stand for hours on the roofs flying their kites with the intense concentration of chess or tennis champions. The kites are flown on lines of stout twine treated with glue and powdered glass. The chief object of the game is to cross your opponent's line and cut through it. When that happens there are screams of joy from the roofs. The severed kite flutters slowly down, and the children pounce on it. It now belongs to them. For a month this game is played in every hour of leisure. Then the season comes to a full stop, and the kites vanish as suddenly as they had appeared.

One day as I was strolling through the bazaar looking at the kites, a very odd thing happened. A complete stranger accosted me and offered to sell me a watch—that is, the remnants of a watch. It was old and rusty and had lost its dial. The man said it was broken and that he could do nothing with it. Being a European, perhaps I could repair it. I could pay anything I liked for it. I took the thing in my hand and at once recognized it. It was Aufschnaiter's wrist watch, which he had sold when we were in Western Tibet—a watertight Rolex. He had had it with him on the Nanga Parbat Expedition. Aufschnaiter had got rid of it with a heavy heart. I thought he would like to have it back, even if it never went again. It would nevertheless be a curiosity. With little hope of success, I gave it to a clever Mohammedan craftsman to tinker with. He was enthusiastic about the mechanism and soon got it to go again. I gave it back to Aufschnaiter as a birthday present. You should have seen his face when he saw it!

In autumn the great horse markets are held. Caravans with hundreds of horses come in from Siling, in northwest China. There is lively bargaining, which the Tibetans are very good at, and high prices are paid for good animals. The nobles like to keep good stables and insist on having a new thoroughbred to ride every year. Of course, only the rich can afford this. The common people, if they ride at all, use Tibetan ponies, but the nobility are expected to spend money on good horses. When they go out riding, they take mounted servants with them. A cabinet minister, for example, is supposed to have six men in uniform with him. The number of horses a noble keeps varies according to his standing—some have as many as twenty.

I have often seen women riding. Their skirts are wide enough for them to ride astride. They often accompany their husbands on journeys that last for weeks, when they go on a pilgrimage or proceed to a new post. They wear a rooflike headdress to protect them against the sun and rub a dark brown plant juice on their faces and cover their mouths with a shawl. When they ride through the streets in this makeup, one woman looks just like another, and I fear I have made many faux pas by not recognizing friends on such occasions.

During these long horseback expeditions, the little children sit on their nurses' laps, and the bigger ones in a sort of cradle with wooden bars, which they grip to keep from falling out.

WE HAD AN EXCITING TIME toward the beginning of December. An eclipse of the moon had been foretold, and since early evening the roofs had been besieged by curious people waiting eagerly for the spectacle. When the shadow of the earth slowly began to creep over the face of the moon, a mutter went through the whole town. Soon all began to clap their hands and cry aloud in order to scare away the wicked demon that stood before the moon. When the eclipse was over, the people returned happily to their houses and played games to celebrate the victory over the demon.

CHRISTMAS WAS DRAWING near, and I had thought of a surprise. I wanted to entertain my friends at a real Christmas party with a tree and presents. I had received so much kindness and hospitality that I wanted to give my friends some pleasure for a change. Preparations kept me very busy. My friend Trethong, whose late father had been a minister, lent me his house for a few days. I hired trained servants and cooks, and bought small presents for my guests, such as electric torches, penknives, table-tennis sets, and family games. I thought of special gifts for my host, Tsarong, and his family. The chief attraction was the Christmas tree. Mrs. Tsarong lent me a juniper tree in a beautiful pot, and I decorated it with candles, apples, nuts, and sweets. It looked very like the real thing.

The party began in the morning, as is usual in Lhasa. Wangdüla supported me as master of ceremonies as I was still afraid of committing some social barbarism. My guests were full of curiosity. They examined the tree from all sides and looked at the packages stacked beneath it. Everyone was full of excitement and anticipation, just like children at home. We passed the day in eating, drinking, and playing games, and when it grew dark I invited my guests to go into another room. I then lit up the Christmas tree and Wangdüla put on his fur coat inside out and played the part of Santa Claus. We put on the record *"Stille Nacht, heilige Nacht,"* the door opened, and with eyes wide with astonishment my guests clustered around the tree. Mr. Liu led the singing, and some of the guests who had been at English schools knew the tune and joined in. It was a strange scene. A medley of races in the heart of Asia gathered around a Christmas tree and singing the dear old Christmas hymn of our homes. I had become pretty good at controlling my emotions, but I must confess that at this moment I could not keep the tears from my eyes, and I had a sudden attack of homesickness.

The cheerfulness of my guests and their pleasure in their Christmas presents—aided by a little alcohol—helped me over my homesickness. When my friends left they told me repeatedly how much they had enjoyed our German "New Year."

A year ago we had thought a couple of pieces of white bread a wonderful Christmas gift in the lonely wastes of the Changthang. Today we sat around a table laden with good things in a company of friendly souls. We had no right to complain of our lot.

We did nothing in particular to celebrate the New Year of 1947. Aufschnaiter had finished his canal and had an important new work to execute. Lhasa had an old electric plant, which had been put up twenty years before by one of the former Rugbians. It was now in a terribly neglected state and gave practically no current. On working days there was just enough power to keep the machines in the mint in motion, but only on Saturdays was there enough current for the needs of private houses.

Tibet produces its own paper money and coinage. The *sang* is the numismatic unit. It is divided and subdivided decimally into the *sho* and the *karma*. Paper money is made with the strong native paper brightly colored and watermarked. The numbers are very skillfully painted on by hand, and all attempts at forgery had hitherto been foiled by the difficulty of imitating the numbers. The bank notes have a very good appearance. Gold, silver, and copper coins are also used. They are stamped with the emblems of Tibet—mountains and lions, which also appear on postage stamps, beside the rising sun.

As the operation of minting was so dependent on the electric current, Aufschnaiter was approached and asked to see if he could repair the old installation. He succeeded in convincing the authorities that there was not much to be gained by doing this and that the proper course was to make use of the water power of the Kyichu River. The existing plant used the weakly flowing waters of a little tributary of the main stream. Fear was expressed that the gods would punish Lhasa if the waters of the holy river were misused for such a purpose, and great credit is due to Aufschnaiter, who succeeded in winning the authorities over. He was instructed to start a survey at once and, in order to avoid a longish journey back and forth every day, he took rooms outside the town in a garden house on a country estate.

We now saw each other much less often. My teaching work kept me in the town, and I was also giving tennis lessons. My pupils, big and small, made quite good progress, but unfortunately Tibetans are not famed for their perseverance. Full of enthusiasm at the start, and ready for anything new, their interest flags before long. For this reason I kept losing pupils and replacing them, which was not very satisfactory for me. The children of good families whom I taught were without exception intelligent and wide awake, and were not inferior to our children in comprehension. In the Indian schools the Tibetan pupils are ranked for intelligence with Europeans. One must remember that they have to learn the language of their teachers. In spite of that handicap, they are often at the head of the class. There was a boy from Lhasa at St. Joseph's College, at Darjeeling, who was not only the best scholar in the school, but also champion in all the games and sports.

Besides my lessons I had found various other ways of adding to my income. In Lhasa one can almost pick up money off the street. One needs only a little enterprise. I might for instance have started a dairy for fresh milk and butter, or sent for an ice machine from India to produce ices for eating. Watchmakers, shoemakers, and gardeners were in great demand, and jobs in business houses, if one knew English, were easy to get. But we had no intention of becoming shopkeepers or merely earning money. We needed work that would at the same time procure us satisfaction. And more than anything, we desired to make ourselves useful to the government and thus in some measure repay their hospitality. We were consulted on all manner of subjects and were very glad to be of use. But we were regarded as maids of all work, and it was sometimes embarrassing to be asked for advice on subjects of which we knew much less than was supposed.

Once we were invited to regild the idols in a temple. By good luck we found in one of the books in Tsarong's inexhaustible library a recipe for preparing gold paint from gold dust. For this we had to order various chemicals from India, for the Nepalese of Lhasa, among whom are skilled gold- and silversmiths, are very jealous of their secrets.

Tibet contains considerable deposits of gold, but modern methods of mining are unknown. Since ancient times they have been scooping out the soil in the Changthang with gazelle horns. An Englishman once told me that it would probably pay to treat by modern methods soil that has already been sieved by the Tibetans. Many provinces must today pay their taxes in gold dust. But there is no more digging than is absolutely necessary, for fear of disturbing the earth gods and attracting reprisals, and thus once more progress is retarded.

Many of the great rivers of Asia have their source in Tibet and carry down with them the gold from the mountains. But not till the rivers have reached neighboring countries is their gold exploited.

Washing for gold is practiced only in a few parts of Tibet where it is particularly profitable. There are rivers in Eastern Tibet where the stream has scooped out bath-shaped cavities. Gold dust collects in these places by itself, and one has only to go and get it from time to time. As a rule the district governor takes possession of these natural gold washings for the government.

I always wondered why no one had thought of exploiting these treasures for personal profit. When you swim under water in any of the streams around Lhasa, you can see the gold dust glimmering in the sunlight. But as in so many other parts of the country, this natural wealth remains unexploited, mainly because the Tibetans consider this comparatively easy work too laborious for them.

Just before our second Tibetan New Year in Lhasa, we received our first letters from home for three years. They had been a long time on the way. One of the envelopes had a Reykjavik postmark and had been around the world. You can imagine our joy at knowing that at last there was a line of communication between our distant, unforgotten homeland and the "Roof of the World" on which we lived. Unfortunately, the line was a very slender one, and the poor postal communication did not improve during all the years of our sojourn in Tibet. The news from Europe was not encouraging. In fact, it strengthened our desire to remain where we were and make a permanent home in Lhasa. Neither of us had very close ties with our old homes. The time we had spent in this peaceful corner of the world had had a formative effect on our characters. We had come to understand the nature and mentality of the Tibetans, and our knowledge of the language had progressed far beyond the stage of merely making ourselves understood. We could now handle all the formulae of polite conversation.

A small radio set kept us in touch with the outside world. It had been presented to me by one of the ministers, who had asked me to pass on interesting political news, particularly that concerning

Central Asia. It gave one a feeling of unreality to get such clear untroubled reception out of this little box. One had to remind oneself that in Lhasa there were no dentists with their electric drills, no trolley cars, no hairdressers with power-driven apparatus—in fact nothing to disturb the radio listener.

I listened to the news the first thing every day and often found myself shaking my head and wondering at the things that men seemed to think important. Here it is the yak's pace that dictates the tempo of life, and so it has been for thousands of years. Would Tibet be happier for being transformed? A fine motor road to India would doubtless raise the people's standard of life very greatly, but by accelerating the tempo of existence it might rob the people of their peace and leisure. One should not force a people to introduce inventions that are far ahead of their stage of evolution. They have a nice saying here: "One cannot reach the fifth story of the Potala without starting at the ground floor."

It is a question whether the Tibetan culture and way of life do not more than balance the advantages of modern techniques. Where in the West is there anything to equal the perfect courtesy of this people? Here no one is made to lose face, and aggressiveness is unknown. Even political enemies treat each other with consideration and politeness, and greet each other cordially when they meet in the street. The women of the upper class are cultivated and elegant. Their clothes reflect their good taste, and they are perfect hostesses. People would have regarded it as a matter of course if we two bachelors had introduced one or more women into our ménage to keep house for us. Our friends did indeed suggest that we ought at least to have one female companion. In moments of loneliness, I often played with the idea, but attractive as I found many of the girls, I could not make up my mind to tie myself up. There were too few points of spiritual contact, without which a joint life would not have satisfied me. I would have been happy to bring out a wife from home, but at first I could not afford to do so and later, politics intervened.

So I lived alone, and my independence proved a great advantage when subsequently I came into close contact with the Dalai Lama. The monks probably would have disapproved still more of our meetings if I had been married. They live in strict celibacy and are forbidden to have anything to do with women. Unfortunately, homosexuality is very common. It is even condoned as giving proof that women play no part in the life of those monks who indulge in it. It also often happens that monks fall in love with women, and ask for their release so as to be able to marry them. This is granted without difficulty. A monk, on leaving holy orders, if he is of noble birth, takes the rank corresponding to that which he held in the cloister; if he is of humble origin he loses his rank but can usually make a living in commerce. Severe penalties are inflicted on monks who get entangled with women without asking permission to leave the order.

In spite of my voluntary loneliness, I found that time passed very quickly. My leisure hours were occupied with reading and visits. Aufschnaiter and I visited each other regularly since we had ceased to live together. We needed to exchange ideas. We were not completely satisfied with our activities and sometimes wondered if we could not make better use of our time. There was so much to be done in the field of exploration in this almost virgin land. We often thought of leaving Lhasa and wandering, as we once had done, through the country as poor pilgrims from station to station and thus getting to know Tibet as no European had ever done before. Aufschnaiter was always dreaming of spending a year by the Namtso, the great, mysterious inland sea, and studying its tides.

OUR LIFE in Tibet gradually lost its sensation of novelty, but that did not prevent us from realizing how lucky we were to be here.

Government offices often gave us letters to translate, coming from all parts of the world and written by persons of the most varied professions. They were mostly applications for permission to enter the country. Many of the applicants offered to work for the government in return for board and lodging, with a view to getting to know the country. Others were sufferers from tuberculosis who hoped for a cure from the mountain air of Tibet. These latter were always answered, and the answers conveyed the blessing and good wishes of the Dalai Lama, and sometimes a present of money. No reply was ever sent to the other applications, and no one received permission to come to Tibet. The unchangeable policy was to present Tibet as the Forbidden Land.

The foreigners whom I met during the five years of my stay in Lhasa were not more than seven in number.

In 1947, on the recommendation of the British Legation, a French journalist named Amaury de Riencourt was officially invited. He stayed three weeks in Lhasa. A year later Professor Tucci, the famous Tibetologist, arrived from Rome. This was his seventh visit to Tibet, but his first to Lhasa. He was reckoned to be the greatest authority on the history and civilization of Tibet, and had translated numerous Tibetan books as well as publishing a number of original works. He always astonished Chinese, Nepalese, Indians, and Tibetans by his knowledge of the history of their countries. I often met him at parties, and once before a large gathering he put me in a very false position by taking sides with the Tibetans against me in an argument about the shape of the earth. In Tibet the traditional belief is that the earth is a flat disk. This was being argued at the party, and I stood up for the spherical theory. My arguments seemed to be convincing the Tibetans and I appealed to Professor Tucci to support me. To my great surprise he took up a skeptical attitude, saying that in his opinion all scientists ought continually to be revising their theories, and that one day the Tibetan doctrine might just as well prove to be true! Everyone chuckled as it was known that I gave lessons in geography. Professor Tucci stayed eight days in Lhasa and then went on a visit to the most famous monastery in Tibet, Samye, after which he left the country, taking with him scientific specimens and many valuable books from the Potala Press.

Other interesting visitors to Lhasa were the Americans Lowell Thomas and his son, who came in 1949. They also remained for a week and attended many receptions given in their honor. They had an audience with the Dalai Lama. Both of them had moving-picture cameras and took some splendid pictures. The son wrote an interesting book, which became a best-seller, and the father, a radio commentator in the U.S.A., made recordings for his future talks. I greatly envied them their splendid photographic equipment and especially their abundance of film. About that time I had joined with Wangdüla in buying a Leica, but we always suffered from a shortage of film. The Americans made me a present of two color films, my first and only ones.

The political situation at this juncture had caused a favorable answer to be given to the petition of the two Americans to be allowed to come to Tibet. The threatening attitude of China, although traditional, had now again become intensified. Every Chinese government, whether imperial, national, or communist, had always professed to regard Tibet as a Chinese province. This pretension was entirely contrary to the wishes of the Tibetans, who loved their independence and were clearly entitled to enjoy it. The Tibetan government had in consequence decided to admit the two Americans, who undertook to make a worldwide publicity campaign in favor of Tibetan independence.

In addition to these four guests of the government, an English engineer and a mechanic came to Tibet on a professional mission. The engineer was employed by the General Electric Company, and his job was to install the new machines for the electric works. He spoke very highly of the work that Aufschnaiter had already done. The mechanic, Nedbailoff, was a White Russian who had been wandering about Asia since the Revolution. He had finally landed in our internment camp at Dehra Dun and in 1947 was about to be repatriated to Russia. In order to save his life, he had fled to Tibet but was rearrested on the frontier. Finally it was decided to let him remain in Sikkim as he was a skilled mechanic. From there he was summoned to Lhasa to repair the machines of the old electric plant, but a few months after his arrival the armies of Red China invaded Tibet, and he had to flee once more. I believe he finally ended up in Australia. His life was one continual flight. He was a natural adventurer and seemed proof against danger and hardship.

India's declaration of independence settled the fate of the British Legation in Lhasa. The British staff were replaced by Indians, but Mr. Richardson stayed on until September 1950, as the Indians had no trained candidate for his post. Reginald Fox was taken over by the Tibetan government as their radio operator. He was instructed to put up radio stations at all important strategic points, as the danger of a surprise invasion by the forces of Red China was growing daily. A trustworthy man was needed for Chamdo, a focal point in East Tibet, and Fox brought in a young Englishman named Robert Ford. I knew him slightly in Lhasa. He was fond of dancing and introduced the samba into Lhasa. At Tibetan parties there was a good deal of dancing. National dances not unlike those of the northern steppes were the most popular, but the fox trot was also favored, though it was frowned on by elderly people, who thought it unseemly that partners should cling so closely to each other.

Ford went off with a large caravan to Chamdo, and one could soon talk with him on the wireless telephone. It appears that radio amateurs all over the world competed for the privilege of talking to the lonely European in his remote outpost, and Ford and Fox received numerous letters and presents. Unfortunately, the notes that Ford made of these harmless conversations later proved his undoing. On his flight before the Chinese invaders, he was cut off and captured. The wildest charges were brought against him. He was accused among other things of poisoning a lama, and the entries in his notebooks were interpreted as espionage. As of 1953, this sympathetic and wholly innocent young man was still a prisoner in the hands of the Reds in spite of the efforts of the British ambassador in Peking to get him released.

I met one other white man in the course of my stay in Tibet—the American Bessac. Later on I shall relate what happened to him.

12

AN ATTEMPTED
COUP D'ETAT

When my second Tibetan New Year in Lhasa came around, I attended all the ceremonies of the festival from the beginning. Tens of thousands of people flocked into the town, and Lhasa looked like a great encampment. This year they celebrated the beginning of the "Fire-Pig-Year." The splendor of the ceremonies was no less than in the previous year, and I was, of course, particularly interested in the events I had missed the year before owing to my illness. The spectacle of which I have the liveliest recollection was the procession of a thousand soldiers in historic costumes. This custom commemorates an historical episode. Long ago a Muslim army marching on Lhasa was overtaken by heavy snowstorms at the foot of the Nyenchenthangla Mountains and completely snowed up. The bönpos of the region brought the arms and armor of the frozen soldiers in triumph to Lhasa. Now they are brought out every year and displayed by a thousand men. The old standards are carried by; one hears the clink of chain mail on men and horses; helmets bearing inscriptions in Urdu reflect the sunshine; the reports of the old muzzle loaders are heard in the narrow streets: altogether a rare pageant of medieval pomp in this old-fashioned city. The parade was staged so beautifully that it gave an impression of absolute reality rather than of an accurate historical revival. The troops led by two generals marched across the Parkhor to an open space on the edge of the city. Tens of thousands of people awaited them there in the warmth of an enormous fire where flames were fanned by countless offerings of butter and grain. The crowd looked on entranced, while monks threw death's-heads and the symbolic effigies of evil spirits into the fire. Cannons buried in the ground fired salutes toward the different mountain peaks. The culminating moment was when the monk of the oracle staggered toward the fire and after a short, wild dance collapsed on the ground. That was the moment for the people to burst out of their frozen immobility into ecstatic cries and gestures.

In 1939, the members of the only German expedition that ever came to Tibet were present at this festival. They barely escaped with their lives, for they had the temerity to try to film the oracle and were at once stoned by the mob. They had to fly from the scene, climbing over garden walls and roofs. There was nothing political in the attitude of the mob nor any trace of hatred of foreigners. It was inspired by the fanatical religious loyalty of the people, which is always capable of producing such outbreaks. Later on, when I was shooting films for the Dalai Lama, I had to be very careful. There was almost always excited scenes, and I was very glad when I succeeded in taking a few shots on my own account.

At this New Year Festival the High Chamberlain informed us that we were on His Holiness's reception list. Although we had seen the young God-King several times and had been honored by his smiling recognition during the processions, we were greatly excited by the prospect of appearing before him at the Potala Palace. I felt that this invitation must have great significance for us and, in fact, it turned out to be the starting point on the road that led me into intimacy with the young God-King.

On the appointed day we put on our fur coats, bought the most expensive scarves we could find in the town, and, in the midst of a gaily clad crowd of monks, nomads, and women in their festal garb, climbed up the long stepway to the Potala. As we climbed, the view over the city became more and more impressive. From here we looked down on to the gardens and the villalike houses. Our road led us past countless prayer wheels, which the passersby kept in movement. Then we passed through the great main gate into the interior of the palace.

Dark corridors, their walls decorated with paintings of strange protecting deities, led through the ground-floor buildings to a courtyard. From there steep ladders, several stories high, took one up to the flat roof. The visitors climbed them carefully and silently. Up above, a dense crowd was already assembled, as everyone has the right to receive the Great One's blessing at the New Year.

On the roof there were a number of small buildings with gilded roofs. There were the apartments of the Dalai Lama. With monks leading the way, a long sinuous line of believers moved slowly toward a door. We two came directly after the monks in the line. When we came into the hall of audience, we craned our necks to get a sight of the Living Buddha over a forest of heads. And he, too, momentarily forgetful of his dignity, looked up eagerly to get a glimpse of the two strangers of whom he had heard so much.

In the posture of the Buddha, leaning slightly forward, the Dalai Lama was sitting on a throne covered with costly brocade. For hours he had to sit and watch the faithful filing by and bless them as they passed. At the foot of the throne lay a mountain of money bags and rolls of silk and hundreds of whites scarves. We know that we must not hand over our scarves directly to the Dalai Lama; an abbot would take them from us. When we found ourselves standing with bowed heads before the Presence, I could not resist the temptation to look up. An eager, boyish smile lit up the charming face of the Dalai Lama, and his hand raised in blessing was laid for an instant on my head. Everything happened very quickly; in a moment or two we were standing before a somewhat lower throne on which sat the regent. He, too, laid his hand on us in blessing, and then an abbot placed red amulet scarves on our necks and we were asked to sit down on cushions. Rice and tea were served and, obedient to the custom, we threw a few grains onto the ground as an offering to the gods.

From our quiet corner we had a wonderful view of all that went on. An endless host of people filed by the young God-King to receive his blessing. With their heads bowed in humble obeisance and their tongues hanging out, they presented a strange picture. None dared look up. A light touch with a sort of silken mop replaced the laying on of hands with which we and the monks had been honored. None of the visitors came empty-handed. Some brought only threadbare scarves, but there were pilgrims with a retinue of bearers laden with gifts. Every offering is immediately registered by the treasurer and, if usable, added to the household stores of the Potala. The numerous silk scarves are afterward sold or given to prize winners in athletic contests. The money offerings remain as the personal property of the Dalai Lama. They flow into the gold and silver rooms of the Potala, in which immense treasures have been accumulated for centuries and inherited by one Incarnation after another.

More impressive than the gifts is the expression of intense devotion on the faces of all these people. For many it is the greatest moment of their lives. They have often come many hundreds of miles on their pilgrimage, throwing themselves in the dust and sometimes walking on their knees. Some have spent months and years, and suffered greatly from cold and hunger on their journey to receive the God-King's blessing. It seemed to me that a touch from the silken mop was a meager reward for such devotion, but one could not but recognize the expression of supreme happiness that lit up their faces when a monk laid a light scarf on the neck of each pilgrim. They carry these scarves to the end of their lives in lockets or sewn into wallets and deem them to be a protection against all evil. The quality of the scarf corresponds with the status of the recipient, but each of them has the mystical triple knot. These knotted scarves are prepared by the monks, but for ministers and the most highly placed abbots the Dalai Lama ties the knots himself. The atmosphere of this crowded room, filled with the scent of incense and the smell of the butter lamps, became very oppressive as time went on, and we were glad enough when the ceremony came to an end.

As soon as the last of the pilgrims had left the room, the Dalai Lama rose and, supported by his servants, proceeded to his private apartments while we stood motionless with bowed heads. As we were leaving, a monk came up and handed to each of us a crisp new hundred-sang note saying, *"Gyalpo Rimpoche ki söre re"* ("This is a gift from the noble king").

We were greatly surprised by this gesture, more especially when we learned that no one had hitherto received a gift in this form. It was typical of Lhasa that everyone in the town knew of the honor that had been done to us before we had mentioned it to a soul. We kept these notes as talismans for many years and when we finally left Tibet we had to admit that they had not disappointed us.

After the audience we took the opportunity to visit the numerous holy places of the Potala in company with the pilgrims. The Potala, one of the most imposing buildings in the world, was constructed in its present form some three hundred years ago by the fifth Dalai Lama. Previously there had been on this site a fortress belonging to the kings of Tibet, which had been destroyed by the Mongols during one of their invasions. From a faraway quarry, gangs of forced laborers carried stone after stone on their backs to the building site; unassisted by any technical devices, skilled stone-masons created the present palace. When the fifth Dalai Lama suddenly died there was a danger that the work would never be completed, but the regent, who could not count on the people's loyalty to himself to finish this formidable work, withheld the news of His Holiness's death. It was first announced that he was seriously ill and then that he had withdrawn from the world for meditation. This deception was continued for ten years until the palace was finished. Today when one looks at this unique building, one can understand and excuse the fraud that made its completion possible.

We found on the roof of the Potala the grave of the ruler to whom the building owes it origin. The remains of the fifth Dalai Lama rest in a shrine near those of the other God-Kings. There are seven of those tombs before which monks sit and pray to the muf-fled sound of drum taps. If one wants to reach the *stupas* (Buddhist shrines) one has to climb up steep ladders—a dangerous venture. There is little light to see by, and the rungs are slippery with the dirt of centuries. The greatest stupa is that of the thirteenth Dalai Lama, which is built several stories deep into the palace. Over a ton of gold was used to supply the gold plate with which the walls of this tower are faced.

After visiting a number of temples we came to the western part of the Potala, where 250 monks are lodged. Namgyetratsang, as this section is called, is narrow and full of corners and not inviting to the European eye, but the view from its little windows makes up for the gloomy and inconvenient interior. I could not help thinking how attractive Lhasa, with its cubical houses and flat roofs, looked from this eminence. We were too high up to see the dirt in the narrow streets.

IN THE FOLLOWING YEARS, I had several opportunities of staying in the Potala as the guest of friends who lived there. Life in this religious fortress resembles, one supposes, that of a medieval castle. Hardly an object belongs to the present day. In the evening all the gates are closed under the supervision of the treasurer, after which watchmen go through the whole Palace to see that everything is in order. Their shouts, ringing along the corridors, are the only sounds in the oppressive stillness. The nights are long and peaceful. Everyone goes to bed early. In contrast to the brisk social life in the city there are no parties or entertainments. From the shrines of the holy dead emanates an atmosphere of mortality, dim and solemn, which makes the whole palace feel like an enormous tomb. I could very well understand that the young ruler was happy when he could move to his Summer Garden. A lonely child without parents or playmates must lead a dreary life in the Potala. He found distraction only in the rare visits of his brother Lobsang Samten, who brought him greetings from his parents and told him all the news of the town.

The Dalai Lama possesses an elephant, the only one in the country, which was presented to him by the Maharajah of Nepal, in whose country there are many religious adherents of the God-King. Many Nepalese enter the monasteries of Tibet and devote their lives to religion. They form separate communities in the cloisters and are reputed to be very apt pupils. The Maharajah originally gave two elephants to the Dalai Lama as a token of his respect, but one of them did not survive the journey over the Himalayas, though the seven-hundred-mile road to Lhasa was carefully cleared of stones. Special stables were prepared at all the halting places for these beasts, one of which, at least, reached the capital in good shape, to the great satisfaction of everyone. No one had ever seen so gigantic an animal. They called him "Langchen Rimpoche." He had a house to himself on the north side of the Potala and, festooned with precious brocade, often took part in processions. Riders, whose horses were not accustomed to such monsters, gave him a wide berth.

During the New Year celebrations, the father of the Dalai Lama died. Everything conceivable had been done to keep him alive. Monks and medicine men had tried every kind of remedy. They had even prepared a doll into which they charmed the patient's sickness and then burned it with great solemnity on the riverbank. It was all to no purpose. To my way of thinking, they would have done better to call in the English doctor, but of course the family of the Dalai Lama must always be a model of orthodoxy and must not swerve from traditional practice in times of crisis.

The body was taken, as usual, to a consecrated plot outside the town where it was dismembered and given to the birds to dispose of. The Tibetans do not mourn for the dead in our sense of the word. Sorrow for the parting is relieved by the prospect of rebirth, and death has no terrors for the Buddhist. Butter lamps are kept burning for forty-nine days, after which there is a service of prayer in the house of the deceased. And that is the end of the story. Widows or widowers can marry after a short time, and life resumes its wonted course.

IN 1947, Lhasa had a minor civil war. The former regent, Reting Rimpoche, who had voluntarily resigned his office, seemed once more ambitious for power. Reting had many adherents among the people and the officials, who stirred up ill feeling against his successor. They wanted to see Reting back at the helm. They decided on action. The coup d'état was to be effected by the modern expedient of a bomb. This was delivered as a present from an unknown admirer in the house of a high monastic official, but before the parcel reached the regent, the infernal machine exploded. Luckily, no one was killed. It was through this unsuccessful outrage that the conspiracy was disclosed. The energetic Tagtra Rimpoche acted with speed and decision. A small army led by one of the ministers marched to Reting's monastery and arrested the former regent. The monks of the Cloister of Sera revolted against this action, and panic broke out in the town. The dealers barricaded their shops and took away their goods for safety. The Nepalese took refuge in their legation, carrying with them all their valuables. The nobles shut the gates of their homes and armed their servants. The whole town was in a state of alert.

Aufschnaiter had seen the columns marching toward Reting and came at top speed from his country home into the town, where he and I organized the defense of Tsarong's mansion. People were less preoccupied with the political crisis than with the fear that the monks of Sera, who numbered many thousands, would break into Lhasa and pillage the town. And there were others who had no confidence in the army, which was to some extent equipped with modern weapons. Military revolutions were not unknown in the history of Lhasa.

The arrival of Reting as a prisoner was awaited with excitement, but in the meantime he had been conveyed secretly to the Potala. The monks, who had planned to set him free, were deceived by this action, but, in fact, from the moment that their leader was arrested their cause was lost. Strong in their fanaticism, they refused to surrender and wild shooting soon began. It was not until the government bombarded the town and monastery of Sera with howitzers and knocked down a few houses that the resistance ceased. The troops succeeded in overpowering the monks, and peace returned to the capital. For weeks the authorities were occupied in bringing the culprits to justice, and many severe floggings were inflicted.

While the bullets were still pinging through the town, the news of the death of the rebellious ex-regent spread like wildfire among the people. Whispered rumors went around about the manner of his death. Many thought he was the victim of a political murder, but more believed that by dint of concentration and his inflexible will he had projected himself into the next world without the formality of dying. The town was suddenly full of the most unbelievable stories of the miracles attributed to him and of the superhuman powers he possessed. On one occasion, when a pilgrim's earthenware cooking pot was boiling over, he is said to have closed it in with his hands by drawing the sides over the top just as if the clay had been still soft and plastic.

The government refused to confirm or deny the rumors. Probably few people knew what had really happened. The late regent had made many enemies during his term of office. On one occasion he caused a minister who was plotting a rebellion to have his eyes put out. Now he had paid for this crime. As usually happens during political upheavals, innocent people often had to pay the penalty for the guilt of others. The former protégés of Reting were dismissed from their posts. One of the prominent men in his party actually killed himself. This was the only case of suicide that I heard of during all my stay in Tibet.

The prison had not room enough for all the condemned persons, so the nobles had to take the responsibility for lodging them and keeping them in custody. As a result, one found in almost every house a convict in chains with a wooden ring around his neck. It was not until the Dalai Lama officially assumed the power of a ruler that an amnesty was granted to political and common-law offenders. Most of the monks of Sera had fled to China. It usually happened that when there was a rising in Tibet the Chinese had a finger in the pie. All the property of the rebels was confiscated by the government and sold at public auction. The houses and pavilions of Reting Rimpoche were demolished, and his beautiful fruit trees transplanted into other gardens. The monastery was thoroughly ransacked by the soldiers, and for many weeks afterward gold cups, brocades, and other valuable objects kept turning up in the bazaars. The sale of Reting's property realized several million rupees for the treasure. Among the effects were hundreds of bales of English woolen goods and eight hundred costumes of silk and brocade. This shows how rich one could become in Tibet. Reting was a man of the people with no background. His career had started when as a boy he was recognized as an Incarnation.

13

COMMISSIONS FROM THE GOVERNMENT

T he religious ceremonies held in commemoration of Buddha's birth and death during the fourth month of the Tibetan year gradually obliterated the memory of the rising. In the autumn we were invited by the government to draw up a new plan of the town. Aufschnaiter interrupted his work, and we began to make a survey. No proper plan of the city had ever been made. In the last century secret agents from India had brought some sketch maps home with them but they had been drawn from memory and were quite inaccurate. Now we were able to make use of Tsarong's theodolite and with our measuring lines went through all parts of the Holy City. We could work only in the early morning for, as soon as the streets began to fill, we were surrounded by a swarm of curious people. We had been given two policemen by the government, as we could not keep the people off by ourselves. But even so we had difficulties. The passersby found it interesting to look into Aufschnaiter's survey glass, from the wrong end, of course, and our operations were considerably hampered. It was no pleasure to trudge through the filthy streets in the biting morning cold, and we needed the whole winter to collect the material for our survey. We had to climb onto the roofs, so as to be able to mark out the houses in the different blocks, and I had to collect more than a thousand different names of householders, all in the Tibetan script. When the copies were ready for the Dalai Lama and all the important government offices, a new parlor game was introduced. People learned how to read the plan and amused themselves by spotting their own houses on it.

At this time the government had the idea of installing a modern drainage and electric system on which they wanted to employ Aufschnaiter and me. Neither of us had studied the technique of these subjects, but my comrade had an excellent knowledge of mathematics, acquired while studying to become an agricultural engineer and, of course, when in doubt we had recourse to the relevant textbooks. Aufschnaiter was already being paid a monthly salary in rupees, and I received my appointment as a salaried official in 1948. I have kept my letter of appointment and am still proud of it.

A few months after our audience with the Dalai Lama, I was summoned in the middle of the night to the Norbulingka Palace and informed that the rising waters of the river threatened to overflow onto the Summer Palace. The monsoon rains convert the gently flowing stream with uncanny speed into a rushing river, in places more than a mile wide. When I arrived on the scene, I found the old embankment on the point of giving way. In pouring rain and by the faint light of lanterns, the bodyguard, under my directions, set to work to build a new dike. We managed to strengthen the old dike sufficiently to keep it unbreached for the moment, and the next day I bought up all the jute sacks that were to be had in the bazaar and had them filled with clay and sods of turf. Five hundred soldiers and coolies worked at high pressure, and we were able to erect new defenses before the old dam burst.

At the same time, the weather oracle was summoned from Gadong, and during the following days he was my neighbor in one of the houses in the palace grounds. Both of us had the same mission—to control the floods. It was fortunate that we had not to rely solely on the oracle and that we had an alternative force of a thousand hands at work. Just as we were throwing the last spadefuls of earth on the dam, the oracle tottered onto the bank and went through his dance. On the same day, the rain stopped, the floods receded, and we both received the commendation of the Dalai Lama.

I was afterward asked if I could do something of a permanent nature to the dam the floods that threatened the Summer Palace every year. I willingly agreed, as I felt confident that with Aufschnaiter's help I could find some means of controlling the floodwater. I knew that the Tibetans always built their dikes with perpendicular walls and realized that that was why they breached so easily.

We began to work in the spring of 1948, and had to complete it before the monsoon. I was given a force of five hundred soldiers and a thousand coolies. No contractor in Tibet had ever had so many hands. I insisted on another innovation and convinced the government that the work would be completed much more quickly if forced labor were not employed. So every man received his pay daily, and good humor reigned in the works. Of course one cannot compare the productivity of Tibetan workers with that of Europeans. The physical strength of the natives was much inferior to that of our workmen. They looked with astonishment at me when I impatiently took a spade and showed them how to dig. And there were many interruptions and pauses. There was an outcry if anyone discovered a worm on a spade. The earth was thrown aside and the creature put in a safe place.

The low productivity of the people must be due to their insufficient diet. The poor man lives generally on tsampa, butter tea, and a few radishes with some paprika. The whole day long they were brewing butter tea in the works: everyone got his portion, and soup was served out at midday.

In addition to my soldiers and coolies I had a fleet of forty yakskin boats. The boatmen—who are associated with the skins of animals and are, consequently, in conflict with the tenets of Buddhism—are regarded, like the leatherworks, as second-class citizens. An example of the way in which they are treated remains in my recollection. One of the Dalai Lamas on his way to the monastery of Samye had crossed a pass over which the boatmen always used to go on their way to the river. The pass became sanctified by the passage of the God-King, and from that time onward on boatman was allowed to use it. With their boats on their backs they were obliged to climb over a much higher and more difficult pass with a corresponding waste of time and energy. The boats weigh over two hundred pounds and the passes are always higher than 16,000 feet. That gives one an idea of the extraordinary power of religion in Tibet over the daily life of the people. It always saddened me to see men trudging by with their boats on their backs. They marched upstream along the bank with slow and measured steps; they could never have rowed against the current. Every boatman was followed by a sheep with a pack on its back. The sheep, as well trained as a dog, needed no lead, and when its master took to the water again it would jump into the boat by itself.

The forty boats employed on the building of my dam had to bring granite from a quarry that lay upstream from us. This was no easy task for the boats; their sides had to be strengthened with boards to prevent the stones from breaking through. The boatmen were men of fine physique, and their pay was higher than that of the other workmen. I noticed that they were not so humble as other "second-class citizens." They had formed a guild of their own and were proud to belong to it.

A happy chance ordained that the bönpo of Tradün should be

one of my collaborators. His duty was to pay the wages every evening. We had the best recollections of each other and often talked about the time when we were in Tradün—a wretched time for me! Today I could laugh about it. When we first met he was on a tour of inspection with twenty servants and treated us with courtesy and friendship. Who would have thought that one day we should be working side by side and that I should be, more or less, his chief? I often could not realize that four years had passed since our first meeting. Four years in which I seemed to have become half a Tibetan! I often caught myself making typical Tibetan gestures, which I saw a hundred times a day and came unconsciously to imitate. As my work served to protect the garden of His Holiness, my chiefs were monks of the highest rank. The government, too, took great interest in my activities. On several occasions the whole cabinet rode out to see the works with their secretaries and servants, and complimented both of us on our success, besides giving us scarves of honor and presents of money. On these occasions the workers were also given money and were granted a half-holiday.

My dikes were actually ready in June; just in time, as the first floodwater came down soon after. That year the river was very high, but the dikes did their job. On the land that used to be flooded we planted willows, whose fresh green leaves gave an added beauty to the Summer Garden.

WHILE I WAS AT WORK erecting embankments to protect the Garden of Jewels, I was often invited by high monastic officials to supper and to stay the night. I was certainly the first European who was permitted to stay in the Potala and the Summer Garden Residence. Thus I had more opportunities to admire the beautiful grounds and the splendid fruit trees and conifers that had been brought from all parts of Tibet. A host of gardeners looked after the flowers and trees, and kept the paths in order. The park is surrounded by a high wall, but it is accessible to visitors wearing Tibetan dress. Two men of the bodyguard inspect arrivals at the gate and see to it that no European hats or shoes find their way into the park. They obligingly exempted me from this rule except for the garden parties, when I used to sweat under the weight of a fur-lined hat. The guard presents arms to nobles of the fourth rank and upward, and I also got a salute.

In the middle of the park is the private garden of the Living Buddha, surrounded by a high, yellow wall. It has two gates strongly guarded by soldiers through which, apart from His Holiness, only the abbots appointed as his guardians may pass. Not even cabinet ministers are admitted. Through the foliage one can glimpse the golden roofs of temples, but the cry of the peacocks is the only sound that escapes to the outside world. No one knows what happens in this inner sanctuary. Many pilgrims come to visit this wall and follow a path that leads clockwise around it. At short intervals there are dog kennels built into the wall, whose savage, long-haired tenants bark when anyone comes too near. The yak-hair leashes prevent the dogs from attacking, but their hoarse growling sounds a discordant note in this peaceful world. Afterward, when I was privileged to enter the secret garden through the gates in the yellow wall, I made friends, as far as one could, with these rough fellows.

Every year dramatic performances are given on a great stone stage outside the inner garden. Vast throngs of people come to see the plays, which go on for seven days from sunrise to sundown. They are performed by groups of male actors and are almost entirely of a religious character. The actors are not professionals. They come from the people and belong to all sorts of professions. When the drama week is over they go back into private life. The same plays are performed year after year. The words are sung in a kind of recitative, and an orchestra of drums and flutes sets the rhythm for the dances. Only the comic parts have spoken lines. The beautiful and valuable costumes belong to the government and are kept in the Summer Palace.

One of the seven groups of actors, the Gyumalungma, is famous for its parodies. It was the only group that I was really able to appreciate. One could not but be astonished at their frankness. It is a proof of the good humor and sanity of the people that they can make fun of their own weaknesses and even of their religious institutions. They go so far as to give a performance of the oracle, with dance and trance and all, which brings down the house. Men appear dressed as nuns and imitate in the drollest fashion the fervor of women begging for alms. When monks and nuns begin to flirt together on the stage, no one can stop laughing, and tears roll down the cheeks of the sternest abbots in the audience.

The Dalai Lama witnesses these performances from behind a gauze curtain at a window in the first floor of a pavilion in the inner garden, behind the yellow wall. The officials sit in tents on either side of the stage. At noon, on their way to a common meal prepared in the kitchen of the Dalai Lama, they file past the window of the ruler.

When the drama week in the Summer Garden is over, the actors are invited to play in the houses of noblemen and in monasteries. In this way the theatrical season lasts for a month. The performances are besieged by the public, and the police often have to intervene to keep order.

DURING THIS YEAR my personal circumstances had improved very greatly. I was self-supporting, and thought myself entitled to a house of my own in which I could live an independent life. I never forgot my indebtedness to Tsarong, who had opened his house to us and helped us to get a footing in Lhasa. Since I had been earning money, I had paid him rent. Recently I had received many offers from friends temporarily transferred to the provinces to let me their houses and gardens with some of their servants thrown in.

I finally decided on one of the houses of the Foreign Minister Surkhang, which was, according to Tibetan ideas, one of the most modern buildings in the town. It had massive walls and a whole frontage of small glass windowpanes, but too many rooms for my needs. That problem was easily dealt with. I closed those I did not need and lived in the others. I chose the room with the most early morning sunshine for my bedroom. By my bed stood my radio, and on the walls I pasted colored illustrations from an Alpine calendar, which somehow—probably with a consignment of Swiss watches—had found its way to Lhasa. The cupboards and chests were brightly painted and carved, as one finds them in European peasants' houses. All the floors were of stone, and my servant took pride in polishing them till they shone like a mirror. He used to smear them with candle grease and then slide about the rooms in woolen shoes, combining business with pleasure. There were colored rugs in every room. As in Lhasa the ceilings are all supported on columns, the individual carpets are generally small. There are in Lhasa celebrated carpet weavers who come to the houses of the nobles and weave carpets of the desired size and shape on the spot. They sit on the ground with a wooden frame in front of them and knot the brightly colored handspun wool into classic designs: dragons, peacocks, flowers, and the most varied forms of ornamentation grow under their practiced fingers. These carpets last for generations. The wool is incredibly durable, and the colors made from bark from Bhutan, green nutshells, and vegetable juices, remain fresh for ages.

I had a writing table and a large drawing board made for my living room. The local carpenters are very clever at restoring old pieces of furniture, but when it comes to making anything new they are lamentably inadequate. In all crafts and professions creative capacity is neglected, and neither in schools nor in private enterprises are experiments encouraged.

In my living room there was a house altar, which my servants tended with particular devotion. Every day seven bowls were filled with fresh water for the gods, and the butter lamps were never allowed to go out. I lived in constant fear of burglars as the idols wore diadems of pure gold and turquoise. Fortunately, my servants were very trustworthy, and in all these years I never missed anything.

My roof, like all others, had a tree for prayer flags in every corner. I fixed the aerial of my radio onto one of these. Every house has a stove for incense and other luck-bringing appurtenances, and I used to take particular care that everything was kept in good order and no national customs infringed or neglected.

My house soon became a real home, and it was always a great pleasure to me to come back after work or paying visits. My servant Nyima would be waiting for me with hot water and tea, and everything was tidy, peaceful, and comfortable. I had some trouble to preserve my privacy, for in Tibet the servants are accustomed to remain within call or to come in without notice and pour out the tea. Nyima respected my wishes, but he attached himself very closely to me and whenever I went out at night, he used to wait for me at the house gate of my host, even though I had told him to go to bed. He feared that I might be set upon as I came home, and that was why he always turned up armed with a revolver and a sword and ready to risk his life for his master. I could not resent this devotion.

His wife and children lived in the house and gave me a fresh object lesson in love of the Tibetans for their children. If one of them fell sick, Nyima spared no expense to bring the best lama to his bedside. For my part, I did what I could to keep my servants in good health, as I liked to see cheerful faces around me. I was able to send them to the Indian Foreign Mission for vaccination and treatment, but I always had to be after them as Tibetans usually pay no attention to sickness in grown-up persons.

In addition to my personal servant, who received a monthly wage of about five pounds, the government gave me a messenger and a groom. Since I had been working at the Norbulingka, I was entitled to ride a horse from the royal stables whenever I needed one. Properly speaking, I was supposed to ride a different horse every day, as the master of the stables had to be careful to see that none of the horses was overworked. He would have forfeited his post if any of them had lost condition. As one may imagine, I found the continual change disagreeable. The horses were always out at grass on the beautiful pastures of the Norbulingka, and when they came into the narrow streets and traffic of the town, they shied at everything they saw. At last I got them to allow me to ride the same horse for a whole week and to ring the changes on three horses only, so that I and my mounts could get accustomed to each other. My horses had yellow reins—the royal color—and when mounted on one of them, I, theoretically, had the right to ride up into the Potala or around the ring, which was forbidden even to ministers.

My stable, kitchen, and servants' quarters were situated in a garden next door to my house—enclosed by a high wall. The garden was of a good size, and I was able to lay out many beds for flowers and vegetables. There was room, too, for badminton and croquet on the lawn, and I put up a Ping-Pong table as well. I grew some vegetables in a small greenhouse and managed to obtain valuable contributions to my meals early in the year. All my visitors had to admire my beds, of which I was very proud.

Mr. Richardson gave me the benefit of his experience, and I devoted my mornings and evenings to gardening, and my industry was soon rewarded. In my first year I managed to grow tomatoes, cauliflowers, lettuces, and cabbages. It was extraordinary how big everything grew without losing quality. But the explanation was really simple. It was essential to see that the roots got enough moisture. The dry air and the warm sunshine then created a hothouse atmosphere in which everything flourished luxuriantly. The problem of watering is not so easy, as there are no pressure pipes here and one cannot use hoses to sprinkle the garden. One has to lay out the beds in such a way that a runnel of water can be carried through them. I had two regular women helpers in the garden. They did all the weeding, and that says a good deal, as weeds grow apace in this soil. So do flowers and fruits, and the rewards of industry are great. From a bed measuring seventy square yards I took over four hundred pounds of tomatoes, some of which weighed half a pound. Other vegetables throve equally well. I do not believe that there are any kinds of European vegetable that would not succeed here, although the summer is short.

ABOUT THIS TIME we began to feel the repercussions of world politics even in the peaceful town of Lhasa. The civil war in China assumed a more and more disquieting aspect, and it was feared that trouble might rise among the Chinese residents in Lhasa. In order to show that Tibet considered itself independent of Chinese politics, the government decided one day to give the Chinese Minister his notice to leave. About a hundred persons were affected by this decision, against which there was no appeal.

The Tibetan authorities acted with typical craft. They chose a moment when the Chinese radio operator was playing tennis to go to his home and take possession of his transmitting set. When he heard about the order to leave that his chief had received, he could no longer communicate with the Chinese government. The post and telegraph offices in the city were closed for a fortnight, and the world thought that Tibet was having another civil war.

The expelled Chinese diplomats were treated with exquisite courtesy and invited to farewell parties. They were allowed to change their Tibetan money for rupees at a favorable rate and were given free transport to the Indian frontier. They did not understand exactly what had happened to them but all were sorry to go. Most of them returned to China or Formosa [Taiwan]. Some traveled direct to Peiping [Peking], where Mao Tse-tung had already established his seat of government.

Thus the century-old quarrel between China and Tibet broke out again. Communist China interpreted the expulsion of the minister and his staff as an affront, not as a gesture of neutrality, which the Tibetans meant it to be. In Lhasa it was fully realized that a Red China would constitute a grave threat to the independence of Tibet and to the Tibetan religion. People quoted utterances of the oracle and pointed to various natural phenomena that seemed to confirm their fears. The great comet of 1948 was regarded as a portent of danger, and freak births among domestic animals were held to be ominous. I, too, felt anxious, but my anxiety was based on a sober estimate of the situation. Asia's future looked black.

About this time, the government decided to send four high officials on a world tour. The members of this mission had been carefully selected for their culture and progressive ideas, as it was desired to show the world that Tibet was a civilized country.

The leader of the mission was Finance Secretary Shekabpa, and the other members were a monk named Changkhyimpa; Pangdatsang, a rich merchant; and General Surkhang, a son of the foreign minister. The two last named spoke a little English and had some idea of Western habits and customs. The government saw that they were outfitted with European suits and overcoats of the best quality and cut; in addition, they took with them splendid silk robes to be worn at official receptions, for they were to travel as a national delegation. They went first to India and from there flew to China. After staying in that country for some time, they traveled by air to San Francisco, via the Philippines and Hawaii. In America they stopped in many places and visited numerous factories, especially those that handled Tibetan raw materials.

Their program in Europe was similar. Their whole journey lasted nearly two years and every letter received from them caused excitement in Lhasa. By the time they returned, they had found new buyers for Tibetan wool, and brought with them a mass of prospectuses for agricultural machinery, looms, carpetmaking machines, and so on. Their baggage also contained a dismantled jeep, which the chauffeur of the thirteenth Dalai Lama reassembled. It was driven once, and then withdrawn from the public eye. Many of the nobles must have wished to buy an automobile just then, but it seems the time was not yet ripe. In America the mission bought gold ingots, which were brought to Lhasa under heavy guard.

While the four delegates were enjoying their world tour, the political situation in Asia had greatly altered. India had been granted independence, the Communists had conquered the whole of China, but all these events had made little impression in Lhasa, where the Dalai Lama's traditional visit to the monasteries was considered more important than world politics.

EVERY YOUNG DALAI LAMA MUST, before officially attaining his majority, visit the monasteries of Drebung and Sera, where he gives proof of maturity by partaking in a religious discussion. The preparations for this journey had been the main topic of conversation for months. His Holiness was, naturally, to be accompanied by the nobles, and the monks of Drebung had constructed a special palace to house him and his retinue.

One day the procession set out in customary splendor on the

five-mile road to the monastery, where the four archabbots of Drebung with a glittering retinue received the divine visitor and led him into his palace. On the same day I, too, rode to Drebung, for some of the monks with whom I had made friends had invited me to stay there during the festivities. I had always wanted to get to know the life of a monastery from the inside. Up to now, like any other pilgrim, I had enjoyed only fleeting glances at the temples and gardens. My friends took me to one of the numerous standard-pattern stone houses, where I was given Spartan lodgings. Pema, a monk who was soon to take his final examinations and already had pupils of his own, acted as my guide to the monastic city and explained to me the layout and organization. No comparison can be drawn between this and any of our religious institutions. Behind these cloister walls the hands of time's clock seem to have been put back a thousand years; there is nothing to show that one is living in the twentieth century. The thick gray walls of the buildings have an age-old appearance, and the overpowering smell of rancid butter and unwashed monks has sunk deep into the stonework.

Every house has from fifty to sixty inhabitants and is divided into tiny cells. There is a kitchen on every floor and plenty of food to eat. The average monk has no other mundane satisfaction, but the more intelligent ones buoy themselves up with the prospect of reaching high positions to reward their zealous studies. They have no private property except for their butter lamps and an icon, or maybe an amulet box. A simple bed is the only concession to comfort. Absolute obedience is the rule. The students enter the monastery as children and immediately don the red cowl, which they are to wear for the rest of their lives. During the first five years they have to perform the most menial services for their teachers. The intelligent ones learn how to read and write, and are admitted to examinations. Only a few succeed in passing out from one grade into another, and most of them remain all their lives in the servant class. The elect are those who after studying the teaching of Buddha for thirty or forty years are able to pass the final tests. They are then qualified for appointment to the highest offices in the Church. The monasteries are the high schools for religious education, and the staff of all purely religious institutions is chosen from their graduates. The monastic officials of the government receive their education in the Tsedrung School.

The final examinations of the monastic schools are held once a year in public in the cathedral. From the whole of Tibet, only twenty-two candidates are admitted to the examination. After a severe oral test held under the auspices of the Dalai Lama's own teachers, the five best candidates are promoted to the highest monastic grade. The student who passes first may become a hermit and devote himself to religious exercises, or he may enter public life with the possibility of one day becoming regent. This happens rarely, because that high post is usually reserved for Incarnations, but cases have occurred in which a man of the people—neither a noble nor a Living Buddha—has been appointed to this great office. The last time this happened was in 1910, when the thirteenth Dalai Lama fled to India before the invading Chinese, and a delegate had to be appointed to represent him.

The ten thousand monks of Drebung are divided into groups, each of which has its own temple and garden. Here they spend the morning hours in communal religious exercises, after which they get their butter tea and soup, only returning to their houses for study in the afternoon. However, they have enough free time to take walks and play simple games. They are also allowed to cook any supplementary food they may receive from their own communities. The groups are organized as far as possible according to their places of origin. In some houses you will find only Mongolians or Nepalese, or students from a particular town such as Shigatse.

Within the monastery, of course, no living creature may be killed, but the cold climate makes it necessary to eat some meat, so the communities send supplies of dried yak meat, and it must be said, fresh meat is often to be had in one of the neighboring villages.

In addition to free food and lodging, the monks receive a little pocket money derived from government grants and the gifts of pilgrims. However, when a monk possesses outstanding gifts, he generally finds a patron among the nobles or the wealthy tradespeople. The Church in Tibet is very rich, owning, as it does, most of the land, and the revenues of enormous estates are enjoyed by the monasteries. Every monastery has its own dealer, who procures provisions and other necessities. One would hardly believe what enormous sums are spent on the upkeep of the monasteries and their inmates. I once helped a monk with his accounts and noted that during the first month of the year, which all the monks spend in Lhasa, the government supplied them with three tons of tea and fifty tons of butter, in addition to pocket money to the value of something over forty thousand pounds.

The red-cowled forms are not all gentle and learned brothers. Most of them are rough, tough fellows for whom the whip is not discipline enough. The worst of them belong to the unauthorized but tolerated organization of the Dob-Dobs, or monkish soldiery. They wear a red armband and blacken their faces with soot. In their belts they stick a huge key, which they can use as a cosh or a missile, and they often have a sharp cobbler's knife in their pockets. Many of them are well-known bullies. Their gait is provocative, and they are quick to strike. Sensible people give them a wide berth. In the war against the Chinese Communists, they formed a battalion that gained a reputation for courage. In peacetime, too, they have opportunities for getting rid of their superfluous energy, as the Dob-Dobs of the different monasteries are always at war with one another. It is fair to add that their differences are not always settled by violence, and that some of their pugnacity is expended in athletic contests between rival monasteries. Drebung is usually the victor, having a larger choice of athletes than its competitors. As a former sports instructor, I often used to go to Drebung, and the monks were always glad to have me taking part in their training. This was the only place in Tibet where I found men with athletic figures and trained muscles.

The great cloisters of Drebung, Sera, and Ganden—the three pillars of the state—play a decisive role in the political life of Tibet. Their abbots, together with eight government officials, preside over the National Assembly. No decision is taken without the assent of these clerics, who naturally are interested, first and foremost, in the supremacy of the monasteries. Their intervention has prevented the realization of many progressive ideas. At one time they looked on Aufschnaiter and me as thorns in their flesh, but when they saw we had no political ambitions and that we fitted ourselves into the customs of the land and carried out undertakings from which they, too, profited, they withdrew their opposition to us.

The cloisters are, as I have said, the high schools of the Church. For that reason every lama—and there are more than a thousand of them in Tibet—must be educated in a monastery. These Incarnations are a constant attraction for pilgrims, who come in thousands to visit them and receive their blessing.

Even during the Dalai Lama's visit to Drebung these Incarnations attended all the ceremonies and sat in the front seats—a regular concourse of the gods! Meanwhile, a religious discussion was held every day in the shady cloister gardens between the ruler and one of the abbots. This is one of the most intimate acts in the religious life of Lamaism, and I never had the slightest hope of being allowed to witness it.

However, one day as I was breakfasting with Lobsang, he asked me if I would like to come with him. I owe it to this unexpected gesture on his part that I was privileged to witness a drama that certainly no other person of another faith has ever witnessed. As I was in the company of the Dalai Lama's brother, no one thought of preventing me from entering the sequestered garden. A strange scene unfolded itself. In front of a dark grove of trees, a great multitude of red-cowled monks, perhaps two thousand of them, squatted on the gravel, while from a high place, the Dalai Lama preached from Holy Writ. For the first time I heard his clear boyish voice. He spoke without any embarrassment and with the assurance of a grown man. This was his first public appearance. The fourteen-year-old boy had been studying for many years, and now his knowledge was being tested before a critical audience. This first appearance might have fateful consequences. It is true that he would never be allowed to renounce his prescribed career, but his performance that day would show whether he was destined to be the instrument of the monks or their ruler. Not all of his predecessors had been as able as the fifth and the thirteenth Dalai Lamas. Many of them remained throughout their lives puppets in the hands of the men who had trained them, and the destiny of the country was controlled by the regents. People spoke of the intelligence of this boy as miraculous. It was said that he had only to read a book to know it by heart, and it was known that he had long taken an interest in all that happened in his country and used to criticize or commend the decisions of the National Assembly.

Now that it came to debating, I saw that his powers had not been exaggerated. The Dalai Lama sat down on the gravel, so as not to emphasize the superiority of his birth, while the abbot in whose monastery the discussion was taking place stood before him and punctuated his questions with the conventional gestures. The Dalai Lama answered all the questions that were put to him, even the "teasers," with readiness and good humor, and was never for a moment disconcerted.

After a while the antagonists changed places, and it was the Dalai Lama who put questions to the seated abbot. One could see that this was not an act prepared to show off the intelligence of the young Buddha; it was a genuine contest of wits in which the abbot was hard put to it to hold his own.

When the debate was over, the young God-King mounted once more onto his golden throne, and his mother, the only woman present, handed him tea in a golden cup. He stole a friendly glance at me as if to assure himself of my approval of his performance. For my part I was deeply impressed by what I had seen and heard, and felt genuine admiration for the presence of mind of this God-Boy from a humble family. He almost persuaded me to believe in reincarnation.

At the end of the religious debate, everyone prayed in chorus. It sounded like a litany and lasted a long time. After that the Dalai Lama, supported by his abbots, returned to the palace. I had always wondered at the senile gait of the Dalai Lama, and now learned that it is part of the ritual and that all these different movements are prescribed. It is supposed to be an imitation of the gait of the Buddha, and at the same time is designed to enhance the dignity of the Dalai Lama.

I would have liked very much to take a few pictures of this unique ceremony, but as it turned out, I was lucky not to have my camera with me. On the next day there was a great fuss when my friend Wangdüla (without my knowing anything about it) tried to photograph the Dalai Lama as he was going around one of the monasteries. He had already taken one successful photo when a zealous monk denounced him. Wangdüla was brought before the regent's secretary and closely interrogated. As a punishment for his offense, he was degraded and told that he was lucky not to be expelled from the monastic order. In addition his camera was confiscated—all this in spite of the fact that he was a nobleman of the fifth grade and the nephew of the former regent. For a while the monks talked of nothing except this incident, but Wangdüla himself took it very calmly. He knew all about the ups and downs of official life.

The next item in the Dalai Lama's program was his progress to the summit of Mount Gompe Utse, a peak over 17,000 feet high, which dominates the monastery of Drebung.

Early one morning a large, mounted caravan set out, consisting of at least a thousand men and several hundred horses. The first objective was a settlement halfway up the mountain. The Dalai Lama's horse was led by two head grooms. On the way, various rest places had been prepared. Each of these was furnished with a throne spread with carpets. Toward evening the caravan reached the halfway station. Incense was burned as a thanks offering for safe arrival, and prayers were said. At this place tents had been pitched, and here the party passed the night. Yaks had been prepared for the next day's journey, and before dawn the Dalai Lama and his high dignitaries set out on the ride up to the summit. The monks of Drebung had already prepared a path of sorts for this pilgrimage. When the party reached the top, prayers were uttered and offerings made to the gods.

Below in the valley the people waited in crowds for the moment when the incense smoke should rise from the peak. They knew that their ruler was up there praying for the welfare of his people. I myself had climbed to the summit the day before and now watched the ceremony from a discreet distance. Among the other spectators were flocks of crows and jackdaws, who could smell the offerings of tsampa and butter, and waited, croaking, for the moment to swoop down on the remains.

For most of those who accompanied the Dalai Lama this was the first time they had even been on a mountaintop. The younger members of the party seemed to take great pleasure in the experience and pointed out to one another different details of the beautiful panorama. In contrast, the older monks and officials, mostly corpulent seniors, had no eyes for the beauties of the landscape, but sat exhausted while their servants ministered to them.

On the same day, the party rode the whole way back to the monastery. A few days later, the Dalai Lama visited the monastery of Sera and engaged in a similar public debate. His advisers had had some misgivings in regard to a visit to Sera, in view of the recent revolt of the monks. But the enthusiastic reception offered him in this monastery was a proof, if one were needed, that he stood high above all cliques and party squabbles.

MEANWHILE, MY LIFE proceeded undisturbed. I was in the service of the government, for whom I translated the news and articles from newspapers, and now and then built small dams and irrigation channels. I regularly went to visit Aufschnaiter at his canal works outside the town. In the course of his excavations he had made some most interesting finds. Workmen had unearthed fragments of pottery, which Aufschnaiter had carefully collected and begun to put together piece by piece. As a result of his repairs, he had a collection of really beautiful vases and jugs, shaped quite differently from those made today. He gave the workmen rewards for what they found, and ordered them to dig with the utmost care and to call him immediately if they uncovered anything of interest. Every week there were discoveries. Graves containing perfectly preserved skeletons with bowls and semiprecious stones beside them were opened. My comrade had found a new occupa-

tion for his leisure hours. He took immense trouble with his collections, which dated back thousands of years. He was very proud
of them and had reason to be, as he had been the first to come upon
proof of a former Tibetan civilization. None of the lamas whom
he consulted could throw light on his finds, and there was no men-
tion in the old history books of an epoch in which the Tibetans
used to bury their dead and put gifts in their graves.

Aufschnaiter wanted to place his discoveries at the disposal of
an archaeological museum in India, and when the Chinese Communists invaded Tibet, we took the collections, carefully packed,
away with us.

NOT LONG AFTERWARD I had an unexpected opportunity to get
out of Lhasa and learn something of a new part of the country.
Some friends had asked me to look at their estates and make sug-
gestions for their improvement. They had managed to get the government to grant me leave of absence, and I was able to visit their
properties one after another. The conditions which I found were
completely medieval. The peasants still used wooden ploughs with
an iron share. These were drawn by dzos. (The dzo is a cross between an ox and a yak, and is a very good draught animal. It looks
very like the yak, and the milk of the cows, which has a high fat
content, is much prized.)

One of the problems that the Tibetans have done little to solve
is that of watering their fields. The springtime is generally very
dry, but no one thinks of carrying water onto the land from the
snow-swollen brooks and rivers.

The estates of the landed gentry are often very large. It sometimes takes a whole day to ride across a property. Many serfs are attached to every estate; they are given a few fields to cultivate for
their own profit, but are obliged to spend a certain time working
for their landlord. The estate managers, who are often merely

trusted servants of the landlord, boss the serfs like little kings. Their own master lives in Lhasa, where he works for the government and has little time to bother about the property. However, his public services are frequently rewarded by gifts of land, and there are noble officials to whom in the course of their careers as many as twenty large farms have been given. The official who falls from grace is equally likely to be dispossessed of his estates, which pass into the hands of the government. Nevertheless, there are many families who have been living in their castles for centuries and bear territorial names. Their ancestors often built these fortresses on the rocky promontories that dominate the valleys. When built on the plain, they are surrounded by moats, but these are now dry and empty. The ancient weapons preserved in the castles testify to the warlike spirit of their former lords, who had constantly to be ready to defend themselves against the attacks of the Mongols.

I was days and weeks on my tour, and riding through unknown country was a welcome change after life in Lhasa. I was not always on horseback. During part of the time I was floating in a yak-skin boat down the mighty Brahmaputra, stopping to visit monasteries that attracted me and taking photographs.

WHEN I GOT BACK to Lhasa, it was already winter. The small tributary of the Kyichu was already frozen—and that caused us to think of something new. With a small group of friends, including the Dalai Lama's brother, we founded a skating club. We were not the first people in Tibet to go in for this sport. The staff of the British Legation had practiced skating to the immense astonishment of the natives. We were actually their heirs, because we acquired their skates, which they had bequeathed to their servants when they left. Our first efforts were very funny, and we always had a good many onlookers to laugh at us and to wonder who would be the next to fall on his head or break through the ice. Par-

ents noted with horror the enthusiasm of their children, determined at all costs to learn how to skate.

The old-fashioned, unsporting noble families could not con-
ceive that anyone would wantonly tie a knife to the sole of his boot
and slither about on it.

14

TIBET
PREPARES
FOR TROUBLE

The Dalai Lama had heard from his brother about our new sport, but unfortunately our rink was invisible from the roof of the Potala. He would have dearly liked to see us disporting ourselves on the ice, but as that was impossible, he sent me his moving picture camera with instructions to film the rink and the skaters for him. As I had never taken a film picture, I made a careful study of the prospectus and instructions before going to work. Then I made my picture and had the film sent to India by the foreign ministry to be developed. In two months it was in the hands of the Dalai Lama. It had come out very well. Through this film I made my first personal contact with the younger ruler of Tibet. It seems curious that a product of the twentieth century should have been the starting point of a relation that, in spite of all conventions, eventually became a close friendship.

Soon after this, Lobsang Samten told me that his brother wished me to film different ceremonies and festival scenes for him. I was astonished to see how great was his interest in these pictures. He always sent me the most precise instructions, sometimes in writing and sometimes verbally through Lobsang Samten. He advised me how to make the most favorable use of the light in certain positions, or, maybe, he would send word to say that this or that ceremony was due to start punctually. I, too, was able to send a message telling him when during a procession to keep his eyes fixed in the direction of my camera.

Naturally, I did my best to avoid being conspicuous during these ceremonies. He, too, regarded this as important and told me to keep in the background, and if I could not do this, to refrain from taking a picture. Obviously, I could not avoid being seen, but as soon as it became known that I was filming and photographing under instructions from His Holiness, I was not interrupted. In fact, the dreaded Dob-Dobs often made the crowd give way to let me have a free field of vision, and when I asked them to pose for me, they obeyed like lambs. In this way I was enabled to make numbers of unique pictures of religious ceremonies. In addition to the moving picture camera, I always had my Leica with me and took many photographs of unusual scenes for myself.

I took some beautiful pictures of the cathedral. The Tsug Lag Khang, as it is called, was built in the seventh century and contains the most precious statue of Buddha in Tibet. The origin of this temple dates from the reign of the famous King Srongtsen Gampo. His two wives were princesses, and both belonged to the Buddhist faith. One of them came from Nepal and founded the second greatest temple of Lhasa, the Ramoche; while the other was a Chinese and brought the golden idol with her from China. The king, who followed the ancient religion, was converted by his wives to Buddhism, which became the state religion. He then caused the cathedral to be built as a home for the golden idol. This building has the same defects as the Potala. Externally it is grand and imposing, but internally it is dark, full of corners, and unfriendly. It is packed with treasure, which is daily added to by refresh offerings. Every minister on appointment must buy new silk-embroidered costumes for the statues of the saints, and a butter dish of solid gold. Loads of butter are burned unceasingly in the lamps, and in summer and winter the air is full of rancid-smelling smoke. The only creatures who benefit by the offerings are the mice, which climb in thousands up and down the heavy silk curtains and gorge on the butter and tsampa in the bowls. It is dark in the temple: not a ray of light penetrates from the outside, and only the butter lamps on the altars shed their flickering gleam. The entrance to the Holy of Holies is usually closed by a heavy iron curtain, which is raised only at stated hours.

In a dark, narrow passage, I found a bell hanging from the roof. I could hardly believe my eyes when I saw on it the inscription "*Te Deum Laudamus.*" It was probably the last surviving relic of the chapel that the Catholic missionaries had built in Lhasa many centuries ago. They had not been able to maintain themselves in Tibet and had been obliged to leave. It may be that the preservation of this bell in their cathedral is due to the deep respect that Tibetans feel for all religions. I would gladly have learned more about the chapel of the Jesuits, but no trace of the building survives.

In the evening the cathedral is filled with worshipers. The curtain is raised, and a long queue waits before the altar of the Buddha. Each worshiper touches the statue with bowed head and makes a small offering. Holy water, tinted with saffron, is poured into his cupped hand by a monk. Part of this he drinks, and the rest he sprinkles over his head. Many monks spend their whole lives in the cathedral. Their duty is to keep watch over the treasures and to fill the butter lamps.

An attempt was once made to install electric light in the cathedral, but a fire occurred owing to a short circuit, and everyone connected with the installation was dismissed. So there was no more talk of artificial light.

Before the cathedral is a terrace of flagstones, polished like mirrors and hollowed out by the prostrations of worshipers over a thousand years. When one looks at these hollows and recognizes the expression of deep devotion on the faces of worshipers, one understands why a Christian mission could never succeed in Lhasa. A lama from the Drebung on a visit to Rome to convert the Catholics would recognize the futility of his mission when he saw the steps of the holy staircase worn down by the knees of countless pilgrims, and would leave the Vatican with resignation. Christianity and Buddhism have much in common. They are both founded on the belief in happiness in another world, and both preach humility in this life. But there is a difference as things are today. In Tibet one is not hunted from morning till night by the calls of "civilization." Here one has time to occupy oneself with religion and to call one's soul one's own. Here it is religion that occupies most of the life of the individual, as it did in the West during the Middle Ages.

Beggars take up their station by the cathedral door. They know very well that man is charitable and considerate when he is in the presence of God. In Tibet, as in most other places, beggars are a public nuisance. While I was building my dam, the government determined to put the sturdy beggars to work. They rounded up the thousand beggars of Lhasa and picked out seven hundred men who were fit for employment. These were put on the job, and received food and pay for their work. On the next day only half of them turned up, and a few days later they were all absent. It is not lack of work or dire necessity that makes these people beggars, nor, in most cases, bodily infirmity. It is pure laziness. Begging offers a good livelihood in Tibet, and no one turns a beggar from the door. And if a beggar gets only some tsampa and a penny or so from each client, the produce of two hours' "work" suffices to keep him going for the day. Then he sits idly by the wall and dozes happily in the sunshine. Many beggars have horrible diseases that deserve sympathy, but they exploit their deformities by thrusting them on the notice of the passerby.

ONE OF THE MOST attractive features in Tibetan life is the habit of going to meet, and seeing off, one's friends. When anyone goes away, his friends often put a tent on his road several miles out of town and wait for him there with a meal to speed him on his way. The departing friend is not allowed to go till he has been loaded with white scarves and good wishes. When he comes back, the same ceremony is observed. It sometimes happens that he is welcomed at several places on his way home. In the morning, maybe, he first catches sight of the Potala, but on his way into the town he is held up at tent after tent by his welcoming friends, and it is evening before he arrives in Lhasa, his modest caravan swollen to stately proportions by his friends and their servants. He comes home with the happy feeling that he has not been forgotten.

When foreigners arrive they are met by a representative from the Ministry of Foreign Affairs, who conveys the greetings of the minister to them and arranges for their lodgings and entertainment. New ambassadors are received with military honors and presented with silk scarves by a delegate of the cabinet. In Lhasa there is a special quarter for guests, where they and their servants and animals are accommodated, and where they find gifts awaiting them on arrival. It would be true to say that in no country in the world are travelers treated with greater attention and hospitality.

During the war, airplanes on their way from India to China often lost their way. This is probably the most difficult air route in the world, as the passage of the Himalayas puts a heavy strain on the skill and experience of the pilot, who, once he has lost his bearings, finds it very difficult to right himself owing to the inadequacy of the maps of Tibet.

One night the droning of motors was heard over the Holy City and caused general alarm. Two days later news came from Samye that five Americans had landed there in parachutes. The government invited them to come to Lhasa on their way back to India. The airmen must have been greatly astonished at being received in tents some way out of the city and offered a hearty welcome accompanied by butter tea and scarves. They said in Lhasa that they had lost their bearings completely and that the wings of their plane had grazed the snow slopes of the Nyenchenthanglha. After this they had turned back, but finding that they had too little fuel to reach India, they decided to scrap their plane and jump. Except for a sprained ankle or two and a broken arm, they came down safely. After a short stay in Lhasa, they were convoyed by the government to the Indian frontier, riding horses and as comfortable as one can be on trek in Tibet.

The crews of other American planes that came down in Tibet during the war were not so lucky. In Eastern Tibet the remains of two crashed planes were found; the members of the crews had all been killed. Another plane must have crashed south of the Himalayas in a province whose inhabitants are savage jungle folk. These people are not Buddhists but naked savages reputed to use poisoned arrows. From time to time they come out of their forests to exchange skins and musk for salt and beads. On one of these occasions, they offered objects that could have come only from an American airplane. Nothing more was ever heard of this disaster. I would have liked to go in search of the site of the accident, but the distance was too great.

THE POLITICAL SITUATION of Tibet was gradually getting worse. The Chinese had already solemnly declared in Peiping that they were going to "liberate" Tibet. Even in Lhasa people were under no illusions about the gravity of this threat. In China the Reds had always carried out what they had taken in hand.

The Tibetan government set to work feverishly to reorganize the army under the supervision of a cabinet minister. Tibet had a standing army, to which every district contributed its quota in proportion to the number of the inhabitants. This conception of compulsory military service differs from ours in that the state is interested only in numbers and not in individuals. A man called up for service can buy a substitute. Often enough these substitutes remain in the army all their lives.

The military instructors have served in India and understand the use of modern weapons. Hitherto the words of command had been given in a mixture of Tibetan, Urdu, and English. The new defense minister's first decision was that all orders were to be given in Tibetan. A new national anthem was composed to replace "God Save the Queen," the tune of which had hitherto been played at important military parades. The text consisted of a glorification of the independence of Tibet and a tribute to its illustrious ruler, the Dalai Lama.

The flat pasturelands around Lhasa were transformed into training grounds for the troops. New regiments were formed, and the national assembly decided to call on the richer classes to furnish and equip another thousand men. It was left to them to enlist in person or to find substitutes. Courses were organized for the training as officers of monks and civil officials. There was a great deal of patriotic enthusiasm.

In the former days, people had not bothered much about the army. The district communities had had to supply their contingents with provisions and supplementary pay. Now the authorities recognized the importance of regular organization, and established fixed rates of pay for officers and men.

It was not easy, at the outset, to supply the needs of the new army. The whole transport system was overworked. The necessary grain had often to be fetched from far-distant depots. These storehouses, which are to be found in all regions where crops are plentiful, are huge, windowless, stone buildings ventilated by holes in the walls. Here the grain can lie for decades without going bad, owing to the dryness of the air. But now they were quickly emptied, for provisions would have to be stored in the neighborhood of the fighting line if it came to war. Nevertheless, the country was not threatened with a shortage of foodstuffs. If a wall were built around Tibet, no one would suffer from cold or starvation, as everything necessary for the needs of the three million inhabitants is found in the country in one form or another. The military kitchens supplied plentiful meals, and the soldiers' pay enabled them to buy cigarettes and *chang*. The troops were contented.

In the Tibetan army it is easy to recognize the difference between officers and men. The higher his rank the more gold decorations an officer wears. There seem to be no proper regulations about dress. I once saw a general who in addition to his gold epaulettes had a collection of glittering objects pinned on his breast. He had probably spent too much time looking at foreign illustrated papers and had devoted himself accordingly, for there are no Tibetan military medals. Instead of mentions and distinctions, the Tibetan soldier receives more tangible rewards. After a victory he has a right to the booty, and so looting is the general rule. He is, however, obliged to deliver the weapons he has captured. A good example of the utility of this system can be found in the battles against the bandits. The local bönpos are entitled to call on the government for aid when they can no longer cope with the robbers. Small military detachments are then sent to help them. In spite of the ruthless manner in which the bandits fight, service in these commandos is very popular. The soldiers have their eye on the plunder and ignore the danger. The soldier's right to the spoils of war has been the cause of a great deal of trouble. In a case with which I was personally connected, it cost the lives of several persons.

When the Chinese Communists occupied Turkestan, the American Consul, Machierman, with a young American student named Bessac and three White Russians, fled to Tibet, having first requested the U.S. Embassy in India to ask the Tibetan government for travel facilities. Messengers were sent from Lhasa in all directions to instruct the frontier posts and patrols to make no difficulties for the fugitives. The party traveled in a small caravan over the Kuen Lun mountains. Their camels stood the journey well, and they obtained fresh meat by shooting wild asses. By ill luck the government messenger was late in arriving at the spot where the party was to cross the frontier. Without challenging or finding out who was approaching them, the soldiers of the outpost, tempted by the sight of a dozen heavily laden camels, fired on the caravan, killing on the spot the American consul and two of the Russians. The third Russians were wounded, and only Bessac escaped unhurt. He was taken prisoner and brought with the wounded man to the nearest district governor. On the way, the two men were insulted and threatened by the soldiers, who had first shared among the spoils and had been overjoyed to find such valuable objects as field glasses and cameras. Before they reached the next bönpo, the government messenger came up with the escort, with orders to treat the Americans and their party as guests of the government. This caused a change of attitude. The soldiers outdid one another in politeness, but the damage could not be undone. The governor sent a report to Lhasa, and the authorities, horrified by the news, did their utmost to express their regret in every possible way. An Indian-trained hospital orderly was sent with presents to meet Bessac and his wounded companion. They were invited to come to Lhasa and asked to bear witness for the prosecution against the soldiers, who had already been arrested. A high official who spoke a little English rode out to meet the approaching travelers. I attached myself to him thinking that it might be some comfort to the young American to have a white man to talk to. I also hoped to convince him that the government could not be blamed for the incident, which it deeply regretted. We met the young man in pouring rain. He was as tall as a bean pole and completely dwarfed his little Tibetan pony. I could well imagine how he felt. The little caravan had been months on the road, always in flight from enemies and exposed to dangers, and their first meeting with the people of the country in which they sought asylum brought three of their party to their death.

New clothes and shoes were waiting for them in a tent by the wayside, and in Lhasa they were put up in a garden house with a book and a servant to look after them. Fortunately, the Russian, Vassilieff, was not dangerously wounded and was soon able to hobble about the garden on crutches. They remained for a month in Lhasa, during which time I made friends with Bessac. He bore no grudge against the country that had at first received him so ill. He asked only that the soldiers who had ill-treated him on the way to the district governor should be punished. He was requested to be present at the execution of the sentence, so as to make sure there was no deception. When he saw the floggings, he asked that the number of lashes should be reduced. He took photographs of the scene, which later appeared in *Life* as a testimonial to the correct attitude of the Tibetan government. Everything was done to pay the last honors to the dead according to Western customs. So it is that three wooden crosses stand today over their graves in the Changthang. Bessac was received by the Dalai Lama, and afterward left for Sikkim, where he was met by fellow countrymen.

The troubled times brought many fugitives to Tibet, but none were so unlucky as this party. Another camel caravan that came through the Changthang belonged to a Mongolian prince, who brought with him his two wives, one a Pole and the other a Mongol. I was full of admiration for these two women who had performed such a tremendous journey, and my astonishment was not lessened when I saw their two charming children, who had stood the hardships of the road equally well.

It is clear that in these critical times the government desired to mobilize not only the material means of defense but also the spiritual force of the people. For this end, religion, the most powerful element in the life of the country, had to be invoked. New ordinances and new officials were employed in the service of this policy. The officials were given plenty of money and a free hand to organize the campaign. All the monks in Tibet were ordered to attend public services at which the Kangyur, the Tibetan bible, was to be read aloud. New prayer flags and prayer wheels were set up everywhere. Rare and powerful amulets were brought out of old chests. Offerings were doubled, and on all the mountains, incense fires burned, while the winds, turning the prayer wheels, carried supplications to the protecting deities in all the corners of heaven. The people believed with rocklife faith that the power of religion would suffice to protect their independence. In the meantime, Radio Peiping was already sending out messages in Tibetan promising that Tibet would soon be freed.

More people than ever streamed to the religious festivals, which, in the early days of 1950, surpassed in pomp and splendor anything I had ever seen. It seemed as if the whole population of Tibet had gathered, in pious enthusiasm, in the narrow streets of Lhasa. But I could not banish the thought that their touching faith would never move the golden gods. If no help came from outside, Tibet would soon be roughly awakened from its peaceful slumbers.

The Dalai Lama had again charged me to take pictures of the festivals, so I was able to see everything from a point of vantage. Four weeks after the "Great" New Year Festival, there is a "Small" Prayer Festival, which lasts for only ten days, but perhaps surpasses the "Great" Festival in splendor. At this moment the spring verdure is beginning to show, and the town presents an unforgettable aspect. The festival is the highlight of the year for the inhabitants of Shö. For two hours an immense banner hangs down from the Potala, of the Shö quarter. This banner is certainly the largest in the world. It takes fifty monks to carry it to its place and unfold it. It is made of fine, heavy silk and adorned with figures of the gods in bright colors. When at last it floats over the town from the Potala, a gay procession moves from Tsug Lag Khang to Shö, and there, after solemn ceremonies, breaks up. It is followed by a curious ritual. Groups of monks perform primitive dances, gyrating slowly to the rolling of drums. They wear masks and are hung with rare, carved ornaments of bone. The people stare entranced at the uncanny figures. Sometimes a whisper runs through the crowd. Someone thinks he has seen the Dalai Lama standing on the roof of the Potala three hundred feet above their heads and looking down through his telescope at the performance.

SHÖ, which stands at the foot of the Potala, is the home of the state printing press—a high, dark building from which never a sound issues into the outer world. There is no humming of machines, and only the voices of the monks echo through the halls. Wooden blocks lie piled on long shelves. They are used only when a new book is printed. The preparation of a new book entails endless work. The monks must first cut out small wooden boards by hand, as there are no sawmills here, and then carve the squiggly letters one by one in the birchwood boards. When they are ready, the tablets are carefully placed in order. Instead of printer's ink they use a mixture of soot, which the monks made by burning yak dung. Most of them get black from head to foot during their work. At last the separate plates are printed off on handmade Tibetan paper. The books are not bound. They consist of loose pages printed on both sides and enclosed by two carved wooden covers. One can either order books in the printing press or buy them from one of the booksellers in the Parkhor. At home they are generally kept in silk wrappers and carefully looked after. As their subject is always religious, they are treated with great respect and usually placed on the house altar. In every better-class house, one finds the complete bible, as well as the two hundred volumes of commentaries. So much reverence is paid to these books that nobody would think of placing one of the volumes on a chair. On the other hand, they think little of the books that interest us. I once found a valuable book on the Tibetan language in a very unsuitable place. The early pages were missing. I took the book away and wrote in the missing pages from another copy, very pleased with my find.

The price of Tibetan books depends on the quality of the paper used. The bible with its commentaries costs as much as a good house or a dozen yaks.

There is another very large printing press at Narthang, in the neighborhood of Shigatse, and almost every monastery has the apparatus for printing books on local saints and the annals of their lamaseries.

The whole culture of Tibet is inspired by religion, as it used to be in early days in Western civilization. The masterpieces of architecture and sculpture, of poetry and painting, glorify the faith and increase the power and reputation of the Church. There is as yet no conflict between religion and science, and consequently the content of most books is a combination of religious law and philosophic knowledge and wisdom gathered from experience. Poems and songs are mainly manuscript, written on loose leaves and not gathered into collections. The poems of the sixth Dalai Lama form an exception to this rule. They are printed as a volume. I bought a copy in the bazaar and have often read them through. They give perfect expression to the poet's yearning for love. I was not the only person to appreciate the verses of this lonely prisoner: many Tibetans love the poems of their long-dead ruler. He was an original figure in the line of the Dalai Lamas. He loved women and used to disguise himself and slip into the town to meet them. His people did not begrudge him his desire to satisfy the needs of his poetic soul.

The manuscripts copied by skilled monks, of which there are very many, cost even more than books. Their subject matter is usually unpretentious and often anecdotal. One of the best-known is the collection of anecdotes written by the most famous Tibetan comic writer, Agu Thönpa, who commented in humorous fashion on the political and religious life of his time and is still immensely popular. At every party someone tells one of his stories to entertain the guests. The taste of the Tibetans for humor and comic situations has caused Agu Thönpa to be appreciated as a classic, and when I lived in Lhasa the leading comedian in the city bore his name.

EVERY YEAR in autumn, all private houses and temples in Lhasa (including even the Potala) are painted and tidied up. It is a dangerous job to paint the high perpendicular walls of the Potala, and the same workmen are employed every year. These men hang on yak-hair ropes and pour the color on the walls from small clay vessels. One sees them sitting in breakneck positions astride the ornaments or a cornice, giving them a fresh polish. Many places from which the rain cannot easily wash away the color acquire a thick crust of limewash. It is a dazzling sight to see the blinding white walls of the Potala rising above Lhasa.

I was very pleased when the Dalai Lama instructed me to make a film showing this work in progress. It gave me a chance of recording something certainly unique in the world. In the early morning, I used to climb the high stone stairway in the midst of a swarm of women carrying pails of whitewash up from the village of Shö. It takes a hundred coolies fourteen days to give the walls their new coat of color. That gave me plenty of time for shots and opportunities to experiment from every possible direction so as to get the most effective pictures. I took a special pleasure in filming the workmen swinging on their ropes between heaven and earth. For the purpose of my work, I was allowed to enter any room in the palace. Many of them were pitch-dark with their windows blocked by piles of lumber accumulated during the centuries, through which I had to fight my way to the light. The effort was worthwhile. I found old, forgotten statues of the Buddha before which no butter lamps now burned and, hidden beneath thick layers of dust, numbers of splendid *tankas*. The museums of the world would account themselves lucky to receive a fraction of the treasures moldering there. In the basement of the palace, my guide showed me still another remarkable feature of this unique building. Wedges had been driven under the pillars that support the roof. The lofty building had sunk in the course of centuries, but the skilled craftsmen of Lhasa had succeeded in restoring it to its original level—a brilliant performance for a people with no modern technique. I succeeded in making a good picture of the painting of the Potala, and sent the film to India to be developed.

LOBSANG SAMTEN SURPRISED ME one day by asking me if I would undertake to build a room for showing films. His brother had expressed the wish that I should do so. Life in Lhasa had taught me that one should not say no even when asked to do things with which one is completely unfamiliar. Aufschnaiter and I were known as "jacks-of-all-trades," and we had already solved a lot of difficult problems. When I had ascertained what amount of current the Dalai Lama's projector would need and how far the projector would have to be from the screen, I declared myself ready to undertake the work. I was then officially commissioned to execute it by the Dalai Lama's abbot guardians. From that time, the gates of the Inner Garden at the Norbulingka were always open to me. I started the job in the winter of 1949–50, after the young king had already returned to the Potala. After looking at all the buildings, I chose an unused house adjacent to the inner side of the garden wall, which I thought I could transform into a motion-picture theater. The best masons in Lhasa and the soldiers of the bodyguard were placed at my disposal. I was not allowed to employ women, whose presence would have profaned the holy place. I used short lengths of iron screwed together into girders to support the ceiling, so as to dispense with the customary pillars. The theater was sixty feet long, and I had to build a platform for the projector. This was accessible both from the inside of the room and from the outside of the building. Some distance away from the theater, I erected a powerhouse for the motor and the generator. I did this at the express wish of the Dalai Lama, who did not want the sound of the motor to be audible in the theater, as he was anxious not to upset the old regent (the installation of a motion picture in the Norbulingka was already revolutionary enough). I built a special room for the exhaust pipes, the noise of which was effectively deadened. As the old gasoline motor was not altogether reliable, I proposed that the engine of the jeep should be made available to propel the generator in case of need. The Dalai Lama approved the suggestion, and as his will was the law, the jeep was adapted to this purpose. We had some trouble at the outset because the garden gate was just too narrow to admit the jeep. However, the young ruler, regardless of tradition, ordered the gateway to be widened. A new gate replaced the old one, and all traces of the operation were removed as soon as possible, so that there should be nothing visible to attract the criticism of reactionary spirits. The strong point about this boy was that he was able to get his ideas put into action without alienating the sympathies of those around him.

So the jeep got its own house and often came to the rescue when the old motor on strike. The chauffeur of the thirteenth Dalai Lama help me to do the wiring, and soon the whole machine was going like clockwork. I took great pains to remove all traces of our building activities from the garden, and made new flower beds and paths on the ground that had been trampled by the workmen. And, of course, I took this unique opportunity to explore the closed garden thoroughly, little thinking that in the future I should often be in it as a guest.

When the spring came, the Norbulingka was a vision of loveliness. The peach and pear blossoms were in full bloom. Peacocks strutted proudly through the grounds, and hundreds of rare plants stood in pots in the sunshine. In one corner of the park, there was a small zoo, but most of the cages were empty. Only a few wildcats and lynxes remained. Formerly there were panthers and bears, but these had soon succumbed in their narrow dens. The Dalai Lama received many presents of wild animals, especially injured ones, which found a safe refuge in the Jeweled Garden.

In addition to the temples there were many small houses scattered about under the trees. Each was used for a special purpose—one was for meditation, another for reading and study, and others served as meeting places for the monks. The largest building, several stories high, stood in the center of the garden and was half a temple and half a residence for His Holiness. The windows were too small for my liking, and I found the title "palace" too flattering for this ordinary house. It was certainly more attractive as a residence than the Potala, which was more like a prison than a palace, but it was rather dark. So was the garden. The trees had been allowed to grow untended for many years, and in places they resembled a dense jungle. No one had ever attempted to clear them out. The gardeners complained that flowers and fruits simply would not grow in the shade of the big trees. I would have been very happy if they had allowed me to tidy up and rearrange the Inner Garden. There were many gardeners, but none with a sense of style. I did succeed in convincing the high chamberlain that certain trees had to be cut down, and I was allowed to supervise the work of felling them. The gardeners had little understanding of this sort of thing, and occupied themselves mainly with cultivating pot flowers, which were left out in the open all day and placed under cover at night.

One of the doors in the wall of the Inner Garden led directly to the stables, which housed the favorite horses of the Dalai Lama and an onager that had been presented to him. These animals lived a contemplative, peaceful life tended by many grooms. They grew fat and soft as their master never rode or drove them.

The teachers and personal servants of the Dalai Lama lived outside the yellow wall in the Norbulingka park. They and the bodyguard, five hundred strong, lived in comfortable and (for Tibet) extraordinarily clean blocks of houses. The thirteenth Dalai Lama had taken a personal interest in the welfare of his troops. He had dressed them in uniforms of European cut and used to watch them exercising from one of his pavilions. I was struck by the fact that these soldiers had their hair cut in Western fashion, in contrast to all other Tibetans. The thirteenth Dalai Lama had probably been favorably impressed by the appearance of British and Indian troops during his stay in India and had modeled his bodyguard on them. The officers lived in nice little bungalows with flower beds blooming all around them. The duties of officers and men were easy. They consisted mainly in mounting guard and turning out to march in ceremonial processions.

Long before the Dalai Lama moved into the Summer Residence, I had finished my building. I wondered if he would be pleased with the theater. I could count on learning his opinion of it all from Lobsang Samten, who was certain to be present at the first performance. The Dalai Lama would probably call on the film man of the Indian Legation to work the apparatus. The legation used frequently to show films, Indian and English, at its pleasant parties, and it was a joy to see the childish enthusiasm with which the Tibetans watched these performances, especially the films showing scenes from distant lands. The question was how the young ruler would react to the pictures.

I was naturally present with my moving-picture camera to see the procession from the Potala to the Norbulingka. I had the usual difficulty in finding a suitable place from which to film the ceremony, but my attendant, a pockmarked giant of formidable aspect, made things easier for me. He carried my cameras, and the crowds opened to let us through. He looked forbidding but was, in fact, a very gallant fellow, as the following anecdote shows.

It sometimes happens that leopards stray into the gardens of Lhasa. They must not be killed, so the people try to lure them into traps or catch them by any sort of device. One day a leopard got through into the Garden of Jewels. Harried on all sides and wounded in the foot by a bullet, it was driven into a corner, where it stood at bay, spitting at anyone who dared to approach it. Suddenly my attendant went for it with his bare hands and held it until other soldiers rushed up with a sack into which they forced it. The man was badly chewed, and the leopard was lodged in the Dalai Lama's zoo, where it soon died.

When the Dalai Lama passed by me in his sedan chair and found me filming, he gave me a smile. My private thought was that he was congratulating himself on his little motion-picture theater, but I am sure that no one else thought as I did; though what could be more natural for a lonely fourteen-year-old boy? Then a look at the humble and rapturous face of my attendant reminded me that for everyone else except myself, he was not a lonely boy but a god.

15

TUTOR
TO THE
DALAI LAMA

After filming the scenes in Norbulingka, I was riding slowly home when, a little way out of Lhasa, I was overtaken by an excited soldier of the bodyguard, who told me that they had been looking for me everywhere and that I must at once ride back to the Summer Garden. My first thought was that the motion-picture apparatus was out of order, as I could hardly imagine that the young ruler, still a minor, would override all conventions and summon me directly to see him. I immediately turned around and was soon back at the Norbulingka, where everything was now peaceful and still. At the door of the yellow gate, a couple of monks were waiting. As soon as they saw me, they signaled to me to hurry up, and when I reached them they ushered me into the Inner Garden. There Lobsang Samten awaited me. He whispered something to me and put a white scarf in my hand. There was no doubt about it. His brother was going to receive me.

I at once went toward the motion-picture theater, but before I could enter the door opened from the inside, and I was standing before the Living Buddha. Conquering my surprise, I bowed deeply and handed him the scarf. He took it in his left hand and with an impulsive gesture blessed me with his right. It seemed less like the ceremonial laying on of hands than an impetuous expression of feeling on the part of the boy who had at last got his way. In the theater three abbots were waiting with bowed heads—the guardians of His Holiness. I knew them all well and did not fail to observe how coldly they returned my greeting. They certainly did not approve of this intrusion into their domain, but they had not dared openly to oppose the will of the Dalai Lama.

The young ruler was all the more cordial. He beamed all over his face and poured out a flood of questions. He seemed to me like a person who had for years brooded in solitude over different problems, and now that he had at last someone to talk to, wanted to know all the answers at once. He gave me no time to think over my answers but pressed me to go to the projector and put on a film that he had long been wanting to see. It was a documentary film of the capitulation of Japan. He came with me to the apparatus and sent the abbots into the theater to act as spectators.

I must have seemed slow and clumsy in handling the projector, as he impatiently pushed me on one side and, taking hold of the film, showed me that he was a much more practiced operator than I was. He told me that he had been busy the whole winter learning how to work the apparatus and that he had even taken a projector to pieces and put it together again. I observed then, for the first time, that he looked to get to the bottom of things instead of taking them for granted. And so, later on, like many a good father who wishes to earn the respect of his son, I often spent the evening reviving my knowledge of half-forgotten things or studying new ones. I took the utmost trouble to treat every question seriously and scientifically, as it was clear to me that my answers would form the basis of his knowledge of the Western world.

His obvious talent for technical things astonished me at our first meeting. It was a masterly performance for a boy of fourteen years to take a projector to pieces and then to reassemble it without any help, for he could not read the English prospectus. Now that the film was running well, he was delighted with the arrangements and could not praise my work too highly. We sat together in the projecting room and looked at the picture through the peepholes in the wall, and he took the greatest pleasure in what he saw and heard, often clasping my hands excitedly with the vivacity of youth. Although it was the first time in his life that he had been alone with a white man, he was in no way embarrassed or shy. While he was putting the next film on the reel, he pressed the microphone into my hands and insisted on my speaking into it. At the same time, he looked through the peepholes into the electrically lit theater in which his tutors sat on carpets. I could see how keen he was to observe the wondering faces of the worthy abbots when a voice should suddenly come out of the loudspeaker. I did not want to disappoint him, so I invited the nonexistent public to remain in their seats as the next film would present sensational scenes from Tibet. He laughed enthusiastically at the surprised and shocked faces of the monks when they heard my cheerful, disrespectful tones. Such light, unceremonious language had never been used in the presence of the Divine Ruler, whose gleaming eyes showed how he enjoyed the situation.

He made me turn the film that I had made in Lhasa while he looked after the switches. I was as curious as he was to see the results, as this was my first full-length picture. An expert could have picked out faults in it, but it seemed quite satisfactory to us. It contained my shots of the "little" New Year Festival. Even the formal abbots forgot their dignity when they recognized themselves on the flickering screen. There was a burst of laughter when a full-length picture appeared of a minister who had gone to sleep during the ceremonies. There was no malice in their laughter, for each of the abbots had sometimes to struggle to keep awake during these endless festivities. All the same, the upper classes must have got to know that the Dalai Lama had witnessed his minister's weakness for afterward whenever I appeared with my picture, everyone sat up and posed.

The Dalai Lama himself took more pleasure than anyone in the pictures. His usually slow movements became youthful and lively, and he commented enthusiastically on every picture. After a while I asked him to turn a film that he had made himself. He very modestly said that he would not dare to show his apprentice efforts after the pictures we had already seen. But I was anxious to see what subjects he had chosen for filming and persuaded him to put his roll onto the screen. He had not, of course, had a large choice of subjects. He had done a big sweeping landscape of the valley of Lhasa, which he turned much too fast. Then came a few under-lighted long-distance pictures of mounted noblemen and caravans passing through Shö. A close-up of his cook showed that he would have liked to take film portraits. The film he had shown me was absolutely his first attempt and had been made without instructions or help. When it was over, he got me to announce through the microphone that the performance was over. He then opened the door leading into the theater, told the abbots that he did not need them anymore, and dismissed them with a wave of the hand. It was again clear to me that here was no animated puppet but a clear-cut individual will capable of imposing itself on others.

When we were alone we cleared away the films and put the yellow covers on the machines. Then we sat down on a magnificent carpet in the theater with the sun streaming through the open windows. It was fortunate that I had long acquired the habit of sitting cross-legged, as chairs and cushions are not included in the Dalai Lama's household furniture. At the start I had wished to decline his invitation to sit down, knowing that even ministers were not supposed to sit in his presence, but he just took me by the sleeve and pulled me down, which put an end to my misgiving.

He told me that he had long been planning this meeting, as he had not been able to think of any other way of becoming acquainted with the outside world. He expected the regent to raise objections, but he was determined to have his own way and had already thought up a rejoinder in case of opposition. He was resolved to extend his knowledge beyond purely religious subjects, and it seemed to him that I was the only person who could help him to do so. He had no idea that I was a qualified teacher, and had he known this it would probably not have influenced him. He asked my age and was surprised to learn that I was only thirty-seven. Like many Tibetans he thought that my "yellow" hair was a sign of age. He studied my features with childish curiosity and teased me about my long nose, which, though of normal size as we reckon noses, had often attracted the attention of the snub-nosed Mongolians. At last he noticed that I had hair growing out the back of my hands and said with a broad grin, "Henrig, you have hair like a monkey." I had an answer ready, as I was familiar with the legend that the Tibetans derive their descent from the union of their god Chenrezi with a female demon. Before coupling with his demon lover, Chenrezi had assumed the shape of a monkey, and since the Dalai Lama is one of the Incarnations of this god, I found that in comparing me with an ape he had really flattered me.

With remarks such as this, our conversation soon became unconstrained, and we both lost our shyness. I now felt the attraction of his personality, which at our earlier fleeting contacts I had only guessed at. His complexion was much lighter than that of the average Tibetan. His eyes, hardly narrower than those of most Europeans, were full of expression, charm, and vivacity. His cheeks glowed with excitement, and as he sat he kept sliding from side to side. His ears stood out a little from his head. This was a characteristic of the Buddha and, as I learned later, was one of the signs by which as a child he had been recognized as an Incarnation. His hair was longer than is customary. He probably wore it so as a protection against the cold of the Potala. He was tall for his age and looked as though he would reach the stature of his parents, both of whom had striking figures. Unfortunately, as a result of much study in a seated posture with his body bent forward, he held himself badly. He had beautiful aristocratic hands with long fingers, which were generally folded in an attitude of peace. I noticed that he often looked at my hands with astonishment when I emphasized what I was saying with a gesture. Gesticulation is entirely foreign to the Tibetans, who in their reposeful attitudes express the calm of Asia. He always wore the red robe of a monk, once prescribed by Buddha, and his costume differed in no way from that of the monastic officials.

Time passed swiftly. It seemed as if a dam had burst, so urgent and continuous was the flood of questions that he put to me. I was astounded to see how much disconnected knowledge he had acquired out of books and newspapers. He possessed an English work on the Second World War in seven volumes, which he had translated into Tibetan. He knew how to distinguish between different types of airplanes, automobiles, and tanks. The names of personages like Churchill, Eisenhower, and Molotov were familiar to him, but as he had nobody to put questions to, he often did not know how persons and events were connected with each other. Now he was happy, because he had found someone to whom he could bring all the questions about which he had been puzzling for years.

It must have been about three o'clock when Sopön Khenpo came in to say that it was time to eat. This was the abbot whose duty it was to look after the physical welfare of the Dalai Lama.

When he gave his message, I immediately rose to my feet meaning to take my leave, but the God-King drew me down again and told the abbot to come again later. He then, very modestly, took out an exercise book with all sorts of drawings on the cover and asked me to look at his work. To my surprise I saw that he had been transcribing the capital letters of the Latin alphabet. What versatility and what initiative! Strenuous religious studies, tinkering with complicated mechanical appliances, and now modern languages! He insisted that I should immediately begin to teach him English, transcribing the pronunciation in elegant Tibetan characters. Another hour must have passed when Sopön Khenpo came again and this time insisted that his master should take his dinner. He had a dish of cakes, white bread, and sheep's cheese in his hand, which he pressed on me. As I wanted to refuse it, he rolled the food up in a white cloth for me to take home with me.

But the Dalai Lama still did not want to end our conversation. In wheedling tones he begged his cupbearer to wait a little longer. With a loving look at his charge, the abbot agreed and left us. I had the feeling that he was as fond of the boy and as devoted to him as if he had been his father. This white-haired ancient had served the thirteenth Dalai Lama in the same capacity and had remained in the service. This was a great tribute to his trustworthiness and loyalty, for in Tibet when there is a change of masters, there is a change of servants. The Dalai Lama proposed that I should visit his family, who lived in the Norbulingka during the summer. He told me to wait in their house till he should send for me. When I left him he shook my hand warmly—a new gesture for him.

As I walked through the empty garden and pushed back the gate bolts, I could hardly realize that I had just spent five hours with the God-King of Lama Land. A gardener shut the gate behind me, and the guard, which had been changed more than once since I came in, presented arms in some surprise. I rode slowly back to Lhasa and, but for the bundle of cakes which I was carrying, I would have thought it was all a dream. Which of my friends would have believed me if I had told him that I had just spent several hours alone in conversation with the Dalai Lama?

Needless to say, I was very happy in the new duties that had fallen to my lot. To instruct this clever lad—the ruler of a land as big as France, Spain, and Germany put together—in the knowledge and science of the Western world, seemed a worthwhile task, to say the least.

On the same evening I looked up some reviews that contained details of the construction of jet planes, about which my young pupil had that day asked me questions to which I did not know the answers. I had promised to give him full explanations at our next meeting. As time went on, I always prepared the materials for our lessons, as I wanted to introduce some system into the instruction of this zealous student.

I had many setbacks on account of his insatiable curiosity, which drove him to ask me questions that opened up whole new fields. Many of these questions I could answer only to the best of my knowledge. In order, for example, to be able to discuss the atom bomb, I had to tell him about the elements. That led to a formal discussion on metals, for which there is no generic word in Tibetan, so I had to go into details about the different sorts of metals—a subject that, of course, brought down an avalanche of questions.

My life in Lhasa had now begun a new phase. My existence had an aim. I no longer felt unsatisfied or incomplete. I did not abandon my former duties. I still collected news for the ministry; I still drew maps. But now the days were all too short, and I often worked till late into the night. I had little time for pleasures and hobbies, for when the Dalai Lama called me, I had to be free. Instead of going to parties in the morning, as others did, I came late in the afternoon. But that was no sacrifice. I was happy in the consciousness that my life had a goal. The hours I spent with my pupil were as instructive for me as they were for him. He taught me a great deal about the history of Tibet and the teachings of Buddha. He was a real authority on these subjects. We often used to argue for hours on religious subjects, and he was convinced that he would succeed in converting me to Buddhism. He told me that he was making a study of books containing knowledge of the ancient mysteries by which the body and the soul could be separated. The history of Tibet is full of stories about saints whose spirits used to perform actions hundreds of miles away from their physical bodies. The Dalai Lama was convinced that by virtue of his faith and by performing the prescribed rites he would be able to make things happen in far-distant places like Samye. When he had made sufficient progress, he said he would send me there and direct me from Lhasa. I remember saying to him with a laugh, "All right, Kundün, when you can do that, I will become a Buddhist, too."

UNFORTUNATELY, we never got as far as making this experiment. The beginning of our friendship was darkened by political clouds. The tone of the Peiping radio became more and more arrogant and Chiang Kai-shek had already withdrawn with his government to Formosa. The National Assembly in Lhasa held one sitting after another, new troops were raised, parades and military exercises were carried out in Shö, and the Dalai Lama himself consecrated the army's new colors.

Fox, the English radio expert, had much to do, as every military unit had to have at least one transmitting set.

The Tibetan National Assembly, by whom all important political decisions are taken, is composed of fifty secular and monastic officials. The assembly is presided over by four abbots from

Drebung, Sera, and Ganden, each of whom has a monk and a finance secretary attached to him. The other members of the National Assembly, whether secular or religious, belong to the different government offices, but none of the four cabinet ministers is a member. The constitution provides that the cabinet should meet in an adjoining chamber and should see all the decisions of the assembly, without possessing the right of veto. The final decision in all questions belongs to the Dalai Lama or, if he is still a minor, to the regent in his stead. Of course, no one would dare even to discuss a proposal coming from such a high authority.

Until a few years ago, the so-called Great National Assembly was convoked every year. This body was composed of officials together with representatives of the guilds of craftsmen—tailors, masons, carpenters, and so on. These annual meetings of about five hundred persons were quietly discontinued. They had really no value except to satisfy the letter of the law. In effect the power of the regent was supreme.

In these difficult times, the State Oracle was frequently consulted. His prophecies were dark and did not help to raise the morale of the people. He used to say, "A powerful foe threatens our sacred land from the north and the east." Or, "Our religion is in danger." All the consultations were held in secret, but the oracular utterances seeped through to the people and were spread abroad by whisperers. As is usual in times of war and crisis, the whole town buzzed with rumors like a beehive, and the strength of the enemy was swelled to fabulous dimensions. The fortunetellers had a good time, for not only was the fate of the country in the balance but everyone was interested in his own personal welfare. More than ever, men sought counsel of the gods, consulted the omens, and gave to every happening a good or bad meaning. Farsighted people already began to send away their treasures to be stored in the south or in remote estates. But the people as a whole believed that the gods would help them and that a miracle would save the country from war.

The National Assembly had soberer views. It had at last become clear to them that isolationism spelled a grave danger for the country. It was high time to establish diplomatic relations with foreign states and to tell the whole world that Tibet wished to be independent. Hitherto, China's claim that Tibet was one of her provinces had remained without contradiction. Newspapers and broadcasters could say what they liked about the country: there was never an answer from Tibet. In conformity with their policy of complete neutrality, the government had refused to explain themselves to the world. Now the danger of this attitude was recognized, and people began to grasp the importance of propaganda. Every day Radio Lhasa broadcasted its views in Tibetan, Chinese, and English. Missions were appointed by the government to visit Peiping, Delhi, Washington, and London. Their members were monastic officials and young noblemen who had learned English in India. But they never got farther than India, thanks to the irresolution of their own government and the intrigues of the great powers.

The young Dalai Lama realized the gravity of the situation, but he did not cease to hope for a peaceful outcome. During my visits I observed what a lively interest the future ruler took in political events. We always met alone in the little motion-picture theater, and I was able to understand often from trifling indications how much he looked forward to my coming. Sometimes he came running across the garden to greet me, beaming with happiness and holding out his hand. In spite of my warm feelings toward him and the fact that he called me his friend, I always took care to show him the respect due to the future king of Tibet. He had charged me to give him lessons in English, geography, and arithmetic. In addition, I had to look after his motion pictures and keep him conversant with world events. He had my pay raised on his own initiative, for although he was not yet constitutionally entitled to give orders, he had only to express a wish for them to be executed.

He continually astonished me by his powers of comprehension, his pertinacity, and his industry. When I gave him for homework ten sentences to translate, he usually showed up with twenty. He was very quick at learning languages, as are most Tibetans. It is quite common for people of the upper class and businessmen to speak Mongolian, Chinese, Nepalese, and Hindi. My pupil's greatest difficulty was to pronounce the letter "F," which does not occur in Tibetan. As my English was far from being perfect, we used to listen to the English news on a portable radio and took advantage of the passages spoken at dictation speed.

I had been told that in one of the government offices there were a number of English schoolbooks stored in sealed cases. A hint was given to the ministry, and on the same day, the books were sent up to the Norbulingka. We made a little library for them in the theater. My pupil was delighted at this discovery, which was something quite out of the ordinary for Lhasa. When I observed his zeal and thirst for knowledge I felt quite ashamed at the thought of my own boyhood.

There were also numerous English books and maps from the estate of the thirteenth Dalai Lama, but I noticed that they looked very new and obviously had not been read. The late ruler had learned much during his long journeys in India and China, and it was to his friendship with Sir Charles Bell that he owed his knowledge of the Western world. I was already familiar with the name of this Englishman and had read his books during my internment. He was a great champion of Tibetan independence. As political liaison officer for Sikkim, Tibet, and Bhutan, he had got to know the Dalai Lama on his flight to India. This was the beginning of a close friendship between the two men, which lasted for many years. Sir Charles Bell was, doubtless, the first white man to come into contact with a Dalai Lama.

My young pupil was not yet in a position to travel, but that did not diminish his interest in world geography, which was soon his favorite subject. I drew for him great maps of the world, and others of Asia and Tibet. We had a globe, with the help of which I was able to explain to him why Radio New York was eleven hours behind Lhasa. He soon felt at home in all countries and was as familiar with the Caucasus as with the Himalayas. He was particularly proud of the fact that the highest summit in the world was on his frontier, and like many Tibetans was astonished to learn that few countries exceeded his kingdom in area.

OUR PEACEFUL LESSONS were disturbed that summer by an untoward event. On August 15, a violent earthquake caused a panic in the Holy City. Another evil omen! The people had hardly got over their fright caused by the comet, which in the previous year had been visible by day and night like a gleaming horsetail in the heavens. Old people remembered that the last comet had been the precursor of a war with China.

The earthquake came as a complete surprise, without premonitory tremors. The houses of Lhasa suddenly began to shake, and one heard in the distance some forty dull detonations, caused no doubt by a crack in the crust of the earth. In the cloudless sky, a huge glow was visible to the east. The aftershocks lasted for days. The Indian radio reported great landslides in the province of Assam, which borders Tibet. Mountains and valleys were displaced, and the Brahmaputra, which had been blocked by a fallen mountain, had caused immense devastation. It was not till a few weeks later that news came to Lhasa of the extent of the catastrophe in Tibet itself. The epicenter of the earthquake must have been in

South Tibet. Hundreds of monks and nuns were buried in their rock monasteries, and often there were no survivors to carry the news to the nearest district officer. Towers were split down the middle, leaving ruined walls pointing to the sky, and human beings, as if snatched by a demon's hand, disappeared into the suddenly gaping earth.

The evil omens multiplied. Monsters were born. One morning the capital of the stone column at the foot of the Potala was found lying on the ground in fragments. In vain did the government send monks to the centers of ill omen to banish the evil spirits with their prayers, and when one day in blazing summer weather, water began to flow from a gargoyle on the cathedral, the people of Lhasa were beside themselves with terror. No doubt, natural explanations could have been found for all these happenings, but if the Tibetans lost their superstitiousness they would at the same time lose an asset. One has to remember that if evil portents can demoralize them with fear, good omens inspire them with strength and confidence.

The Dalai Lama was kept informed of all these sinister events. Though naturally as superstitious as his people, he was always curious to hear my views on these things. We never lacked matter for conversation, and our lesson time was all too short. He actually spent his leisure hours with me, and few people realized that he was using his free time for further study. He kept punctually to his program, and if he awaited my coming with pleasure, that did not prevent him from breaking off as soon as the clock told him that our conversation was over, and that a teacher of religion was waiting for him in one of the pavilions.

I once learned by chance what store he set by our lessons. One day, on which many ceremonies were to take place, I did not expect to be called to the Norbulingka and so went with friends for a walk on a hill near the town. Before I started, I told my servant to flash me a signal with a mirror if the Dalai Lama sent for me. At the usual hour, the signal came, and I ran at top speed back into the town. My servant was waiting with a horse at the ferry, but fast as I rode, I was ten minutes late. The Dalai Lama ran to meet me and excitedly grasped both my hands, calling, "Where have you been all this time? I have been waiting so long for you, Henrig." I begged him to pardon me for having disturbed him. It was only then that I realized how much these hours meant to him.

On the same day, his mother and youngest brother were present, and I showed them one of the eighty films the Dalai Lama possessed. It was very interesting for me to see the mother and son together. I knew that from the moment of the official recognition of the boy as the Incarnate Buddha the family had no more claim on him as a son or brother. For that reason his mother's visit was a sort of official event, to which she came in all her finery and jewels. When she left, she bowed before him, and he laid his hand on her head in blessing. This gesture well expressed the relation of these two persons to each other. The mother did not even receive the two-handed blessing, which was accorded only to monks and high officials.

It very seldom happened that we were disturbed when we were together. Once a soldier of the bodyguard brought him an important letter. The huge fellow threw himself three times to the ground, drew in his breath with a panting sound as etiquette demands, and delivered the letter. He then withdrew from the room, walking backward, and closed the door silently behind him. In such moments, I was very conscious how greatly I myself offended against the protocol.

The letter I have mentioned came from the eldest brother of the Dalai Lama, the Abbot of Kumbum in the Chinese province of Chinghai. The Reds were already in power there and they were now hoping to influence the Dalai Lama in their favor through his brother Tagtsel Rimpoche. The letter announced that Tagtsel was on the way to Lhasa.

On the same day, I visited the Dalai Lama's family. His mother scolded me when I arrived. Her mother's love had not failed to notice how much he depended on me and how often he had looked at the clock as he waited for my coming. I explained why I had not come in time and was able to convince her that my unpunctuality had not been due to casualness. When I left her, she begged me never to forget how few chances of enjoying himself in his own way her son had. It was perhaps a good thing that she herself had seen how much our lesson hours meant to the Dalai Lama. After a few months, everyone in Lhasa knew where I was riding about noon. As was to be expected, the monks criticized my regular visits, but his mother stood up for her son's wishes.

The next time I came through the yellow gate into the Inner Garden, I thought I noticed the Dalai Lama looking out for me from his little window, and it seemed he was wearing glasses. This surprised me as I had never seen him with spectacles on. In answer to my question, he told me that he had for some time been having difficulty with his eyes and had therefore taken to wearing glasses for study. His brother had procured him a pair through the Indian Legation. He had probably damaged his eyes when he was a child, when his only pleasure was to look for hours together through his telescope at Lhasa. Moreover, continuous reading and study in the twilight of the Potala were not exactly calculated to improve his sight. On this occasion he was wearing a red jacket over his monastic robe. He had designed it himself and was very proud of it, but he allowed himself to wear it only in his leisure moments. The chief novelty about this garment was the fact that it had pockets. Tibetan clothes do not have any, but the designer had noticed the existence of pockets in the illustrated papers and in my jackets, and had realized how useful they might be. Now, like every other boy of his age, he was able to carry about with him a knife, a screwdriver, sweets, etc. He also now kept his colored pencils and fountain pens in his pockets and was, doubtless, the first Dalai Lama to take pleasure in such things. He was also much interested in his collection of watches and clocks, some of which he had inherited from the thirteenth Dalai Lama. His favorite piece was an Omega calendar clock, which he had bought with his own money. During his minority, he could dispose of only the money that was left as an offering at the foot of his throne. Later on, the treasure vaults of the Potala and the Garden of Jewels would be open to him, and as ruler of Tibet, he would become one of the world's richest men.

16

TIBET

IS INVADED

Now for the first time one heard voices saying in public that the majority of the Dalai Lama should be officially declared before he reached the normal age. In these difficult times, the people wanted to have a young, unimpeachable sovereign on the throne and no longer to be at the mercy of the corrupt and unpopular clique that surrounded the regent. The present régime was in no wise fitted to be a support and an example to a people on whom war was being forced.

About this time something unprecedented occurred in Lhasa. One morning we found posters on the walls of the street leading to the Norbulingka with the inscription, "Give the Dalai Lama the Power." In support of this appeal, there followed a series of accusations against the regent's favorites. Naturally, we talked about these posters at my next meeting with His Holiness. He had already heard about them from his brother. It was guessed that the monks of Sera were responsible for them. The Dalai Lama was not at all pleased with the turn things were taking; he did not consider himself ripe for the throne. He knew that he still had much to learn. For that reason he did not attach much importance to the posters and was more interested in carrying out our program of studies. His greatest worry was whether his knowledge equaled that of a Western schoolboy of the same age, or whether he would, in Europe, be classed as a backward Tibetan. I was able to assure him quite honestly that he was above the average in intelligence and that it would be easy for him to catch up with the greater knowledge of European boys. It was not only the Dalai Lama who had an inferiority complex. One constantly hears Tibetans saying, "We know nothing. We are so stupid!" But, of course, the fact that they say so proves the contrary. Tibetans are anything but dull-witted, and in making this judgment, they are confusing education with intelligence.

With the help of the Indian Legation, I succeeded from time to time in getting drama films for our moving pictures. I wanted to build up a more comprehensive repertory in order to please the Dalai Lama. The first of the drama films I secured was *Henry V*, and I was very curious to see what the young ruler's reaction to it would be. He allowed his abbots to be present at the performance, and when it grew dark, the gardeners and cooks who worked inside the yellow wall slipped into the theater. The public squatted on the carpets on the floor of the theater, while the Dalai Lama and I sat as usual on the steps leading from the auditorium to the projection room. I whispered to him a translation of the text as it was spoken and tried to answer his questions. Luckily, I had taken some trouble to prepare myself, because it is not so easy for a German to translate Shakespeare's English into Tibetan. The public were somewhat embarrassed by the love scenes, which I cut the next time we turned the film. Kundün was enthusiastic about the picture. He was deeply interested in the lives of great men, and his interest was not limited to kings. He wished to know all about generals and men of science, and to study their exploits. He watched a documentary film about Mahatma Gandhi several times. The Mahatma was a highly honored figure in Tibet.

I already had reason to approve of his taste. Once when we were selecting an assortment of films, he put all the comic and purely entertaining pictures on one side and asked me to change them. His interest was in educational, military, and cultural pictures. Once I thought to please him by showing him a particularly beautiful film about horses, but I had to admit that the subject did not attract him. "It is funny," he said, "that the former body"—meaning thereby the thirteenth Dalai Lama—"was so fond of horses, and that they mean so little to me."

At this time he was growing very quickly and displayed the usual characteristics of the awkward age. Once he let his exposure meter fall and was as unhappy about it as a poor child who has broken his only toy. I had to remind him that he was the ruler of a great dominion and that he could buy as many exposure meters as he liked. His modesty was a source of perpetual wonder to me. The average child of a rich tradesman was certainly far more spoiled than he was. His manner of life was ascetic and lonely, and there were many days on which he fasted and kept silence.

His brother Lobsang Samten, the only person who could freely keep him company, though older than he, was far less developed mentally. At the beginning of our lessons, the Dalai Lama had insisted on his brother joining us, but for Lobsang this obligation was a torment, and he constantly asked me to make excuses for his absence. He admitted to me that he could hardly understand anything of our conversation and that he always had to struggle to keep awake. On the other hand, he had a much more practical understanding of government business and was already able to help his brother in carrying out his official duties.

Kundün received his brother's frequent excuses with resignation, at which I was surprised as Lobsang had told me how quick-tempered he had been as a child. No trace of this quality remained; in fact, he was really too collected and serious for his age. But when he laughed, he laughed as heartily as any ordinary child, and he was very fond of harmless jokes. Sometimes he used to pretend to box with me and often used to enjoy teasing me.

Open as he was to the influence of Western thought, he nevertheless had to conform to the centuries-old traditions of his office. All objects that had served for the personal use of the Dalai Lama were regarded as sovereign remedies against illness or charms against evil spirits. There was great competition for the cake and fruits that I used to bring home with me from His Holiness's kitchen, and I could not give my friends greater pleasure than by sharing these things with them.

I knew how much the young king desired to lead his people one day out of the fog of gloomy superstition. We dreamed and talked endlessly about enlightenment and future reforms. We had already drawn up a plan. We proposed to bring to Tibet experts from small, neutral countries who had no interests in Asia. With their help we would build up systems of education and public health, and train Tibetans to carry on the work. A great task was reserved for my friend Aufschnaiter. As an agricultural engineer in Tibet, he would have more than enough to do for the rest of his life. He himself was enthusiastic about these ideas and asked for nothing better than to go on working here. For my part, I wished to devote myself to organizing education and dreamed of undertaking the great work of creating a university with its different faculties. But the future held out no prospect of realizing our visions, and Aufschnaiter and I were clear-sighted enough not to feed on false hopes. It was inevitable that Red China would invade Tibet, and then there would be no place for us two friends of Tibetan independence.

WHEN WE WERE already on intimate terms with each other, I asked Kundün if he would not tell me something about his recognition as an Incarnation. I already knew that he had been born on July 6, 1935, in the neighborhood of Lake Kuku-Nor, but when I congratulated him on his birthday, I was the only person who did so. Birthdays are unimportant dates in Tibet. They are generally not known and never celebrated. For the people, the date of their king's birth is quite without interest. He represents in his person the return to earth of Chenrezi, the God of Grace, one of the thousand Living Buddhas, who have renounced Nirvana in order to help mankind. Chenrezi was the patron god of Tibet, and his reincarnations were always the kings of Bö —as the natives call Tibet. The Mongolian ruler Altan Khan, who had embraced Buddhism, gave the title of Dalai Lama to the Incarnations. The present Dalai Lama was the fourteenth Incarnation. The people regarded him as the Living Buddha rather than as a king, and their prayers were directed to him not as ruler so much as patron god of the land.

It was not easy for the young king to satisfy the demands made on him. He knew that he was expected to give divine judgments, and that what he ordered and what he did were regarded as infallible and would become a part of historical tradition. He was already striving by means of week-long meditation and profound religious study to prepare himself for the heavy duties of his office. He was much less self-assured than the thirteenth Incarnation. Tsarong once gave me a typical example showing the dominating character of the late ruler. He wished to enact new laws but met with bitter opposition from his conservative entourage, who quoted the utterances of the fifth Dalai Lama on the same context. To which the thirteenth Dalai Lama replied, "And who was the fifth former body?" The monks thereupon prostrated themselves before him, for his answer had left them speechless. As an Incarnation, he was, of course, not only the thirteenth but also the fifth and all the other Dalai Lamas as well. It entered my mind when I heard this story how lucky Tibet had been never to have had a ruler like Nero or Ivan the Terrible. But to a Tibetan such a thought could never have occurred, for how could an Incarnation of the God of Grace be other than good?

The Dalai Lama could give no satisfactory answer to my question about how he was discovered. He was only a small child when it happened, and he had only a hazy remembrance of the event. When he saw how deeply I was interested in the matter, he advised me to ask one of the nobles who was present at his recognition.

One of the few living eyewitnesses of the event was the Commander in Chief of the Army, Dzasa Künsangtse. One evening he told me the story of this mysterious event. Some time before his death, in 1933, the thirteenth Dalai Lama had given intimations regarding the manner of his rebirth. After his death, the body sat in state in the Potala in traditional Buddha posture, looking toward the south. One morning it was noticed that his head was turned to the east. The State Oracle was straightaway consulted, and while in his trance the monk oracle threw a white scarf in the direction of the rising sun. But for two years, nothing more definite was indicated. Then the regent went on a pilgrimage to a famous lake to ask for counsel. It is said that every person who looks into the water of Chö Khor Gye can see a part of the future. When the regent, after long prayers, came to the water and looked in its mirror, he had a vision of a three-storied monastery with golden roofs, near which stood a little Chinese peasant house with carved gables. Full of gratitude for the divine direction, he returned to Lhasa and began to make preparations for a search. The whole nation took a lively interest in the business, feeling itself an orphan with no divine patron to protect it. With us it is generally, but mistakenly, believed that each rebirth takes place at the moment of the predecessor's death. This does not accord with Buddhist doctrine, which declares that years may pass before the god once more leaves the fields of Heaven and resumes the form of a man. Search groups set out to explore in the year 1937. Following the signs that had been vouchsafed, they journeyed eastward in quest of the Holy Child. The members of these groups were monks, and in each group there was one secular official. They all carried with them objects that had belonged to the thirteenth Dalai Lama.

The group to which my informant belonged journeyed under the leadership of Kyetsang Rimpoche till they reached the district of Amdo in the Chinese province of Chinghai. In this region there are many monasteries, as the great reformer of Lamaism, Tsong Kapa, was born here. The population is partly Tibetan and lives peacefully side by side with Muslims. The group found a number of boys, but none of them corresponded to the specifications. They began to fear that they would fail in their mission. At last after long wanderings, they encountered a three-storied monastery with golden roofs. With a flash of enlightenment, they remembered the regent's vision, and then their eyes fell on the cottage with carved gables. Full of excitement they dressed themselves in the clothes of their servants. This maneuver is customary during these searches, for persons dressed as high officials attract too much attention and find it hard to get in touch with the people. The servants, dressed in the garments of their masters, were taken to the best room, while the disguised monks went into the kitchen, where it was likely they would find the children of the house.

As soon as they entered the house, they felt sure that they would soon find the Holy Child in it, and they waited tensely to see what would happen. And, sure enough, a two-year-old boy came running to meet them and seized the skirts of the lama, who wore around his neck the rosary of the thirteenth Dalai Lama. Un abashed the child cried "*Sera Lama, Sera Lama!*" It was already a matter for wonder that the infant recognized a lama in the garb of a servant and that he said that he came from the Cloister of Sera—which was the case. Then the boy grasped the rosary and tugged at it till the lama gave it to him; thereupon he hung it around his own neck. The noble searchers found it hard not to throw themselves on the ground before the child, as they had no longer any doubt. They had found the Incarnation. But they had to proceed in the prescribed manner.

They bade farewell to the peasant family and returned a few days later—this time not disguised. They first negotiated with the parents, who had already given one of their sons as an Incarnation to the Church, and then the little boy was awakened from his sleep and the four delegates withdrew with him to the altar room. Here the child was subjected to the prescribed examination. He was first shown four different rosaries, one of which—the most worn—had belonged to the thirteenth Dalai Lama. The boy, who was quite unconstrained and not the least bit shy, chose the right one without hesitation and danced around the room with it. He also selected out of several drums one that the last Incarnation had used to call his servants. Then he took an old walking stick, which had also belonged to him, not deigning to bestow a glance on one that had a handle of ivory and silver. When they examined his body, they found all the marks that an Incarnation of Chenrezi ought to bear: large, outstanding ears, and moles on the trunk, which are supposed to be traces of the four-armed god's second pair of arms.

The delegates were now sure that they had found what they sought. They telegraphed in a secret code via China and India a message to be conveyed to Lhasa, and immediately received instructions to observe the utmost secrecy, to avoid intrigues that might inperil the success of their mission. The four envoys took a solemn oath of silence before a *tanka* on which a likeness of Chenrezi was embroidered, and then went off to inspect other boys as a blind. One must remember that the search was being conducted on Chinese territory, which made caution essential. It would have been fatal to betray the fact that the real Dalai Lama had been discovered, for the Chinese could then have insisted on sending an escort of troops with him to Lhasa. The delegates accordingly asked the governor of the province, a certain Ma Pufang, for permission to take the boy to Lhasa, where the Dalai Lama would be identified out of a number of candidates. Ma Pufang asked a hundred thousand Chinese dollars for the surrender of the child and this sum was at once paid over. This was a mistake, as the Chinese now perceived what importance the Tibetans attached to the child. They then asked for another three hundred thousand dollars. The delegates, conscious of their previous mistake, gave only a part of this sum, which they borrowed from local Mohammedan merchants, promising to pay the balance when they came to Lhasa to the merchants who accompanied the caravan. The governor agreed to this arrangement.

In the late summer of 1939, the four delegates, together with their servants, the merchants, and the Holy Child and his family, started for Lhasa. They traveled for months before reaching the Tibetan frontier. There a cabinet minister was waiting for them with his staff. He gave the boy a letter from the regent containing official confirmation of his recognition. Then for the first time homage was paid to him as Dalai Lama. Even his parents, who had certainly guessed that their son must be a high Incarnation, only now learned that he was no less than the future ruler of Tibet.

From this day the little Dalai Lama distributed blessings as naturally as if he had never done anything else. He has still a clear recollection of being borne into Lhasa in his golden palanquin. He had never seen so many people. The whole town was there to greet the new embodiment of Chenrezi, who at last after so many years returned to the Potala and his orphaned people. Six years had passed since the death of the "Previous Body," and of these, nearly two had elapsed before the god reentered a human body. In February 1940, the enthronement of the Dalai Lama was celebrated during the Great New Year Festival, when he received new names such as "The Holy One," "The Tender, Glorious One," "The Mighty of Speech," "The Excellent Understanding," "The Absolute Wisdom," "The Defender of the Faith," and "The Ocean."

Everyone was astonished at the unbelievable dignity of the child and the gravity with which he followed ceremonies that lasted for hours. With his predecessor's servants, who had charge of him, he was as trusting and affectionate as if he had always known them.

I was very glad to have heard this account more or less at first-hand. During the lapse of time, many legends had collected around these extraordinary events, and I had already heard several garbled versions.

WITH THE APPROACH of autumn, the hours of our companionship were more and more frequently interrupted. Even our quiet corner of the Jeweled Garden felt the breath of the coming storm. As the crisis intensified, the initiation of the young king into the business of government proceeded apace. The National Assembly transferred itself to the Norbulingka so as to be able to communicate important events to His Holiness without delay. The young king in spite of his inexperience surprised the whole official world by his farsightedness and his cleverness in opposing unsuitable policies. There was no doubt that the destinies of the state would soon be entrusted to him.

The situation grew ever more serious. News came from East Tibet that Chinese cavalry and infantry were concentrating on our frontier. Troops were sent to the east, though it was clearly recognized that they were too weak to hold up the enemy. The government's attempts to arrive at a settlement by diplomatic means were in vain. The delegations that had been sent out for propaganda purposes had got stuck in India. Tibet could count on no aid from outside. The example of Korea showed clearly enough that even the support of the United Nations was of uncertain avail against the Red armies. The people became resigned to the prospect of defeat.

On October 7, 1950, the enemy attacked the Tibetan frontier in six places simultaneously. The first engagement took place, but Lhasa received no news of the fighting for ten days. While the first Tibetans were dying for their country, festivals were being held in Lhasa, and the people waited for a miracle. After the news of the first defeats, the government sent for all the most famous oracles in Tibet. There were dramatic scenes in the Norbulingka. The gray-headed abbots and veteran ministers entreated the oracles to stand by them in their hour of need. In the presence of the Dalai Lama, the old men threw themselves at the feet of the prophetic monks, begging them for once to give them wise counsel. At the climax of his trance, the State Oracle reared up and then fell down before the Dalai Lama, crying, "Make him king!" The other oracles said much the same thing, and as it was felt that the voice of the gods ought to be listened to, preparations for the Dalai Lama's accession to the throne were at once put in hand.

In the meantime, the Chinese troops had penetrated hundreds of miles into Tibet. A few Tibetan commanders had already surrendered, and others had ceased to resist, seeing no future in a fight against overwhelming force. The governor of the principal town in East Tibet had sent a wireless message to Lhasa asking for permission to surrender as resistance was useless. The National Assembly refused his request, so after blowing up his guns and ammunition dumps, he fled in the direction of Lhasa with the English radio operator, Ford. Two days later he found his way barred by Chinese troops, and both men were captured. I have already referred to the fate of Robert Ford.

The National Assembly now sent an urgent appeal to the UN for help against the aggressors, claiming that their country had been invaded in peacetime on the pretext that the Red People's Army could not tolerate the influence of imperialistic powers in Tibet. The whole world knew, they pointed out, that Tibet was utterly free from any foreign influence. Here there were no imperialistic influences and nothing to liberate. If any nation deserved the help of the UN, it was Tibet. Their appeal was rejected, and the UN expressed the hope that China and Tibet would unite peacefully.

It was now clear to the meanest intelligence that as no outside help was forthcoming, Tibet must surrender. Everyone began to pack up. Aufschnaiter and I knew that our hour was come and that we had lost our second home. The thought of departure was bitter, but we knew that we must go. Tibet had treated us with hospitality and had given us tasks to perform into which we had put our whole hearts. The time during which I had been privileged to give lessons to the Dalai Lama had been the best of my life. We had never had anything to do with the military activities of Tibet, as many European newspapers asserted.

The Dalai Lama began to be anxious about our personal prospects. I had a long conversation with him, as a result of which it was agreed that I should now take my leave as I had long planned to do. This would give me greater freedom of movement and allow me to slip away without comment. In a few days, the Dalai Lama was to move to the Potala, where for the time being he would have no time for my lessons. My plan was to travel first to

South Tibet and visit the town of Shigatse, after which I should go on to India.

The ceremony at which the Dalai Lama was to be declared of age was imminent. The government would have liked to hurry it on, but the propitious date had to be determined by the omens. At the same time, it was of pressing importance to decide what was to be done with the young ruler. Was he to remain in Lhasa or to flee? It was usual, when difficult questions had to be decided, to be guided by the conduct of previous Incarnations. It therefore seemed relevant to remember that, forty years ago, the thirteenth Dalai Lama had fled before the invading Chinese and that things had gone well for him thereafter. But the government could not undertake singlehandedly to make such a critical decision. The gods must have the last word. So in the presence of the Dalai Lama and the regent, two balls of kneaded tsampa were made, and after being tested on a pair of gold scales to ensure that they were of exactly the same weight, they were put in a golden basin. Each of these balls had rolled up inside it a slip of paper: on one of these was written the word "yes," and on the other "no." Meanwhile, the State Oracle had hypnotized himself and was performing his dance. The basin was placed in his hands, and he rotated it with ever-increasing speed until one of the balls jumped out and fell on the ground. When it was opened, it was found to contain the "yes" paper, and so it was decided that the Dalai Lama should leave Lhasa.

I had postponed my journey for a while, for I wished first to know the Dalai Lama's plans. I hated leaving him in these unhealthy times, but he insisted on my departure and consoled me by saying that we should meet again in the south. The preparations for his own flight were being hurried on, but great secrecy was maintained to avoid alarming the people. The Chinese were still some hundreds of miles to the east of Lhasa and for the moment were not moving, but it was feared that an unexpected advance might cut off the Dalai Lama's chance of escape to the south.

The news that the ruler was getting ready to leave was bound to leak out. The fact could not be concealed that his private treasures were being taken away. Every day, caravans of heavily laden mules were seen leaving the town in the charge of men of the bodyguard. Consequently, the nobles hesitated no longer and began to move their families and treasures into safer places.

Outwardly, life in Lhasa followed its normal course. It was only by the shortage of means of transport that one noticed that many people were keeping back their pack animals for their own purposes. Market prices rose a little. Reports came in of the gallant deeds of individual Tibetan soldiers, but it was generally known that the army was routed. The few units that still held their ground were soon obliged to yield to the enemy's superior tactics.

In 1910, the invading Chinese had plundered and burned when they came to Lhasa, and the inhabitants were paralyzed by the fear that these outrages would be repeated. Nevertheless, it is fair to say that during the present war, the Chinese troops had shown themselves disciplined and tolerant, and Tibetans who had been captured and then released were saying how well they had been treated.

17

I LEAVE TIBET

I left Lhasa in the middle of November 1950. I had been hesitating about going, when an opportunity of securing transport made up my mind for me. Aufschnaiter, who had originally intended to accompany me, hesitated at the last moment, so I took his baggage with me, leaving him to follow a few days later. It was with a heavy heart that I left the house that had been my home for so long, my beloved garden, and my servants, who stood around me weeping. I took with me only my books and treasures, and left everything else to my servants. Friends kept dropping in with presents, which made my going harder. It was a small consolation to think that I would see many of them again in South Tibet. Many of them still firmly believed that the Chinese would never come to Lhasa and that after my leave was over I would be able to return in peace. I did not share their hopes. I knew that it would be long before I saw Lhasa again, so I bade farewell to all the places that I had come to love. One day I rode out with my camera and took as many photos as I could, feeling that they would revive happy memories in the future and perhaps win the sympathy of others for this beautiful and strange land.

The sky was overcast when I embarked in my little yak-skin boat, which was to take me down the Kyichu as far as its junction with the Brahmaputra. This six-hour river journey saved me a ride of two days. My baggage had gone on ahead of me by road. My friends and servants stood on the bank and waved to me sadly. As I took a snapshot of them, the current caught the boat, and they were soon out of sight. Floating down the river, I could not keep my eyes off the Potala; I knew the Dalai Lama was on the roof looking at me through his telescope.

On the same day, I caught up with my caravan, consisting of fourteen pack animals, and two horses for me and my servant. The faithful Nyima had insisted on accompanying me. Once more I was on the march, up hill and down dale, over mountains and passes, till after a week we reached Gyangtse, on the great caravan route to India.

Not long before, one of my best friends had been appointed governor of the region. He received me as a guest in his house, and here we celebrated the accession to the throne of the Dalai Lama, which was kept as a feast day throughout Tibet. The news of this event had been circulated throughout the country by runners. New prayer flags fluttered over all the roofs, and for a short time the people forgot to think about the dismal future, and danced and sang and drank in a burst of old-time happiness. At no time had a new Dalai Lama inspired so much confidence and hope. The young king stood high above all cliques and intrigues, and had already given many proofs of clear-sightedness and resolution. His inborn instinct would guide him in the choice of his advisers and protect him from the influence of scheming men.

Alas! as I knew, it was too late. He had come to the throne at the very moment when Fate had decided against him. Had he been a few years older, his leadership might have altered the history of his country.

During this month I visited Shigatse, the second largest town in Tibet, famous for the great monastery of Trashilhünpo. There I met a number of friends anxious for news from the capital. In this place people thought less about running away, as the cloister was the seat of the Panchen Lama.

This high Incarnation had been for generations supported by the Chinese as a rival to the Dalai Lama. The present incumbent was two years younger than the Dalai Lama. He had been educated in China and proclaimed in Peiping as the rightful ruler of Tibet. In reality, he had not the slightest claim to this position. He had legal rights in the monastery and its lands, but nothing more. It is true that in the ranking of the Living Buddhas, Ö-pa-me stood higher than Chenrezi, but in fact the first Incarnation had originally been only the teacher of the fifth Dalai Lama, who, out of gratitude to him, had declared him to be an Incarnation and given him the monastery with its enormous benefices.

At the time of the selection of the last Panchen Lama, there had been a number of candidates. One of the children was discovered in China, and on that occasion the Chinese authorities had refused to allow him to be taken to Lhasa without a military escort. The Tibetan government had been unable to resist this proposal, and one day the Chinese simply declared this child to be the true Incarnation of Ö-pa-me and the only rightful Panchen lama.

They had thus dealt themselves an important card in their game of politics with Tibet and intended to make the best possible use of their trump. The fact that they were Communists did not prevent the Chinese from making violent radio propaganda in favor of his religious and temporal claims; nevertheless, he had few supporters in Tibet. These were mainly inhabitants of Shigatse and the monks in his monastery, who saw in him their chief and wanted to be independent of Lhasa. These people awaited the "Army of Liberation" without fear. It was, indeed, rumored that the Panchen Lama would make common cause with the Chinese. There is no doubt that the people of Tibet would be glad to have his blessings, for as the Incarnation of a Buddha, he is held in high honor. But even if he were forced upon them by the Chinese, the Tibetans would never recognize him as their ruler.

This position is uncontestably reserved for the Dalai Lama as the Incarnation of the patron god of Tibet. So it came about that, when the moment arrived to play their trump card, the Chinese failed in their attempt to impose the Panchen Lama as ruler on the people of Tibet. His authority is limited, as formerly, to the Monastery of Trashilhünpo.

During my trip to Shigatse, I took occasion to visit the cloister and found yet another large town inhabited by thousands of monks. I unobtrusively managed to take a few photographs. Among other curiosities I found in a temple a most impressive gilded idol as high as a house of nine stories, with a gigantic head.

The town of Shigatse stands on the Brahmaputra at no great distance from the monastery. It reminds one a little of Lhasa, being also dominated by a fortress. There are ten thousand inhabitants, among whom are to be found the best craftsmen in Tibet. Wool provides the staple industry. It is brought by caravans from the neighboring plains of the Changthang. Shigatse stands higher than Lhasa, and the climate is markedly colder. Nonetheless, the best grain in the country comes from here, and the Dalai Lama and the nobles of Lhasa get all their flour from this place.

AFTER A FEW DAYS, I rode back to Gyangtse. There my friend the governor was waiting to tell me the glad news that the Dalai Lama was expected to pass through Gyangtse before long. An order had come instructing all caravan stations to be ready to receive guests and to have the roads put in order—that could have only one meaning. I put myself at the disposal of the governor to assist in the preparations.

Plentiful supplies of peas and barley were stored in the caravansaries as fodder for the animals, and an army of workers collected to tidy and improve the roads. I went with the governor on one of his tours of inspection in the province. When we returned to Gyangtse, we learned that the Dalai Lama had left Lhasa on December 19 and was now on his way here. We met his mother and brothers and sisters on their way through Gyangtse—all except Lobsang, who was traveling with the king. I also met Tagtsel Rimpoche for the first time in three years. He had been forced by the Chinese to take an escort of Chinese troops and carry a message to his brother. The Chinese had gained nothing by this, and Tagtsel had not sought to influence the Dalai Lama. Tagtsel was very pleased to have escaped from the Chinese. His escort had been arrested, and the wireless transmitter that they carried confiscated.

The caravan of the Holy Family was a very modest one. The mother was no longer in her first youth and had the right to be carried in a palanquin, but she rode like the others and covered long distances every day. Before the governor and I rode to meet the Dalai Lama, the Holy Mother with her children and servants had continued their journey southward.

My friend and I rode for about three days along the Lhasa road, and on the Karo Pass we ran into the advance party of His Holiness's caravan. Looking down from the pass, we could see the long column crawling up the road in a thick cloud of dust. The Dalai Lama had an escort of forty nobles and a guard of some two hundred picked soldiers with machine guns and howitzers. An army of servants and cooks followed, and an unending train of fifteen hundred pack animals brought up the rear.

In the middle of the column, two flags were waving, the national flag of Tibet and the personal banner of the fourteenth Dalai Lama. The flags denoted the presence of the ruler. When I saw the young God-King riding slowly up the pass on his gray horse, I unwillingly thought of an ancient prophecy that people sometimes used to quote under their breath in Lhasa. An oracle had long ago declared that the thirteenth Dalai Lama would be the last of his line. It seemed that the prophecy was fulfilling itself. Since his accession, four weeks had passed, but the young king had not taken up the reins of power. The enemy was in the land, and the ruler's flight was only a first step toward greater misfortunes.

As he rode by me, I took off my hat, and he gave me a friendly wave of the hand. At the top of the pass, incense fires were burning to greet the young God-King, but an unfriendly clattering blast was agitating the prayer flags. The convoy moved on without delay to the next stopping place, where all was prepared and a hot meal was waiting for the travelers. The Dalai Lama passed the night in a neighboring monastery, and before I went to sleep I thought of him sitting in an unfriendly guest room with dusty idols for company. He would find no stove to warm him, and the paper-covered window frames were his only protection against storm and cold, while a few butter lamps provided just enough light to see by.

The young ruler, who in his short life had known no home but the Potala and the Jeweled Garden, was now forced by misfortune to learn something of the country he ruled. In what dire need he stood of comfort and support! But, poor boy, he had to raise himself above all his troubles and use all his strength in blessing the countless throngs who came to draw comfort and confidence from him.

His brother Lobsang, seriously ill with a heart attack, was traveling with the convoy in a litter. I was horrified to hear that the doctors had used the same rough methods on him as they do on a sick horse. On the day the convoy was to leave, he had lain in a swoon for several hours, so the Dalai Lama's physician recalled him to life by applying a branding iron to his flesh. He told me later all the details of this memorable journey.

The Dalai Lama's flight had been kept strictly secret. The authorities did not want to disturb the people and feared lest the monks of the great cloisters would do their utmost to deter him from his resolution. Accordingly, the high officials who had been chosen to accompany him were informed only late in the evening that the caravan would leave at two o'clock the next morning. For the last time, they all drank butter tea in the Potala, and then their cups were refilled and left standing as a charm to bring about a speedy return. None of the rooms that the departing king had inhabited was to be swept on the following day, for that would bring ill luck.

The column of fugitives moved silently through the night, proceeding first to the Norbulingka, where the young ruler stopped to say a prayer. The caravan had not been a day on the road before the news of the flight had spread right and left. The monks of the Monastery of Jang swarmed in thousands to meet the Dalai Lama. They flung themselves before his horse's hoofs and begged him not to leave them, crying that if he went away they would be left without a leader, at the mercy of the Chinese. The officials feared that the monks would try to prevent the Dalai Lama from going any further, but at this critical moment he showed the strength of his personality and explained to the monks that he could do more for his country if he did not fall into the hands of the enemy, and that he would return as soon as he had concluded a suitable agreement with them. After demonstrations of affection and loyalty, the monks cleared the way for the caravan to proceed.

News of the Dalai Lama's approach soon reached Gyangtse. Small white stones were laid along the sides of the streets to keep away the evil spirits. Monks and nuns flocked from the convents, and the whole population stood for hours waiting to receive their king. Indian troops, stationed not far away, rode to meet the caravan to do honor to the Dalai Lama. On arriving at all the larger places, the convoy took the form of a procession. The Dalai Lama dismounted and seated himself in his palanquin. We had got into the way of starting regularly soon after midnight to avoid the sandstorms that blew throughout the day over the unprotected plateau. The nights were icy cold. The Dalai Lama wrapped himself snugly in his fur-lined silk mantle and wore a great bearskin cap that covered his ears. Before dawn there were often fifty degrees of frost, and though the air was still, riding was a penance.

The Dalai Lama often jumped off his horse before his abbots could help him and hurried with long strides far ahead of the others. Naturally, all the other riders also had to dismount, and many corpulent noblemen who had never walked in their lives fell miles behind. For two days we rode through a blizzard, shivering in the bitter cold, and we felt the greatest relief when we had left the Himalaya passes behind us and descended into warmer, well-wooded country.

Sixteen days after leaving the capital, the caravan reached its provisional destination, the headquarters of the district governor of Chumbi. On arrival the Dalai Lama was carried in his yellow chair through the dense crowds into the governor's modest house, which at once acquired the title of "Heavenly Palace, the Light and Peace of the Universe." No mortal man would ever again inhabit it, for every place in which the Dalai Lama spent a night was automatically consecrated as a chapel. Henceforward, the faithful would bring their offerings there and pray for the god's blessing.

The officials were lodged in the houses of the peasants of the surrounding villages and had to accustom themselves to doing without their usual comforts. Most of the soldiers were sent back to the interior as there was no accommodation for them in Chumbi. All the approaches to the valley were guarded by military posts, and only persons carrying a special pass could come in and go out. There was at least one representative of every government office in the Dalai Lama's suite, and so a provisional government was set up, which observed routine office hours and held regular meetings. A service of couriers was established between Lhasa and the provisional government. The Dalai Lama had brought his great seal, with which he validated the decisions of the authorities in Lhasa. The messengers covered the distance between Lhasa and Chumbi at incredible speed, one of them performing the double journey (nearly five hundred miles over mountainous country) in nine days. The couriers, who were the only link between Lhasa and the outside world, brought the latest news of the Chinese advance. Later on, Fox arrived with his instruments and established a radio station.

The wives and children of the officials who had accompanied them traveled straight on to India. There was no accommodation for them in Chumbi. Many of them took the opportunity to make pilgrimages to the holy places of Buddhism in India and Nepal. Even the family of the Dalai Lama, with the exception of Lobsang Samten, had gone south and were now living in bungalows in the hill station of Kalimpong. Many of the refugees had their first sight of railways, airplanes, and motorcars when they came to India, but after the first excitement of seeing these marvels, they longed to be back in their own country, which, if backward in the devices of civilization, represented for them the firm ground of existence.

DURING THESE DAYS I lived in Chumbi as the guest of a friend, an official. My work was at an end, and I often felt bored, but I could not bring myself to say good-bye to my friends. I felt like a spectator at a play, who foresaw the tragic denouement and was saddened by the inevitable end, but had to sit out the last act. To deaden my anxiety, I used to go daily up into the mountains, and made many sketch maps.

I had only one official duty to perform, and that was to keep the foreign minister supplied with the news, which I got through my little radio. I learned that the Chinese had not advanced any farther and were now calling on the Tibetan government to come to Peiping and negotiate a settlement. The Dalai Lama and the government concluded that it would be good policy to accept the invitation, and a delegation with plenary powers was dispatched. As armed resistance would have been senseless, the government used the person of the Dalai Lama as a bargaining counter, for they knew that the Reds were very anxious to have him back in Tibet. Delegations drawn from all classes of the population kept arriving in Chumbi to beg the ruler to return. The whole of Tibet was sunk in depression, and I now realized to the full how closely the people and their king were bound to each other. Without the blessing of his presence, the country could never prosper.

At last no alternative was left to the Dalai Lama but to accept the conditions of the Chinese and return to Lhasa. After long negotiations, treaty terms had been formulated in Peiping. These secured the internal administration of the country to the Dalai Lama, and guaranteed that religion would be respected and freedom of worship granted. In return for these concessions the Chinese insisted on taking over the foreign relations of Tibet and being responsible for the defense of the country. They would have the right to send as many soldiers into the country as they wished, thereby to assure the realization of any future demands they might make.

As the governor's house was situated in a cold and sunless valley, the Dalai Lama moved to the romantic-looking Dungkhar cloister. There he lived withdrawn from the world, attended by the monks and his own servants, and I hardly ever found an opportunity of conversing with him alone. Lobsang Samten lived in a room in the monastery, where I often visited him. We went out frequently with the Dalai Lama on his long walks. He used to visit the neighboring cloisters on foot, and everyone wondered at the speed with which he walked. Nobody could keep up with him. This was the first time he had opportunities for physical exercise, and he made full use of them. His energy, moreover, was good for the health of his staff, who had to be in training to keep pace with him. The monks gave up snuff, and the soldiers tobacco and strong drink. In spite of the general depression, the religious feasts were regularly observed, but the materials were lacking to reproduce the pomp and ceremony of the Lhasa celebrations. An agreeable interlude was provided by the visit of an Indian savant, who brought the king a genuine relic of the Buddha in a golden urn. On this occasion, I took my last and best photo of the Dalai Lama.

The standard of life of the nobles became lower and lower the longer we stayed in the Chumbi Valley. Almost everybody went about on foot, as, with few exceptions, all the horses had been sent away. It is true they still had their servants and did not need to do anything for themselves, but they had to go without their comforts, their palatial houses, their parties, and their entertainments. They took to intrigue in a small way and found relaxation in gossiping and spreading rumors. They began to realize that the period of their supremacy had come to an end. They could no longer make any decisions for themselves and had to refer everything to the Dalai Lama. Moreover, they could not be sure that the Chinese would give them back their property when they returned, although they had promised to do so. The curtain had rung down on feudalism, and they knew it.

I remained in the Chumbi Valley till March 1951, and then decided to go on to India. I had long realized that I would not be able to return to Lhasa, but I was still an official of the Tibetan government and had to ask for leave of absence before going away. It was at once granted. The passport delivered to me by the cabinet was valid for six months and contained a clause asking the Indian government to assist me should I return to Tibet, but I knew that I would never be able to make use of it. I was sure that in six months the Dalai Lama would be back in Lhasa, where he would be tolerated as the Incarnation of Chenrezi but never more recognized as the ruler of a free people.

I had long been racking my brains to find a solution to my own personal problem, and after careful consideration I decided on going to India. I had been corresponding with Aufschnaiter for some time and had actually met him at Gyangtse, where he confided to me that he meant to stay in Tibet as long as possible and then to move across to India. When we parted, we had no idea that we should not see each other for years. I took his baggage with me to Kalimpong and deposited it there. After that I did not hear from him for a year. It seemed as though he had completely disappeared. All sorts of rumors went around, and many people believed he was dead. It was not until I was again in Europe that I heard he had gone to stay in our fairyland village of Kyirong and had waited there until the Chinese came. He stayed literally until the last minute and got out with even greater difficulty than I had six years before. I was very happy to get a letter from him, posted in Nepal, telling me that he was alive.

He is still a willing exile in the Far East, endeavoring to satisfy his insatiable thirst for exploration. There are few men alive with such a thorough knowledge of the Himalayas and the Forbidden Land as he possesses. What will he not have to tell when he returns to Europe after all these years?

I left with a heavy heart but could not remain any longer. I felt deep anxiety about the fate of the young king. I knew that life in the Potala would be darkened by the shadow of Mao Tse-tung. Instead of peaceful prayer flags, I thought of the Red flag with its hammer and sickle and its claim to world dominion floating in the wind. Perhaps Chenrezi, the eternal God of Grace, would survive this soulless régime, as he had survived so many Chinese invasions. I could only hope that the most peaceful nation on earth would not have to suffer too much and would not be demoralized by revolutionary changes. It was almost seven years to the day since my entry into Tibet, when I found myself looking at the cairns and prayer flags of the frontier pass that led out of India. Then I had been hungry and tired, but full of joy at reaching the land I longed for. Now I had servants and horses and savings enough to tide me over in the near future. But I was prey to the deepest depression and felt none of the tingling expectation that used to possess me at the frontier of a new country. I looked back mournfully at Tibet. The giant pyramid of Chomolhari rising in the distance seemed to give me a farewell greeting.

In front of me was Sikkim, dominated by the enormous mass of Kinchinjunga, the last of the Himalayan giants for me to see. I took my horse's reins in my hand and walked slowly down toward the Indian plain.

A few days later, I was in Kalimpong and once again among Europeans after many years. They looked strange to me, and I felt a stranger in their company. Reporters of many newspapers hurried to meet me, hungry for news from the Roof of the World. It took me a long time to acclimatize myself to all the bustle and paraphernalia of civilization. But I found friends who helped me over the bridge. I still could not reconcile myself to leaving India, where I felt in touch with the fate of Tibet, and kept on postponing my departure for Europe.

In the summer of that year, the Dalai Lama returned to Lhasa, and the Tibetan families who had fled to India also went back to their homes. I had the experience of seeing the Chinese Governor-General of Tibet passing through Kalimpong on the way to take up his post at Lhasa. Until the autumn of 1951, the whole of Tibet was occupied by Chinese troops, and news from that country was scanty and unclear. As I write these concluding lines, many of my fears have been realized.

There is famine in the land, which cannot feed the armies of occupation as well as the inhabitants. I have seen in European papers photos of enormous posters bearing the picture of Mao Tsetung stuck up at the foot of the Potala. Armored cars roll through the Holy City. The loyal ministers of the Dalai Lama already have been dismissed, and the Panchen Lama has made his entry into Lhasa with an escort of Chinese soldiers. The Chinese have been clever enough to recognize the Dalai Lama as the official head of the government, but the will of the occupying power is paramount. They have dug themselves in quite comfortably in Tibet and with their powerful organization have already built roads hundreds of miles long, which connect this once trackless land with their own country.

I follow all that happens in Tibet with the deepest interest, for part of my being is indissolubly linked with that dear country. Wherever I live, I shall feel homesick for Tibet. I often think I can still hear the wild cries of geese and cranes and the beating of their wings as they fly over Lhasa in the clear cold moonlight. My heartfelt wish is that this book may create some understanding for a people whose will to live in peace and freedom has won so little sympathy from an indifferent world.

WHEN HE ENDED his original account, in 1952, Heinrich Harrer thought that no one would ever be able to share his experience of the rare qualities of the Tibetan people. Since 1959, however, he finds the

Tibetan diaspora in India, Europe, and America proving his praises to be no exaggeration. The mayor of a little Swiss village told Harrer, "If only I could exchange all my guest workers for Tibetans." Though news from the Roof of the World continues to sadden him, Harrer takes bittersweet comfort in the fact that his own friendship with the Dalai Lama and his family has only deepened since their flight. On the occasion of the opening of a Tibet exposition in Vienna organized by Harrer, the Dalai Lama sent him the letter on page 323.

OFFICE OF **TIBET**
BUREAU DU

GENEVA (SWITZERLAND)   8-10, RUE DU PORT   TÉL. (022) 25 89 52

To my friend Heinrich Harrer,

I wish you with all my heart every success at the opening of the Tibet exposition. I am sending you on this occasion my personal representative in Europe, Thubten Phala, my sister Dschetsuen Pema, and my brother Lobsang Samten. You lived for seven years in Tibet, and during that time you became one of us. You have thence the best knowledge of our country and so are in a position to bring Tibetan art and culture to the Austrian people in as lively a way as possible.

    I include in my prayers the wish that the exposition may be a complete success.

> Dalai Lama
> Eleventh Month Twentieth Day
> Year of the Wooden Serpents
> [January 1, 1966]

EPILOGUE: 1996

It was more than half a century ago that I had the privilege to live in Tibet, at a time when it was still a happy and free land. In one of his introductions, His Holiness the Dalai Lama said I had "become one of us." He continued: "Now, as we grow older, we remember those happy days we spent together in a happy country. A sign of genuine friendship is that it does not change, come what may. Once you get to know each other, you retain your friendship and help each other for the rest of your life. Harrer has always been such a friend to Tibet. His most important contribution to our cause was his book *Seven Years in Tibet,* which introduced millions of people to my country. Today, he is still active in the struggle for the Tibetan people's freedom and rights, and we are grateful to him for it."

When Peter Aufschnaiter and I reached Lhasa after nearly two years of walking over mountain passes as high up as 20,000 feet, we had frostbite and blisters, and we were starved and ill. Lhasa was known as the Forbidden City, and therefore it would not have surprised us if the Tibetan government had brought us back to the border. However, the opposite happened. They took pity on us;

they gave us food, new and warm clothes, a home, and work, and we became friends.

Who on earth would have thought at that time that we would have to flee from that peaceful country on the roof of the world? However, the Chinese invaded the Land of Snow, and the Dalai Lama, with more than a hundred thousand people, had to turn to India and elsewhere in the free world for asylum. What has since happened in Tibet is hardly to be believed. More than 1.2 million Tibetans lost their lives and of about six thousand monasteries, temples, and shrines, 99 percent were either looted or totally destroyed.

In these days when Tibetans suffer and need help, I try my best to find support for the Dalai Lama and the refugees from his land. I give fund-raising lectures and publish the old black-and-white pictures, because almost all Tibetans, whether in Tibet or as refugees elsewhere, have never seen how beautiful and happy their country once was. It makes me very proud that this book has been printed in Tibetan letters as well. What will bring still more attention to the cause of the refugees is the fact that *Seven Years in Tibet* will be made into a film. The producer's intention of emphasizing the invasion, destruction, and genocide in Tibet has resulted in the Chinese putting pressure on all neighboring countries to refuse permission to film in their land for the movie version of *Seven Years in Tibet*.

The fear goes on in conformity with the solution of the human rights commission, which at the last meeting in Geneva, in April 1996, condemned all other nations but China. The producer will now shoot in other countries with ice-covered mountains, and some friends in Asia are of the opinion that this will give even more interest and attention to the movie than before.

As for myself, I would like to inform the reader that after many decades and a number of expeditions to other remote regions of our globe, motives change as one grows older.

However, with Asia, and Tibet in particular, it is different. For hundreds of years, it has fascinated missionaries, explorers, and traders. The lure of the East, with all its secrets, mystics, and forbidden cities—even up to the present time, of Shangrila—captivates and attracts the minds of intellectuals as well as adventurers.

In the time between the two wars, a British colonial officer said that with the invention of the airplane the world has no secrets left. However, he said, there is one last mystery. There is a large country on the Roof of the World, where strange things happen. There are monks who have the ability to separate mind from body, shamans and oracles who make government decisions, and a God-King who lives in a skyscraper-like palace in the Forbidden City of Lhasa.

Ever since I was a youngster, I read only geography books, and my great role model was the Swedish explorer Sven Hedin, who had written fascinating books on his adventures in Tibet. When my prisoner-of-war camp in India was moved to the foothills of the Himalaya range, my ambition to escape naturally focused on the direction north of Tibet, which I felt must be "out of this world."

To make one thing clear, the British treated us exactly according to the Geneva Convention. To stay inside the barbed wire was actually quite pleasant. We had books and sporting activities, and we did not suffer from hardships, repression, or hunger. There was no reason to get away from something unbearable or dreadful. I wanted to get away to reach something, maybe even to reach that forbidden country lying beyond the highest mountains of the world.

This book ends in spring of 1951, when I said farewell to my young friend the Dalai Lama and to my homeland Tibet. This time it was not of my own free will to get away, it was just the opposite. The last picture I took of His Holiness before crossing the border into Sikkim and India was the last picture taken of him in free Tibet. Soon afterward, it became the first *Life* cover in color and spread the news that Tibet had been overrun by the Chinese. The Dalai Lama returned with his ministers to Lhasa, in the belief that the Chinese would adhere to the promises of the seventeen-point agreement.

In a nutshell, this is what happened: life with the conquerors went from bad to worse. In March 1959, during an uprising in Lhasa, the Dalai Lama fled by night and finally, after many weeks, reached India safely. It was exactly fifteen years after I fled from India to Tibet that the Dalai Lama fled Tibet and reached India. The Indian government very generously extended asylum to the Tibetans, and the unofficial exile government of the Dalai Lama settled on the India hill station Dharamsala.

The great mother of His Holiness died there in 1962, and some years later his elder brother Lobsang Samten, only fifty years of age, who had been my friend in Lhasa, died in New Delhi of an infection. To lose these two family members was an extremely hard blow for His Holiness.

The admiration and reverence for the Dalai Lama has grown widely in the world in the past years. To the dismay of the Chinese, popular demand for Tibet's independence has been increasing throughout the world, due mainly to the endeavors and charisma of the Dalai Lama. Slowly the world has come to realize the extent to which Tibet's culture has been mutilated.

No doubt the greatest recognition for the Dalai Lama and his cause came in 1989, when he received the Nobel Peace Prize.

It is not difficult to imagine my personal pride and gratitude in having one of the truly great men of our time as a friend and as my lasting contact with the equally great nation that took me in when I was a penniless fugitive.

It is a wonderful coincidence that we both have July 6 as our birthday, and it certainly was one of the greatest days in my birthplace, Hüttenburg, in the province of Carinthia, in Austria, that His Holiness, the Fourteenth Dalai Lama, came to bless and open the H. H. Museum.

Today the destruction in Tibet continues. The holy city of Lhasa has become a Chinese town; only 2 percent of the typical Tibetan houses are left. However, thousands of Chinese shops, and hundreds of brothels, gambling houses, and amusement establishments built to please the soldiers of the occupation army have disappeared. Decades of destruction, suppression, genocide, sterilization, and political indoctrination could not break the Tibetans' will for freedom, or their deep-rooted religious beliefs.

On March 10, 1996, in New Delhi, the thirty-seventh anniversary of the bloody Lhasa uprising, the Dalai Lama said that he regrets that repression in Tibet continues. The human rights commission emphasized that torture and cruelty to children is a daily routine for the Chinese occupation authorities. The support for the cause of Tibet is growing, and the Dalai Lama and his people will never give up. My vision is that all those who love Tibet and freedom will accompany the Dalai Lama when he returns to the monument of Tibetan genius, the Potala.

Though vocal support for Tibetan freedom is growing throughout the world, materialistic aims in most countries are given preference over human rights.

ABOUT THE AUTHOR

HEINRICH HARRER
CURRENTLY RESIDES
IN LIECHTENSTEIN.